RELIGION AND BELIEF

SKILLS-BASED SOCIOLOGY

Series Editors: Tony Lawson and Tim Heaton

The *Skills-based Sociology* series is designed to cover all the key concepts, issues and contemporary debates in Sociology, emphasises contemporary developments in sociological knowledge, with a focus on recent social theories. Each title thoroughly addresses a particular topic area within sociology, and offers contemporary examples, up-to-date references and pedagogical features to aid learning and focus upon the development of essential analytical skills.

Published
CULTURE AND IDENTITY
Warren Kidd

STRATIFICATION AND DIFFERENCE
Mark Kirby

Forthcoming
POLITICAL SOCIOLOGY
Warren Kidd, Philippe Harari and Karen Legge

THEORY AND METHOD (*Second edition*)
Mel Churton and Anne Brown

EDUCATION AND TRAINING (*Second edition*)
Tony Lawson, Anne Brown and Tim Heaton

MASS MEDIA (*Second edition*)
Marsha Jones, Emma Jones and Andrew Jones

CRIME AND DEVIANCE (*Second edition*)
Tony Lawson and Tim Heaton

HEALTH AND ILLNESS (*Second edition*)
Michael Senior, Chris Liverey and Bruce Viveash

THE FAMILY (*Second edition*)
Liz Steel, Anne Brown and Warren Kidd

Skills-based Sociology
Series Standing Order ISBN 0–333–69350–7
(*outside North America only*)

You can receive future titles in this series as they are published. To place a standing order please contact your bookseller or, in the case of difficulty, write to us at the address below with your name and address, the title of the series and the ISBN quoted above.

Customer Service Department, Macmillan Distribution Ltd, Houndmills, Basingstoke, Hampshire RG21 6XS, England

Religion and Belief

Joan Garrod and Marsha Jones

First published 2009 by
PALGRAVE MACMILLAN
Houndmills, Basingstoke, Hampshire RG21 6XS and
175 Fifth Avenue, New York, N.Y. 10010
Companies and representatives throughout the world

PALGRAVE MACMILLAN is the global academic imprint of the Palgrave Macmillan
division of St. Martin's Press, LLC and of Palgrave Macmillan Ltd. Macmillan® is a
registered trademark in the United States, United Kingdom and other countries.
Palgrave is a registered trademark in the European Union and other countries.

ISBN-13: 978-0-333-68763-5
ISBN-10: 0-333-68763-9

This book is printed on paper suitable for recycling and made from fully
managed and sustained forest sources. Logging, pulping and manufacturing
processes are expected to conform to the environmental regulations of the
country of origin.

A catalogue record for this book is available from the British Library.

A catalog record for this book is available from the Library of Congress.

Library of Congress Cataloging-in-Publication Data

Garrod, Joan.
  Religion and belief / Joan Garrod and Marsha Jones.
    p. cm. -- (Skills-based sociology)
  Includes index.
  ISBN 978-0-333-68763-5
  1. Religion and sociology--Textbooks. I. Jones, Marsha. II. Title.
  BL60.G37 2009
  306.6-dc22   2008043231

10   9   8   7   6   5   4   3   2   1
18   17 16 15 14 13 12 11 10 09

Printed and bound in China

Contents

List of Tables
and Figures

Tables

Figures

Acknowledgements

The authors and publishers would like to thank the following for permission to reproduce copyright material:

Abrams *et al.* (1985), *Values and Social Change in Britain*, reproduced with the permission of Abrams, Gerard and Timma and Palgrave Macmillan.

Crown copyright material is reproduced with the permission of the Controller Office of Public Sector Information (OPSI) and the Controller of HMSO.

Every effort has been made to trace all copyright holders, but if any have been inadvertently overlooked, the publishers will be pleased to make the necessary arrangement at the first opportunity.

Chapter 1

Introduction: the Philosophy behind the Book

This book is intended to provide a brief introduction to the sociology of religion and belief. It makes no claim to be a comprehensive and in-depth guide. Rather, it introduces some of the major debates within this exciting topic, in particular that concerning the nature and role of religious beliefs and institutions in contemporary societies, including Britain. As with all areas in sociology, it is important that you learn to understand and use the relevant concepts, and, to this end, you will find it useful to have access to a dictionary of sociology. At the end of each chapter, the most important concepts used in that chapter are listed. If you were writing an essay on this aspect of the sociology of religion, you would be expected to use these concepts in an informed and relevant manner. You should therefore look though them and ensure that you are clear about the meaning of each, as it applies to the topic under discussion. A summary of the main points covered in each chapter is also provided.

Also at the end of each chapter there is a 'Critical Thinking' section. This will contain some points to consider, sometimes an activity or two to help develop your knowledge and skills, and some guidance on writing an essay on the material covered in the chapter. Taken together, it is hoped that these will help you to engage with the text, and to reflect on some of the issues raised.

This book is part of Palgrave Macmillan's 'Skills-based Series'. As the name implies, the series is designed to do more than simply impart knowledge (K), though this is, of course, an important aim. It is intended that using the books to reflect on the points raised, learning the appropriate concepts and undertaking the exercises, including writing the essays, will enable you to develop and practise important skills, particularly those of interpretation (I), analysis (A) and evaluation (E).

SUBJECT CONTENT

The content of this book is divided into eight chapters. Chapter 1 introduces you to some of the definitional problems of the sociology of religion. Chapter 2 examines some of the theories of the role of religion in society produced by what are known as the classical sociologists. Chapter 3 looks at how more recent sociologists have examined the role of religion, particularly in late-modern and postmodern societies. Chapter 4 examines the similarities and differences between various religious organisations, their appeal and member-ship. Chapter 5 explores some of the arguments and evidence regarding whether religion acts as mainly a conservative force in society or as an agent for social change, as well as looking at situations where religion has been associated with conflict. Chapter 6 addresses the question of the continuing strength or decline of religion in contemporary societies – in other words, examines the secularisation debate. Chapter 7 looks at some of the social characteristics associated with religious belief and participation, particularly those of ethnicity and gender. Chapter 8 discusses some of the issues and debates that have come to prominence regarding religious groups, beliefs and practices in the context of the changes brought about by globalisation.

THE SOCIOLOGY OF RELIGION

What exactly *is* the sociology of religion? As with most questions raised in sociology, there is no simple, or even single, answer. However, in broad terms we may say that it is a branch of sociology that examines the role and the significance of the *diversity* of organised religions and individual religious beliefs both in particular societies and globally. The sociology of religion also studies and explores the *nature* of religious beliefs held by societies and groups of people within those societies. Also of great importance is to investigate and try to measure and understand the *effects* – on individuals, groups, societies and increasingly clusters of societies – of people holding particular beliefs.

Any student of history will be aware of the significance of the impact of religion throughout human history. Religion both shapes, and is shaped by, many different social forces in society, and sociologists are interested in exploring these. Religion and religious beliefs are arguably now more to the forefront of events in the contemporary world than at any time in the recent past, and understanding their nature and the influences that shape them seems an increasingly important and worthwhile endeavour.

Malcolm Hamilton (1995) suggests that the sociology of religion has two main themes, or central questions. These are:

1   Why have religious beliefs and practices been so central a feature of culture
    and society?
2   Why have religious beliefs and practices taken such diverse forms?

While this book does not presume to have definitive answers to either of these
important questions, it will help you to explore them.

RELIGION, FAITH AND BELIEF

God isn't compatible with machinery and scientific medicine and universal
happiness. You must make your choice. Our civilisation has chosen
machinery, medicine and happiness.   (Huxley, 1965, p. 183)

The modern western world is not a religious place. It is possible to
exaggerate the faith of pre-industrial Europe and it is possible to overlook
the continued attraction of the supernatural, but there is compelling
evidence in every index of the popularity of religious belief and behaviour
that modern Westerners are little interested in God or Gods.   (Bruce 1992).

The quotations above show that neither Huxley or Bruce view religious faith
as playing an important part in modern Western societies. There are, of course,
many who would disagree with them in this respect. Is such disagreement
simply the result of different interpretations of the available evidence, or do the
two sides in the debate use fundamentally different criteria to decide what
'religion' and 'religious' mean? The evidence and arguments presented in the
following chapters should help you to draw your own conclusions.

Much of the work undertaken by sociologists of religion in the West has
been focused on Christianity to the exclusion of other faiths. This is an
ethnocentric position (one that looks at something only from the point of view
of the writer's own culture) and as we shall see later in the chapter, has only
recently been challenged by a more multi-faith approach.

When asked in surveys, most people claim to have some kind of faith, or
belief, and most people, if asked, can give the name of a religion to which they
'belong' – though such belonging may not be formalised in the sense of being a
member of a religious community. However, in many (though by no means all)
Western societies the number of people regularly participating in some kind of
act of worship outside the home represents only a very small proportion of the
population of that society, and the proportion in many countries has been
falling for the past century.

In the 2001 census, 71.6 per cent of the population said that they were 'Christian'. However, a MORI poll of 503 adults in England, taken in April 2001, in which the vast majority of the respondents were Christian, showed that only 9 per cent intended to go to church on Good Friday, and 14 per cent on Easter Monday, and 66 per cent said that Christmas was more important to them than Easter, although Easter, with its celebration of Christ's resurrection, is the most important festival in the Christian calendar. Only 33 per cent correctly identified Palm Sunday as the day on which Jesus rode into Jerusalem to his death, and just over half (52 per cent) knew that Good Friday was the day on which Jesus was crucified. Another survey of 1018 people in Northern Ireland, carried out in December 2007, showed that only 42 per cent knew that there were four gospels, and only 54 per cent could name the parts of the Holy Trinity. We can see, therefore, that professing a faith, or belief, in a particular religion does not necessarily mean that the person has an understanding and knowledge of some of the most important and central parts of that religion.

Glock and Stark (1965) distinguish between three kinds of belief. These are:

1 **Warranting** beliefs – these acknowledge the existence not only of the divine, but of a particular *type* of divinity, e.g., a Trinitarian God (Father, Son and Holy Ghost).
2 **Purposive** beliefs – these explain what the 'divine purpose' is, and where humankind fits into that plan.
3 **Implementary** beliefs – these set out the ethics of how believers should behave, both with respect to their God and to their fellow humans.

While some people may simply 'believe', or 'have faith' in a general sense, others have a strong religious *commitment*, that may, for example, cause them to participate in acts of worship at regular intervals, or live their lives in a particular manner even if at times this is at odds with other groups in society. Stark and Glock (1968) claim that a fundamental dimension of religious commitment is that the person will hold a certain theological outlook, and will acknowledge the truths of the religion. They say that 'every religion maintains some set of beliefs which adherents are expected to ratify'.

In the Western world, the extreme and often violent religious conflicts of the past, particularly those of the 17th century, showed clearly the need for 'managing' religion in a way that would not tear societies apart. The response to this need was the emergence of the political doctrine of liberalism. Religious beliefs became increasingly a private, personal and individual matter, and the legal separation of church and state ensued. It was felt important for the maintenance and stability of society that there should be a system of shared values and a broad consensus, even if (or perhaps particularly if) members of that society held different religious beliefs.

However, such consensus and shared values are increasingly felt to be threatened by the growth in international migration, which has brought issues of religious belief and practice to the forefront in many societies. What happens when a society contains members who hold mutually exclusive belief systems? Important issues and potential conflicts flow from this when a person's religious belief is inextricably linked to their sense of identity. Many religious identities are now transnational, and offer an alternative to a single state-based identity. Increasingly, the idea of a national identity based on secular citizenship and shared by all members of a society seems under threat, and many Western governments are putting increasing emphasis on 'assimilation', rather than the celebration of cultural and religious differences that formed part of the idea of multiculturalism.

For a while, the sociological study of religion fell almost into neglect. As we shall see, the classical sociologists saw religion and religious beliefs either as an ideology of capitalist societies that would disappear with the presumed failure of capitalism, or as a superstition that would die away in the face of rational, science-based knowledge systems. However, now religion is firmly at the centre of political debate, its study seems more important than ever.

DEFINITIONS OF RELIGION

Attempting to establish what, in the UK, constitutes the legal definition of religion is far from easy. There are, however, two interesting examples. One is from the Charity Commission. In November 1999, the Charity Commissioners for England and Wales published their decision on whether they should accept the request of the Church of Scientology (England and Wales) to be recognised as a charity (such recognition has important tax benefits). The Commissioners said that their definition took into account whether the Church of Scientology was an organisation that was:

i   established for the charitable purpose of the advancement of religion and/or
ii established for the charitable purpose of the promotion of the moral or spiritual welfare or improvement of the community.

The Commissioners concluded that, for the purposes of registration, the Church of Scientology (CoS) could *not* be considered as an organisation established for the advancement of religion. They decided this because, although they accepted that the CoS had a belief in a supreme being (one of the criteria for establishing a religion for charitable purposes), as the 'core practices' of Scientology were auditing and training, these did not constitute 'worship' (another criterion) 'as they do not display the essential characteristic of reverence or veneration for a supreme being'.

However, during the consultation for the Charities Act 2006, the Charity Commissioners stated the following:

> Belief in a Supreme Being is a necessary characteristic of religion in charity law which is why the criteria that we use include reference to a Supreme Being rather than a god. The existing law allows theistic, non-theistic and polytheistic faiths to be regarded as religions in charity law and the precise nature of a Supreme Being is not defined. A Supreme Being does not necessarily have to be in the form of a creator god; it may be in the form of one god or many gods or no god at all in the accepted understanding of the term. (*www.charity-commission.gov.uk/spr/corcom1.asp*)

This revised definition has led some to suggest that the Church of Scientology now has a stronger claim to be defined as a religion.

The other legal example comes from the Equality Act 2006, from the part that relates to the prohibition of discrimination on grounds of religion or belief. The Government issued guidance notes, which said that the Act prohibited discrimination on the basis of:

▪ a person's actual religion or belief;
▪ a religion or belief they are thought to have;
▪ the religion or belief of someone else with whom they are associated (e.g. a friend or member of their family).

The guidance notes also include the following statement:

> Thus, the concept of religion will include, but not be limited to, those religions widely recognised in this country such as the Baha'I Faith, Buddhism, Christianity, Hinduism, Islam, Jainism, Judaism, Rastafarianism, Sikhism and Zoroastrianism. The concept of belief includes beliefs such as Humanism, or other philosophical beliefs similar to a religion. However, other categories of beliefs, such as support for a political party, are not included. (*http://www.religionlaw.co.uk/07relguide.pdf*)

This appears to make an interesting distinction between 'religion' and 'belief', though both of these are covered by the Act.

We can see therefore that one of the many problems facing the student new to the sociology of religion is how religion is to be defined. Many people hold a common-sense understanding of what religion is, but sociologists have to be more exact. Unless we are clear about what we mean by religion from the outset we will be unable to answer such questions as whether or not religion has declined in modern societies, or whether religious beliefs have been replaced by something else. There is therefore a need to have a working definition that will allow systematic investigation to be undertaken. It is important to note that any definition adopted will have some effect both on the type of data collected and on the interpretation of that data, so it is necessary to tread carefully.

It is interesting to note that sociologists do not agree on a single definition of religion. It is important, therefore, that whenever we read the work of sociologists in this field we should ask ourselves exactly what definition has been used by this sociologist. For clarity, definitions of religion are usually divided into two broad classifications – **inclusivist** and **exclusivist**.

Inclusivist definitions make reference to belief systems, but do not specify a belief in a God or gods. In other words, such definitions allow us to include beliefs not conventionally viewed as religious, such as communism or psychoanalysis. Probably the earliest sociological definition to form the basis of research was that of Emile Durkheim in *The Elementary Forms of the Religious Life*. His definition of religion was: 'A unified system of beliefs and practices relative to sacred things, that is, things set apart and forbidden, beliefs and practices which unite into one moral community called a church, all those who adhere to them' (1965, p. 47).

Despite Durkheim's reference to 'sacred things', and a 'moral community called a church', what is omitted is any reference to a god or supernatural being. It is an **inclusivist** definition because it could encompass other types of belief. Giddens (1997, p. 436) also uses an inclusivist definition of religion. He sees a religion as having the following characteristics:

- a set of symbols, invoking feelings of reverence or awe;
- a set of rituals or ceremonials engaged in by a community of believers (these rituals can be very diverse, ranging from praying to fasting and feasting, but they are linked to the sacred rather than the ordinary);
- beliefs which do not necessarily involve gods, but 'some beings inspiring attitudes of awe or wonder'.

If a definition refers explicitly to belief in a deity (god) or several deities, then we have an **exclusivist** definition of religion. We can see an example of this type of definition in the work of Stark and Bainbridge (1987). They argue that religions involve some conception of a supernatural being, world or force, and the notion that the supernatural is active, that events and conditions here on earth are influenced by the supernatural. Note the important point that this definition makes specific reference to some kind of supernatural entity or force, and one which is able to influence earthly matters. We must be aware, therefore, especially when we come to discuss the process of secularisation, exactly which kind of definition of religion has been used at the outset.

THE WORLD'S MAJOR RELIGIONS

It might be helpful here to give a very brief summary of the major religions found in Britain today.

Christianity

Christianity is one of the world's largest religions. Although its origins are in the Middle East, it is now found especially in Western Europe, North and South America, Australia and New Zealand, and large parts of Africa, particularly in the south. It is the majority faith in the UK. However, while the 2001 census revealed that 71.6 per cent of adults considered themselves to be Christian, a survey in 2005 showed that only 6.3 per cent were regular church attenders.

What Christians believe

- There is only one God, but He is seen as a Trinity -- as Father, Son and Holy Spirit.
- Jesus the Son of God took human form two thousand years ago, lived on earth and was put to death by crucifixion. By this sacrifice, humans were saved from death and sin.
- For those who accept God, there is eternal life after earthly death.
- The Holy Book is the Bible, and particular emphasis is given to the books of the New Testament, which contain Jesus' teachings.
- Christians try to live their life according to the ten commandments, revealed by God to Moses on Mount Sinai.
- The most important date in the Christian calendar is Easter, which celebrates the crucifixion and resurrection of Jesus.

Islam

The Muslim community in Britain originates from many different countries and cultures; these include Pakistan and Bangladesh, East Africa, some of the Arab countries, Iran and India. It is clear that because of their very different backgrounds, it is difficult to regard the Muslim community as a single whole. Muslim settlement, however, is highly concentrated. Almost half the Muslim community lives in London. Other groups live in the West Midlands, Yorkshire and Manchester. Three-quarters of the Pakistani and Bangladeshi community live in Birmingham.

What Muslims believe

- Islam means 'submission to God', the one God being Allah. Mohammed is its main and final prophet and it is on his teachings that the faith is founded.
- Prayer is obligatory and formal prayers are said five times daily. The mosque plays an important role in the faith; informally, it is used as a meeting place, a place for eating and residence as well as formally for prayer. It is mainly men and boys who are allowed to pray in the mosque. Women may enter the mosque, but they pray separately.
- Muslims observe a month of fasting, Ramadan, and each Muslim aspires to make a pilgrimage to the Holy City, Mecca.
- Muslims are divided into two groups: the Sunni, who are the majority, and the Shi'ites, who represent about 15 per cent of Muslims.
- Islamic law is all-encompassing. The religious leaders are skilled in the interpretation of the Holy Book, the Qur'an. Dietary requirements are rigorously followed.

Judaism

Judaism dates from 1000 BCE in the Middle East. A monotheistic faith (belief in just one God), it demands obedience to a strict moral code. Since the Middle Ages there have been Jewish communities in Britain, and Jews are the longest-established religious minority in the UK. There are three major branches of modern Judaism. Orthodox Jews believe in the strict interpretation of the Jewish laws, including those governing dress, separation of the sexes, observing the Sabbath (Saturday) as a day of rest, and eating kosher food. Reform Jews are more 'modern' in their views, and Progressive Jews believe in merging Jewish beliefs with modern liberal social and political ideals. In the 2001 census, 267,000 people said that they were Jewish. Almost a third of the Jewish population in Britain live in north-west London. In the 19th century there was a thriving community in Belfast, but today there are only about 400 Jews in Northern Ireland.

Jewish communities have suffered many periods of persecution throughout the past, culminating in genocide under the Nazi regime during the 1930s and 1940s. When the State of Israel was created in 1948, Judaism became its official religion.

There is some difference of opinion as to whether Jews are a nation, race or simply a religious group. On one side are those who see themselves as belonging to one of a multiplicity of religious faiths in a religiously heterogeneous society. On the other are those who see themselves as a nationality. The two main branches of European Jewry are the Ashkenazi and the Sephardi. In medieval Europe, the Ashkenazi were the Jews living along the Rhine in northern France and Western Germany, while the Sephardi are the descendants of the Jews originating in North Africa who were expelled from Spain in 1492.

What Jews believe

- Jews are the descendants of Abraham, who received a covenant from God almost two thousand years BCE.
- There is one God who judges, rewards and punishes (a monotheistic religion).
- The Holy Book is the Torah, five books which describe the Jews' history and lay out a set of laws.
- The religious leader is the Rabbi who interprets the Torah to his congregation. There are important dietary practices associated with Judaism.
- Prayers, family and congregational, are central to Jewish life. The Sabbath is kept holy.
- Jews are born into the faith, although conversion is accepted. Jewishness is passed down the maternal line (through the mother).

Hinduism

Many Hindus moved to Britain as a consequence of the policy of Africanisation of the East African states. Approximately 70 per cent of Hindus in Britain are Gujarati, 15 per cent are Punjabi and the rest are from Uttar Pradesh, Bengal and some of the southern states of India. Hindus do not necessarily attend a place of worship and practise their religion at home. However, there are many Hindu temples in Britain which act as important community centres. Hindus are divided by ethnic background and by caste which comes from the stratification of the traditional Hindu caste system. The castes are hierarchical occupational groupings, based on rituals of purity and impurity. Caste is ascribed: the Brahmin are the intelligentsia and priesthood; the Kshatriyas are administrators and military; Vaishyas are the merchants and agriculturists and the Sudras are the manual labourers. Outside these are the Harijan who have the lowest status in Hindu society.

Hinduism is the most ancient of all the major religions, dating back approximately 6000 years. Any definition of Hinduism is difficult because it is such a diverse faith. Some observers define it as what it is not. According to Nesbitt (1990), for practical purposes Hinduism is best defined as a vast religious tradition comprising all those systems of thought, beliefs and practices which originated in the Indian subcontinent, other than Jainism, Buddhism, Sikhism and tribal religions.

What Hindus believe

- Hindus believe in one god, Brahman, who has many incarnations. These include Indra (God of rain), Surya (Sun), Chadra (Moon), Ganesha (the remover of obstacles), Yama (Death), Sarasvati (Goddess of Learning) and Lakshmi (Goddess of Wealth).
- At the heart of Hinduism is the belief in 'dharma' which is 'universal law', applying to every individual's specific social status and life-stage.
- There is a common belief in reincarnation – that believers are part of an ongoing process of birth, death and rebirth. This belief in reincarnation is underpinned by an acknowledgement of 'karma', which refers to action and the consequences of action. So, reincarnation is a moral rebirth dependent upon the accumulation of good karma.
- There is no single Holy Book, but a large number of religious sources. The Vedas dating from 300 BC contain hymns, ritual instructions and philosophical observations. There are two great epic stories: the Ramayana and the Mahabharata.

Sikhism

By the early 1970s, the Sikh community was well established in Britain. Most come from the Punjab, East Africa and other British colonies. Many of the Sikhs in Britain continue to be concerned with events in their Punjab homeland, especially the massacre which took place at the Golden Temple of Amritsar in 1984.

What Sikhs believe

Defining Sikhism is less difficult a task than with Hinduism, as it is of more recent origin and its adherents are mainly Punjabi.

- Sikhs have ten 'spiritual masters', led by Guru Nanak Dev who was born in the Punjab in 1469.

- Sikhism has a code of conduct which defines a Sikh as 'any person whose faith consists of belief in one God, Akal Purakh, the ten Gurus, the Adi Granth, and other scriptures and teachings of the ten Gurus. He or she must also believe in the necessity and importance of 'Amrit' (the Sikh baptism ceremony).
- Sikhism is monotheistic, but Sikhs believe that the one God can be called by many names, including Allah.
- Orthodox Sikhs signify their faith by wearing the five 'K's. They leave their hair uncut, wear a comb in the hair to symbolise spirituality, a steel bracelet for spiritual allegiance and brotherhood, a long undergarment for modesty and finally a dagger to symbolise readiness to fight.

Buddhism

Buddhism originated in India over 2500 years ago as an offshoot of Hinduism, but it grew in popularity and spread all over Asia. According to the 2001 census, there are almost 152,000 Buddhists in Britain, but this is certainly an underestimate. This is because the religion does not demand commitment to Buddha alone, and many people who belong to other faiths, e.g. Christians and Jews, also class themselves as Buddhists. Buddhists do not worship gods or deities, and the religion has a focus on personal spiritual development.

What Buddhists believe

- Everything is subject to change (the law of impermanence), though some things may last longer than others.
- Nothing occurs by pure chance (the law of causation). As well as the influence of natural forces, it is our karma that is responsible for what happens. 'Karma' is the idea that all actions have consequences, so our lives are conditioned by our past actions.
- The soul is indestructible. Consciousness continues after death, and finds expression in a future life.
- Suffering is universal; it is caused by desire and yearning but it can be prevented and overcome by conquering cravings and desires. Following the path of Buddha allows one to escape the cycle of craving and suffering. This leads to the state of nirvana, or complete enlightenment, where one is liberated from karma.

Important concepts
Ethnocentricity • Inclusivist definitions of religion • Exclusivist definitions of religion

Summary points

- Much of the earlier work on religion by Western sociologists adopted an ethnocentric position. This is now changing, mainly due to increasing globalisation.
- The existence of a number of different faiths in one country, some of them having beliefs and practices that may call into question the idea of a value consensus, and which may be strongly linked to a person's identity, is posing challenges for some Western governments. Ideas of the assimilation of different groups, rather than a celebration of cultural differences, are beginning to assert themselves.
- No truly sociological study of religion can be undertaken without establishing how religion is to be defined.

Critical thinking

Points to consider

- In what ways might a focus on Christianity in contemporary Britain be criticised as ethnocentric?
- Is it possible to have religious faith, or belief, yet not belong to an organised religion? What might be the consequences of this for the study of religion?
- How would *you* define religion?
- Using your definition, think about how you could try to measure the extent to which people in Britain today are 'religious'.
- Identify some of the problems that you might encounter if you were to carry out this research.
- To what extent would you agree with the Charity Commissioners' reasons in 1999 for their decision not to recognise the Church of Scientology as a religion?

Activity

Using Stark and Bainbridge's exclusivist definition (above), complete the table by showing which of the following would be classed as a religion. Give brief reasons for your answer.

Belief system	Religion ✓	Religion ×	Brief reasons for your answer
Communism			
Buddhism			
Transcendental meditation			
Hinduism			
Belief in UFOs			

Chapter 2

The Role of Religion in Society: the Classical Sociologists

After studying this chapter, you should:

- have knowledge and understanding of the views of the classical sociologists on the role of religion in society;
- be able to assess the strengths and weaknesses of the arguments and evidence put forward in this debate;
- have knowledge and understanding of a number of important concepts that are relevant to the debate.

Given that all societies have some beliefs and practices which could be termed as 'religious', many sociologists have sought answers to the question of the nature of the role played by religion in society. In other words, they want to find an answer to the questions 'What is religion for?' and 'What does it do for individuals and for society?'

Sociologists writing in the 19th and early 20th centuries were concerned about the impact on traditional forms of religion brought about by the development of science and scientific thinking and of new technologies. Until the development of scientific ways of studying natural phenomena and explanations based on observations and experiments, religion provided a framework for people to incorporate these phenomena into their view of the world. Usually, such explanations were based on magic or superstition and notions of powerful, supernatural gods or beings, or of one omnipotent god.

The classical theorists, Comte, Saint-Simon and Durkheim, saw the contribution of religion as one of maintaining social integration and social stability in a context of rapid social transformation, such as was taking place in 19th-century European societies. The more conservative thinkers maintained that religion would inevitably play a central role in the future well-being of societies.

The more liberal thinkers believed that in the future social order would need either strong religious institutions or institutions acting as religious substitutes, while the more radical social thinkers thought that as societies became more industrially advanced, the need for religion would eventually decline. This is what we now refer to as the modernity thesis; the idea that as societies advance scientifically and technologically, then the need for less rational or unscientific explanations decreases. Comte assumed that religion would inevitably decline as societies became more complex, and that the discipline of sociology would be sufficient to provide explanations of society in the future. Durkheim, however, maintained that religion in some form would survive, though not in the traditional sense of belief in god or gods. He wrote: 'There is something eternal in religion which is destined to survive all the particular symbols in which religious thought has successfully enveloped itself. There can be no society which does not feel the need of upholding and reaffirming at regular intervals the collective sentiments and the collective ideas which give it its unity and individuality' (1915, pp. 474–5).

However, this is not to assume that Durkheim thought that religious belief was inevitable. Rather, for him, religion had two major elements – the provision of a set of moral regulations and also a framework for making sense of the world. It was this latter element that he thought would be overtaken by scientific thought, though in future the rationalist aspects of scientific thought would also pervade the sphere of morality.

Weber's work is most closely associated with the decline of religion and magic and the rise of rationality. For him, modernity was to be best understood as the triumph of rational thinking. Modern capitalism is the result of a rationalisation process, but Weber does not see this as a triumph. 'A world dominated by rationality – a world where efficiency, calculability and predictability are the dominant goals – means a world bereft of meaning, or of mystery, or of a concern with spiritual fulfilment' (Jones, 1993, p. 73).

Functionalists believed that they were able to demonstrate that religion itself was an important sub-system in any modern society, and distinctions were made between the **content** of religion, which could be variable, and the **functions** of religion, which were not.

AUGUSTE COMTE (1798–1857)

Comte is important not least because he was the first to use the word 'sociology' and argue for the development of a science to study human society. He was born into a devoutly Catholic and monarchist family, but at the age of 14 he informed his parents that he had 'naturally ceased believing in God' and had also become a Republican. An extremely intelligent and able student, at the age of 16 he was awarded a place at the prestigious Ecole Polytechnique in Paris. This had been founded in 1794 to train military engineers, and had become a school for the teaching of advanced science. Under Napoleon it became the most important scientific institution in France. Although he was expelled after two years for leading a student protest, it was his time at the Ecole Polytechnique that was influential in forming Comte's model of the society of the future, which he saw as being led and sustained by a new elite of scientists and engineers.

Comte became the secretary to the Utopian socialist Saint-Simon, and both men began work on defining and establishing a science of human behaviour. It was Comte's belief that each science, in its development, goes through three distinct stages. Comte also stated that each science was dependent on the knowledge developed by the previous one, and that as the phenomena studied become more complex, so too do the methods needed to study them. Comte first called his new science of human society 'social physics', which he later changed to 'sociology'. It would be sociology that held all the other sciences together, and it would be modelled on them, not only in its methods of enquiry and theoretical basis, but also in the service that it would provide for humans. The study of society would be in two parts – social statics, which would involve the study of socio-political systems and the conditions for social order, and social dynamics. Social dynamics would be the study of human evolution and progress, through the study of the three stages. These three stages, applied to both the natural sciences and sociology, were as follows:

1 *Theological stage*. In this stage, humans view nature as having a will of its own. The theological stage itself is in three stages. Firstly there is *animism*, in which objects are seen as having their own 'soul' and their own will. This is followed by *polytheism*, which sees the will of the gods imposed on objects. The last stage is *monotheism*, where it is the will of just one God that imposes itself on all other objects.
2 *Metaphysical stage*. This is a more logical and abstract phase, in which desires are replaced by knowledge of causes and forces.
3 *Positivist stage*. In this stage, the search for absolute knowledge and final causes is abandoned, and is replaced by the study of laws. The only

legitimate means of obtaining knowledge is the combination of observation and reasoning. Every scientific theory must be based on observed facts, though Comte acknowledged that facts cannot be properly observed without the guidance of theory.

The aim of all sciences, including social science, is to understand the world around us and to transform it to our advantage. Once the laws of the progress of human evolution are established, and the basis for social order and harmony are identified, then it will be possible for people to use these for their own collective (and beneficial) purposes. Comte believed that the acquisition of this social knowledge would lead to a stable society, with opinions being shared and people far less likely to fight over differing political and religious opinions. True freedom lay in the rational submission to scientific laws.

It is important to remember that Comte insisted that nothing was absolute, and knowledge was relative. He believed that scientific enterprise would be self-corrective as further knowledge was obtained, and that human understanding was subject to continued progress.

Comte and Religion

Comte was born during the last years of the French Revolution and the subsequent social upheaval, leading eventually to the establishment of Napoleon as Emperor in 1804. Comte believed that the Revolution was essentially good, as it swept away the *ancien régime* with its absolute monarchy and the enormous power and influence of the Catholic Church, but he thought that it was also negative in that it destroyed the old order without creating what he would consider a proper new one.

Comte viewed religion as providing a unifying principle to human society, and as being at the root of social order. It legitimises the governance of the people, as Comte believed that no temporal power can endure without spiritual power. He saw that there was therefore a need for a new religion and a new faith. However, the new 'priests' would be members of a scientific-industrial elite (the technocrats) able to explain the laws of the new social order. This new religion would be a 'positive religion' arising out of the new positive science. It would be a non-theistic religion (without a god) and would be a religion of man (*sic*) and society. Positive religion would bring about a new moral order, and would urge people to 'live for others'. Comte even drew up a calendar of positive saints, who included Dante, Shakespeare, Frederick the Great of Prussia and Adam Smith, the economist. Comte was to be the High Priest, and indeed took to signing his circulars 'The Founder of Universal Religion, Great Priest of Humanity'. While such things may strike us as almost comical, it is worth reminding ourselves of what Comte saw as his overall purpose. 'The object of all my labour has been to re-establish in society something spiritual that is capable of counter-balancing the influence of the ignoble materialism in which we are at present submerged.'

KARL MARX (1818–1883)

Marx's analysis of religion, which predated Durkheim's by about half a century, was similar to that of Durkheim in that Marx too saw religion as a social construction. By this he meant that the ideas and beliefs of religion arose from the thoughts and desires of humans, rather than from an external, supernatural, source. In Marx's own writings there is little systematic analysis of the role of religion; his ideas stem mainly from the work of writers such as Feuerbach. For Feuerbach, religion is constructed from the ideas and values of different societies and projected on to supernatural forces or deities. He makes use of the term 'alienation' to account for the distance created between people and the gods they have created. Only when individuals realise that the values and ideas which have been projected on to religion are really socially constructed, can they become free. It was this view of religion that Marx adopted.

Marx believed that religion, particularly in a capitalist society, had an ideological role. That is, a major part of its function was to support and justify the social inequalities on which capitalism is based. In addition, its promise of an end to all suffering in the next life, and the belief that suffering is a way of God's testing the depth of one's faith, offered comfort to those suffering oppression. Religious beliefs, according to Marx, relieved the suffering from alienation brought about by capitalism. By providing the justification for an unequal and hierarchical society as deriving from 'God's will', and also by providing comfort to deaden the suffering of exploitation, religion made it less likely that the oppressed in society would rise up and challenge, or try to change, their situation. For individuals, then, religion brought hope and the ability to accept one's lot in life, while for capitalist society, it provided a justification for the inequalities of capitalism, and helped to maintain the status quo.

Marx, however, believed that those aspects of religion that were based on supernatural beliefs were incompatible with rational scientific thought, and that therefore the traditional forms of religion would be likely to disappear once such scientific and rational thought became more widespread. However, because Marx thought that religion and religious beliefs reflected class inequalities, and arose out of alienation, he believed that religion would not actually disappear until capitalism itself was overthrown. He argued that under

Superstructure			
Family	Education	Legal system	Politics
Mass media		Religion	Ideology
Infrastructure			
Social relations of production + Forces of production The economy			

Figure 2.1 Diagram illustrating the relationship between superstructure and infrastructure

capitalism, the ideological role of religion was too important for it to cease to exist. However, Marx saw that some aspects of religion might have to change as a result of the growth of science and rational thinking.

Sociologists have largely inferred that Marx saw religion as operating within the superstructure to legitimate the power of those who own the means of production. This means that it keeps the system as it is. As Figure 2.1 demonstrates, the elements in the superstructure arise from the infrastructure. They act to legitimate the power of those who control the infrastructure – namely the bourgeoisie. This is a deterministic model because it assumes that the areas in the superstructure have little or no independence or autonomy from the economic base of society. In other words, the infrastructure determines or moulds the elements in the superstructure.

Whereas Durkheim viewed religion as a form of 'social cement' helping to provide social solidarity, Marx saw religion as an instrument of oppression used by the powerful to legitimate the inequalities of class, gender and race. He referred to it as the 'opium' of the masses. He saw it as 'the sigh of the oppressed creature, the heart of a heartless world, just as it is the spirit of a spiritless situation. It is the opium of the people.' Marx used opium as a metaphor for the way in which something was needed as a drug to escape from the harsh realities of the poverty, squalor and disease-ridden lives of the 19th-century urban proletariat. Religion, however, acted as a double-edged sword. On the one hand, it offered comfort from the oppression of an alienating world, but on the other, it concealed the very causes of that oppression. Religion in the 19th century not only reflected the suffering of the proletariat, it offered an escape from this suffering by offering the rewards of the afterlife.

For Marx, religion was, therefore, both the expression of real misery and the protest against that very misery. It served an ideological function by obscuring the causes of distress, and at the same time reinforcing the status quo. Religion, atheism and communism were all stages or features of development rather than its goal, which Marx saw as some form of 'positive humanism'.

Engels

In his essay, 'On the History of Early Christianity' (1894), Engels noted the similarities between the early religious movements and the early socialist movements. 'Both Christianity and the workers' socialism preach forthcoming salvation from bondage and misery; Christianity places this salvation in a life beyond, after death, in heaven; socialism places it in this world, in a transformation of society' (1894, p. 209). However, for Engels, religion was false; it was a 'spiritual gin' producing a state of false consciousness which could not free a society from alienation.

Historically, there is little evidence in support of Marx's view. It does not appear that members of the 19th-century working class were strongly religious; in fact the Christian churches were largely filled by the middle and upper classes.

EMILE DURKHEIM (1858–1917)

Durkheim was particularly interested in the role of religion as an integrating force in society, reinforcing shared norms and values and helping to reduce conflict. Many of Durkheim's views were formed by his studies of religion in small-scale, traditional societies, although he has been criticised for making very generalised statements about these. Like Marx, Durkheim believed that religion has a *social* basis; that is, it has a particular function linked to the maintenance and stability of society.

Durkheim identified various societies in which particular objects, such as totem poles and trees, were given religious properties and meanings. These objects were 'sacred' to the members of those societies. Durkheim described all other, non-sacred, objects as 'profane'. His argument was that in coming together in shared religious rituals, the members of society developed a sense of 'belonging', in sharing in something greater than their individual experiences. Durkheim also believed that through the rituals and acts of worship, the central values of society would be constantly reinforced.

Durkheim, though, like the other sociologists of this period, was living at a time of huge social change, where those societies that were at the forefront of the Industrial Revolution were becoming increasingly complex. Patterns of life that had existed with relatively little change for centuries were overturned, and the effects of these fundamental changes were felt in many different areas of society, particularly family life, work and community. It was obvious that the way that religion operated in simple, small-scale societies would be different from religion in complex industrial societies. Nevertheless, Durkheim believed that in going back to look at religion in simple societies, he had identified its central role and purpose, which was that of helping to create and maintain social solidarity. This function, he argued, would remain even when societies became more complex.

However, as such increasing complexity occurred, and rational thought began to replace beliefs in magic and superstition, Durkheim predicted that ideas of the sacred would become more abstract, and less focused on objects. Religion in a modern world would be organised around a 'cult of man', that is, around ideas of *individualism*. The 'sacred' in society would come to refer more to abstract ideas, such as justice and freedom, than to totems and other physical objects of worship. However, while Durkheim acknowledged that the nature of religion would change, he believed strongly that such is its fundamental role of establishing a moral code and keeping society together, it would never disappear.

An interesting piece of research published in 1982 (Stark et al.) into the power of religion to prevent acts of crime and suicide showed that membership of a religious organisation does indeed tend to promote conformity to the wishes of others and to provide a measure of stability. However, the researchers conclude that this was an effect not of the religious doctrines themselves, but of the importance of social bonds encouraged by integration into a religious group. This lends some support to Durkheim's views on the integrating force of religion.

Although he considered himself a radical and a progressive, we nowadays refer to Durkheim's work as more characteristically conservative. He was concerned with the maintenance of social order, especially with the move towards modernity. He argued that religion would become antiquated, but that there would be a need for an alternative agent to maintain the moral consensus, that is a kind of new non-religious moral order.

There are three major propositions in Durkheim's work on religion:

- that religion is society becoming conscious of itself;
- that the representations created in religion are the original source from which all subsequent forms of human thought have emerged;
- that as creations of the superior being which is society, religious symbols are accorded a peculiar respect or veneration -- denied to those of the profane world.

Durkheim predicted that although the traditional religious institutions would decline, the social functions of religion would remain. Social integration and solidarity would, therefore, become less dependent on religion in the public domain, and religion would become more of a personal choice. His study 'The Elementary Forms of the Religious Life' (1915) is a classic examination of the origin of religion and the role religion plays in society. In order to undertake this study, Durkheim looked for the origins of religion in one of the earliest societies still in existence at that time. He argued that religion derives from a double source:

i   the need to make sense of the world;
ii   people's need for sociability.

Indigenous Aboriginal religion

Durkheim's analysis of 'simple' religions was based on a native Australian tribe (see below). There are two groups of indigenous peoples in Australia – the Aborigines and the Torres Strait Islanders. In the 2006 Australian census, 455,016 respondents described themselves as indigenous, 18.3 million said that they were non-indigenous, and 1.13 million did not give a classification. It is not really possible to speak of 'the' Aboriginal and Torres Strait Islander religion, partly because indigenous beliefs and cultural practices vary according to region and to tribe. However, there are some shared beliefs, one of the most central concerning the period of creation, known in English as the Dreamtime.

It is important to note, however, that the Aboriginal concept of time is circular, rather than linear, so the Dreamtime is not only in the past, as we might imagine it, but has a spiritual connection to the present. In the Dreamtime, the Ancestral Beings taught the first people to make tools and weapons, hunt animals and the correct way to conduct ceremonies. Though regarded in some sense as ancestors, Ancestral Beings may not necessarily be in human form, as Aborigines believe that a person's spirit may return in human, animal or plant form after death. Each Ancestral Being has its own Creation story, and each played a specific role in the Dreamtime, including laying down laws and creating a part of the landscape. The stories of the Dreamtime form the basis not only of Aboriginal religion, but of law, social order and behaviour.

This information is contained in the body of songs, stories, dances and paintings of each tribe. Dreams are seen as very important because they can transport people to the Dreamtime, and are sometimes seen as the memory of things that occurred at that time. Stories about the Dreamtime are told to children and sung and acted out during ceremonies. Images of the Dreamtime appear on weapons, utensils, body painting, ground designs, bark paintings and rock art. As adolescents pass through their various initiation rites, they are introduced to the more important and secret parts of sacred songs and dances.

Durkheim's analysis was based on secondary data about an Australian Aboriginal society, the Arunta, collected in the 19th century by the social anthropologists Spencer and Gillen. Arunta society was assumed to be based on totemism, which in turn was founded on clan relationships. The social organisation of the Arunta was based on bands and clans. A band consisted of a small group who lived together, whereas the clan was a much larger group containing members of several bands.

A totem was a sacred object for the Arunta. Each clan was represented by a specific totemic object. No two clans within the same tribe could have the same totem. The totem was 'the very prototype of sacred things'. The totems themselves were ordinary objects – animals, plants or fish – but their representation was more significant. According to Durkheim, 'the totem is above all a symbol, a material expression of something else'. By this he meant that it was a 'sacred' object. In totemism there are three sorts of sacred object:

- the emblem or representation of the totem;
- the totem itself;
- the clan, which commands obligation and respect.

According to Durkheim 'the essence of religion lies in the rigid and elementary distinction made in all societies between the sacred and the profane'. He discovered, through an examination of the structure of their language, that the Arunta divided the world into the sacred and the profane (the non-sacred). The sacred element was set apart and forbidden, while the profane referred to everyday events and objects.

The ritual

Periodically the clan organised a ceremonial ritual. Rituals form an important part of a Durkheimian understanding of the role of religion in society. The ceremonial and ritual are essential because of the way in which they serve to bind people together. While they are participating in these rituals, individual clan members feel some power greater than themselves – the emergence of 'effervescences' which give proof to individuals of the existence of a superior power. These collective ceremonials also served to create a collective sentiment or what Durkheim called the 'conscience collective'. The conscience collective refers to the shared beliefs of a society. It promotes a feeling of belonging, of solidarity and a sense of the continuity of the group as a whole.

Why does the totem take on a sacred character? Durkheim believed that it is because it stands for the clan itself. 'The reverence which people feel for the totem actually derives from the respect they hold for central social values' (Giddens, 1997). In religion, the object of worship is the totem, the totem represents the clan, the clan is the society, hence the collective worship is of the society itself as represented by the totem. When Durkheim said that 'society worships itself' he meant that religion is a positive response to the very 'socialness' of social life – that is, it celebrates and thereby reinforces the fact that people can form societies. The sacred, therefore, represents things which have the capacity to bind people together in a moral community.

This is indeed a radical thought, because Durkheim seems to deny the existence of any god or supernatural being by emphasising the fact that society itself is the object of worship. Although classified as a positivist and functionalist sociologist, Durkheim seems to be arguing here from a more interpretivist position. This is similar to his work on suicide, where he interprets the meanings of religious and family membership to potential suicide victims. When he argues that individuals in the very act of worshipping together in religious rituals are in effect creating the social meaning of religion itself, he is taking a Realist position.

Some sociologists have compared the sentiments felt and expressed by crowds at civic rituals to the 'effervescences' noted by Durkheim when the clan members came together in worship. Bocock (1985) argues that civic rituals could be a new form of the 'sacred' in societies where religion seems less prominent. These contemporary rituals might include royal weddings and funerals, and remembrance days. During the first week of September 1997, Britain witnessed an event of this nature. The sudden death and then the funeral of Diana, Princess of Wales united the country in a public display of mourning previously unknown. However, not everyone in the country took part in the collective grief over her death. Bocock points out that this is not uncommon. Not everyone necessarily accepts the same values; neither did those who witnessed the funeral feel part of a sacred ritual, but rather took the opportunity to express what they felt as a personal grief.

Durkheim has often been criticised for his focus on the positive, functional side of religion, particularly with regard to its helping to maintain consensus in society. However, it is hard to disagree with the view that, where members of a group share the *same* religious beliefs and values, they tend to live in harmony. If we look at examples of situations in which religion is associated with conflict, we see that the underlying cause is often that members have come to *disagree* about the meaning of their religion and how it should be practised, or it is the case that the people involved do not share the same religion to begin with. Conflicts between Protestants and Roman Catholics, for example, from the 16th century onwards, have been founded on violent disagreements regarding how the church should be organised and how God should be worshipped.

Indeed, Durkheim recognised that the totem, which bound together members of the clan and the animal or plant species or natural phenomena which shared that totem, also, by definition, excluded those who did not share the totem. Therefore totemic religious beliefs acknowledged exclusion and even hostility as well as consensus. As Raymond Aron (1967) puts it: 'Hence, if a religious cult is aimed at societies, there exist only national tribal religions. In that case, the essence of religion might be to inspire in human beings a fanatical attachment to partial groupings and to dedicate the attachment of each individual to a collectivity and, at the same time, to manifest his hostility to other groupings.'

Durkheim's analysis of religion is often used as an example of religion playing a *conservative* role in society. If religion functions to maintain social solidarity, then it is difficult to argue that religion also acts a change agent, promoting social change. Later functionalists such as Talcott Parsons and Bronislaw Malinowski also argued that religion was a form of social cement which functioned to maintain social solidarity. Malinowski's work, like Durkheim's, was based on social anthropological evidence of small, non-literate societies such as those of the Trobriand Islands, where Malinowski did his own fieldwork. He was especially interested in the role played by religion during life crises, when individuals are most likely to be experiencing anxieties. Death and bereavement produce the greatest levels of personal anxiety, and a funeral ritual for death helps to support the bereaved and maintain cohesion between the group members. Other anxiety-creating events are often managed by some form of religious ritual. For the Trobriand Islanders, whose existence relied on fishing, a ritual to ensure safe sailing on open seas helped to reduce the tension associated with fears of storms and rough seas.

Although still related to the functions of religion, Parsons' analysis of religion emphasised the part played by the *explanatory* nature of religion. The ultimate questions which individuals ask about the nature of being and the purpose of life find responses in religion. In providing answers to such fundamental questions, religion again lessens tensions and anxieties and hence helps to promote social order and control.

Hirschi and Stark (1969) assessed an aspect of the functionalist approach to religion in their study of the effect of religion as an agent of social control. In an interesting quantitative research study, they tested the assumption that religion played a part in sustaining the personal values and ethics which govern people's conformist behaviour. They tested three major hypotheses:

1 Religious training prevents delinquency by promoting the development of moral values.
2 Religious training prevents delinquency by promoting the acceptance of conventional authority.
3 Religious training prevents delinquency because it promotes belief in the existence of supernatural sanctions.

They administered a questionnaire to more than 4000 students and controlled for gender and race. In relation to their hypotheses they found the following:

1 Frequent church attenders were no different from infrequent church attenders in attitudes towards morality.
2 Frequent church attenders were little different in their attitudes to the law and the police than infrequent church attenders.
3 There was no relationship between belief in supernatural sanctions and delinquent behaviours.

'Hirschi and Stark argued that the data supported the findings that religiosity had no effect on delinquency. They maintained that the findings of this raise doubts about the functionalist view of religion. As religion appears to have no impact on delinquency, the idea that religion serves to maintain social control is undermined. This is reinforced by the apparent lack of effect that belief in religious sanctions has on ensuring conformity to social norms' (Harvey and MacDonald, 1993, p. 134).

Although this is an interesting study to have undertaken, it does leave several questions unanswered.

MAX WEBER (1864–1920)

Religion and social change: Weber and the Protestant ethic

As part of his study of worldwide religions, Max Weber made extensive studies of Hinduism, Buddhism, Taoism and Judaism. However, his essay on the rise of Protestantism and its effect on economic behaviour and on social change (*The Protestant Ethic and the Spirit of Capitalism*), first published in 1904/5, is more relevant here.

Weber agreed with Marx on the general socio-economic factors which lead to capitalism, but his analysis looked at the relevance of **rationality** to capitalism as it developed in Western Europe. Rationality may be defined as 'a distinguishing characteristic of modernity which suggests that actions in modern societies are governed by logic and order' (Lawson and Garrod, 1996, p. 222). Weber was interested in the meanings which individual social actors imposed on social action in order to make sense of the world. In *The Protestant Ethic and the Spirit of Capitalism* we can see how Weber's interpretive sociology, or 'verstehen sociology', becomes central to solving this historical puzzle.

The thesis

In Western Europe during the late 17th century by far the majority of the successful entrepreneurs and skilled tradespeople were Protestant. In addition, only some European countries successfully practised capitalism. Other writers had already supposed some connection between the Reformation and modern capitalism, for example that the abandonment of traditional, pre-capitalist forms of economic activity went together with the abandonment of tradition in other areas of social life such as religion. Weber rejected this view, arguing that it was not the case that the Reformation had inevitably weakened the control of the Church in everyday affairs. Rather, he argued, the Church had gained strength. Protestantism actually demanded much more of its members than did Catholicism, especially in the area of economic behaviour and consumption.

Weber's originality lay in his sociological unpacking of the 'spirit of capitalism'. He used the works of Benjamin Franklin to produce an *ideal type* of this new form of economic behaviour. An ideal type is a model of a specific phenomenon which is created by bringing together its most recognisable characteristics. It is a very useful device for sociologists because it acts as a yardstick against which we can measure actual examples of the thing in question.

Weber's ideal type of the 'spirit of capitalism' in Western Europe was characterised by:

- 'the pursuit of profit, and forever renewed profit, by means of continuous, rational, capitalistic enterprise'. This meant that entrepreneurs had to plan systematically, weigh up risks and apply the rules of calculation and book-keeping to their businesses;
- the strict avoidance of all spontaneous enjoyment;
- the view that those who were time-wasters and lazy were wasting God's work on earth; and that
- the capitalist 'is dominated by acquisition as the purpose of his life'.

So a new form of economic activity emerged which was characterised by a dedication to profit, together with the avoidance of the use of this wealth for personal pleasure. The capitalists were to be devoted to producing wealth as if it were their vocation – or 'calling'. Weber found that the early entrepreneurs and tradespeople were often Protestant and in many cases, followers of John Calvin. Weber concentrated on the Calvinist teachings, which he took from the work of Richard Baxter, an English Puritan. He used these teachings to produce an ideal type of the main characteristics of Calvinist faith:

- The universe was created for the greater glory of God; 'God does not exist for men, but men for the sake of God';
- God was transcendental, beyond human comprehension;
- life was to be frugal and ascetic, avoiding all spontaneous enjoyment;
- a belief in predestination (however, this was predestination from birth; only a small group were chosen to be 'the Elect', and individuals could not alter their possibility of salvation by their behaviour in life);
- work was to be a calling; time-wasting was an affront to God.

Weber's sociological problem, therefore, was to understand the links, if any, between the content of a specific type of religious belief and a particular type of economic behaviour at a given historical moment. By using verstehen sociology (attempting to reach an empathetic understanding), Weber argued that the consequence of Calvinist belief on its followers was 'an unprecedented inner loneliness'. He interpreted the position of the Calvinist as one of deep insecurity, because Calvinism made paradoxical demands. Calvinists had to work in a calling for the greater glory of God, but could not spend the profit made on pleasurable activities. They were without the help of a mediating priest so stood alone before God and had no certainty about their destiny. Each Calvinist had, therefore, to make sense of his/her life by gaining some sign from God that they were one of the Elect or saved. The situation of such grave uncertainty could not be sustained. Its resolution, according to Weber, led to the 'elective affinity' between capitalism and Protestantism.

What did Weber mean by this? The Protestant entrepreneurs, in keeping with their faith, worked 'religiously' to be successful in their 'calling'. However, as they could not spend their profits on luxuries, they reinvested them into their businesses, thus becoming even more successful. They took this worldly success as a sign that they must be one of the Elect, arguing that surely God would have chosen only those who prospered in their calling. Therefore, rationality in business promoted success. The rational conduct of life on the basis of the idea of a calling was born – from the spirit of Christian asceticism. This was referred to as 'the Protestant ethic'.

It is important to note that Weber was *not* reversing Marxism by arguing that religious ideas determined economic activity. He used the term 'elective affinity' rather than causation, thus allowing some relative autonomy to religion, which, in this case, led to the establishment of rationality in Western capitalism. Once this economic mechanism was set in motion, the necessity for its encouragement through religious faith declined, but the Protestant ethic lived on. Weber argued that these early Protestants *chose* to work in a calling. Now, we are *forced* to do so: 'The idea of duty in one's calling prowls about in our life like the ghost of dead religious beliefs.'

Weber's ideas on religion are not without their critics. The term 'elective affinity' is vague and has led some to assume that it referred to a causal relationship. Marshall (1991) argues that Weber's argument is tautological (circular or self-fulfilling), as he defines his ideal types in terms of each other. However, support for Weber's thesis has come from Robert K. Merton when writing about the beliefs of ascetic Protestantism on the development of science in 17th-century England. Merton (1968) points out that although the Puritans constituted a minority in the English population, they accounted for 62 per cent of members of the Royal Society, which was instrumental in pioneering rational, scientific endeavour. As Merton argues, 'The deep-rooted religious interests of the day demanded in their forceful implications the systematic, rational, and empirical study of Nature for the glorification of God in His works and for the control of the corrupt world.'

Is Weber's thesis applicable to society today?

Although there have been many criticisms of Weber's analysis, what interests M. Jones (1996) is the relevance of the work for today. She has questioned whether individuals have really inherited the discipline of work in a calling. According to Weber, a calling necessitates for the individual 'an incentive methodically to supervise his own state of grace in his own conduct ... a rational planning of one's life in accordance with God's will'. In our apparently secularised society with its emphasis on leisure, consumption and pleasure, it seems that the Protestant ethic has little place. However, as Jones maintains, there is evidence of the insidious nature of the Protestant ethic in the most public and the most private domains of modern life.

The Protestant ethic and the public domain: work

It has become commonplace to refer to some professional and managerial workers as 'workaholics', compulsive workers whose work life is so demanding that it leaves little space for leisure and family time. This may not be solely a result of the Protestant Ethic, but rather of a series of structural changes which have affected the workplace. Increased technology has led to forced redundancies; companies have been down-sized and delayered. Downward social mobility has become a reality for many middle-class workers. Pahl (1996) points out that there is plenty of anecdotal evidence for workers staying late at work, fearing to leave the office before the others. However, so far relatively little sociological research has been undertaken. Pahl quotes an NOP poll which showed that over 70 per cent of British workers who work over 40 hours per week want to work less but are either obliged or *are self-compelled not to do so* (our emphasis).

This striving for success is punitive; it produces anxiety and stress which in turn produce more striving and insecurity and more workaholism. This situation is becoming more and more commonplace for the middle-class women who have begun to occupy more and more managerial and professional posts. Their anxieties are compounded by guilt over decisions about having children and the provisions for childcare.

A *Guardian* newspaper report in February 2006 reported that in the previous year, almost 5 million employees in the UK worked on average almost seven-and-a-half hours a week without being paid (*Guardian*, 'Open All Hours', M. Keating, 18 February 2006). Many workers feel overworked and stressed, and envious of their European counterparts who work fewer hours, do less unpaid overtime and get longer holidays. Similarly, a British Social Attitudes report (Crompton and Lyonette 2007) said that both full-time and part-time employees are finding it increasingly difficult to achieve what they regard as a satisfactory balance between work and life outside work. Although working hours have fallen for men, an increase in the hours worked by women means that longer hours are being worked in two-earner families. Furthermore, both men and women appear to be expected to work harder. It seems certain, then, that many workers are straitjacketed by the work ethic and it seems that unless there is a complete reversal of attitudes towards work, this situation will continue.

The Protestant ethic and the private realm: sex

This self-compulsion can be found in the private realm too. We are encouraged to become good at parenting, good at marriage and, more recently, good at sex. Sex has not previously been associated with the Protestant ethic, not least because for the early Protestant, the idea of sexual pleasure in itself was sinful. As Weber remarked: 'Rational ascetic alertness, self-control, and methodical planning of life are seriously threatened by the peculiar irrationality of the sexual act, which is ultimately and uniquely unsusceptible to rational organisation' (quoted by Turner, 1991, p. 112).

However, sexual activity and imagery are ubiquitous aspects of contemporary popular culture. Sex is about pleasure. It is one way that modern individuals can express themselves and find release from the pressure of the modern workplace, but this is another area where the work ethic reigns. The idea of 'performance' has intruded even into the most intimate parts of our lives. Although we are now encouraged to talk openly about sex, in the wake of this increased openness has come stress and anxiety. Magazines challenge us on our sexual performance. *More!*, which is read by teenage girls, is a clear example of this. Like other adolescent magazines, it encourages consumption – fashion, cosmetics and music – but part of its appeal lies with sex. It doesn't simply talk about sex, it encourages 'great sex'. It is no longer sufficient to be 'doing it', but readers must be 'working at it'. For example, a series of issues of *More!* illustrated a 'position of the fortnight'. These sexual positions have difficulty ratings, making sex into some kind of athletic competition, encouraging us to improve our scores. *More!* is not the only magazine to promote good sex; many of the popular women's magazines openly encourage women to be more sexually assertive and to demand better performances from their partners. However, while undoubtedly improving sexual relations, we face guilt and anxiety if we are not getting enough sex or not enough great sex. Our performance is measurable. It is ironic, then, that in those private areas where we believe ourselves to be most liberated, we are in fact compelling ourselves to 'duty in a calling'. The Protestant ethic has forced us to do so.

Philip Jones (1993, p. 73) sees despair in Weber's analysis, which was qualitatively different from those of Marx or Durkheim:

It is ... the story of the social destruction of the human spirit by modernity. Durkheim and Marx constructed versions of a social theory which could specify the societal route to a future of progress and human emancipation. ... But Weber ... has no cure for rationalisation. ... A world dominated by rationality – a world where efficiency, calculability and predictability are the dominant goals – means a world bereft of meaning, or of mystery, or of a concern with spiritual fulfilment. ... For Weber, the triumph of capitalism as a form of life signals the end of the line for progress; the train bearing the hopes for humanity's spiritual welfare has run into the buffers of terminal rationality.

CONCLUSION

The classical sociologists, then, grappled with trying to understand the particular role of religion and religious beliefs for individuals and societies, and with trying to predict what would happen to that role, or roles, as industrialising societies became more complex and the nature of work and social organisation underwent fundamental changes. While their beliefs in the nature of the role played by religion differed in some – and often some important – respects, they all acknowledged that the functions of religion would change as societies changed.

Important concepts

positive religion • social construction • alienation • capitalism • ideology • social solidarity • Protestant ethic • elective affinity

---

Summary points

- The classical sociologists held different views regarding the role of religion in society.
- Comte saw 'old' religion as being at the root of social order. As societies progressed to the positivist stage, there would be a need for a new religion and a new moral order.
- For Marx, religion was used to justify capitalism and provide some comfort to those oppressed by it. While capitalism existed, the ideological role played by religion was too important for it to disappear. However, religion might have to change with the growth of rationalist ideas.
- Durkheim emphasised the integrating function of religion by providing social solidarity through shared rituals and beliefs. As societies grew more complex, there would be a growth in ideas of individualism, and the 'sacred' would refer more to abstract ideas than to physical objects of veneration.
- Weber's analysis showed that, under certain circumstances, religion could be a powerful force for social change. He believed that he had demonstrated an important link between a particular type of religious belief (Calvinism) and a particular type of economic behaviour (capitalism).
- In some respects, elements of the Protestant ethic live on in people's lives today.

Critical thinking

Points to consider

- Consider the extent to which religious beliefs might be seen as justifying social inequalities. Think of particular examples.

- Think of at least two examples of religious practices which might serve to reinforce important norms and values in the society in which they occur.
- How far do the majority of people in the UK appear to live their lives according to the Protestant ethic? Is there anything to suggest that its importance is waning? If so, what?

Activity

In order to test your understanding of how Weber connected a religious belief to a form of economic activity, answer the following questions:

1 In what way(s) did Weber see Western capitalism differently from Marx?
2 What is meant by the 'spirit of capitalism'?
3 What are the main characteristics of Calvinism?
4 What is meant by 'verstehen sociology'?
5 How did Weber use this in his essay?
6 Why did Calvinists feel an 'unprecedented inner loneliness' before God?
7 How did they resolve this?
8 How did this affect Western capitalism?
9 What does 'elective affinity' mean?

Essay guidance

The following is an example of a full-length essay question. The list of questions will help you to practise the skills of 'unpacking' a question to make certain of exactly what it is that you are being asked to do, and will also help you to plan a logically structured answer. Remember that there is no single 'right way' of answering a question – there are several different approaches that would enable you to get high marks. The structure suggested here is just one way.

'The main function of religion in society is to maintain the power of the upper classes.' Assess the arguments and evidence for this view.

1 Look carefully at the way that the question is laid out. When there is a statement in quotation marks, as in the question above, it usually means that this is expressing a particular point of view. The first important task is therefore to identify the sociological perspective from which this view is taken. What kind of sociologist would make the statement in the question?
2 Now look at the second sentence in the question title. What is the 'command word' – what is the main skill you will have to display in answering this question?
3 You will have identified that you are being asked to 'assess' something. Now look again at the sentence. What exactly are you being asked to assess – is it one thing or more?
4 Again, you will have identified that in this particular question you are being asked to assess two separate things – 'arguments' and 'evidence'. While they may be related, they are not the same thing. What is the difference between them?

5   You will have worked out that 'arguments' relate to the theoretical position(s) held, while 'evidence' refers to any kind of data that could be used to support or refute the view in question.

6   Having now 'unpacked' the question, you are in a position to plan your answer. It is always a good idea to make a brief plan. This will enable you to impose a logical structure on your answer, so that your points lead from one another to make a coherent argument, and will also help to ensure that, particularly if writing under the pressures of an exam, you are less likely to forget something, by always being able to refer back to your plan. You are likely to have your own particular way of writing a plan, one that you find most helpful to you. Some people prefer a series of brief, written points, while others work best from a diagram, such as a spidergram. For the purposes of this exercise, the plan will be in the form of brief written notes. Look at the grid below. The left-hand side suggests the structure, with some guidance, and you should make brief notes in the right-hand column to develop the ideas further – but remember that this is a plan, so don't write too much. Under exam conditions, reading the question and writing your plan should take 5–7 minutes – certainly no more than that. However, as this exercise is designed to develop the skill of interpreting a question and writing a plan, doing the exercise may well take you longer than that.

Introduction Identify the perspective. Jot down just one or two points which you could use to summarise the view expressed in the statement.	
Development points: **1** What arguments are put forward to support this view? (Think about the concept of 'ideology'.)	
2 How is religion supposed to work in this way? What is it in its message that enables it (allegedly) to fulfil this function?	
3 What *evidence* is there that could be used to *support* the view expressed in the statement?	

4 There are, of course, critics of the view expressed in the question – what *alternative* views are there of the role of religion? What *criticisms* of the expressed view have been made (remember to keep the focus on 'arguments')?	
5 What criticisms have been (or could be) made of the evidence you put forward in paragraph 3? What evidence could you use from different societies?	
6 Make notes for a brief conclusion that sums up the arguments and evidence you have presented. On balance, do they support or refute the view expressed in the question? You may think it impossible to decide, but you should be able to explain why.	

Chapter 3

The Role of Religion in Society: Contemporary Debates

By the end of this chapter, you should:

- have knowledge and understanding of a range of more recent sociological views on the role of religion in society;
- be able to assess the strengths and weaknesses of the different views;
- use your knowledge and understanding to write an essay on the role of religion in contemporary societies.

Sociological interest in the role of religion has not diminished since the days of the classical sociologists, and a number of other views on the importance and significance of religion (or its decline) have since been proposed. Beckford (1989) argues that the boundaries of the sociology of religion have been shaped by specific ideas about the development of industrial society, and that this has created considerable difficulties for contemporary sociologists of religion when analysing the place of religion in 'advanced' industrial societies.

NEO-MARXISM

Although the classical Marxist view is a largely deterministic view of the role of religion, other Marxist thinkers have allowed religion some independence or relative autonomy from the economic base. Neo-Marxist writers have examined and reinterpreted one of the central tenets of the classical Marxist view of religion, namely that the ideological role of religion is to underpin capitalism and support the status quo.

Gramsci (1971) used the concept of **hegemony** to show how the cultural institutions of society, including religion, come to shape people's perceptions of the social world. Religious beliefs can therefore foster a particular way of thinking about the organisation of society that can be exploited by powerful groups and used to their own ends. An example of this would be the belief held by many Christians that the world reflects God's divine plan, and it is not our place to question it. The inequalities in society can thus be explained as 'God's will', and people will have the position in society that God intended for them. However, if the ruling class had complete hegemony, then religions and religious ideas would always support the status quo. Gramsci acknowledged that few, if any, groups were able to achieve complete hegemonic control in society, therefore there was always the possibility that other ideas and other interpretations of social institutions were possible, leaving the way open for dominant ideas to be challenged. Gramsci believed that there was an important role for intellectuals, namely helping the working classes to see these different interpretations, and thus bring about social revolution. Poulantzas also believed that individuals within a social institution, such as a religious organisation, could come to interpret their role in a way not intended by those in power.

This leads to the interesting concept of liberation theology, initially found in the 1960s and 1970s in Latin America in response to the growth of military dictatorships. While associated primarily with Roman Catholic clergy, but also involving Protestant leaders, liberation theology is the name given to a movement in which priests, far from upholding the status quo, argue that it is their duty to see that the Church addresses the legitimate grievances of the poor and oppressed. Both popular movements and Christian groups joined together in their demand for social justice. The harsh military regimes found in Latin America led to extreme political repression and the suppression of dissent. The liberation theologists argued that there was a need to examine the relationship between faith and poverty, the gospel and social justice. Between 1959 and 1965, members of the Catholic left in Brazil published a series of texts on the need for a Christian ideal of history, linked to popular action and urging followers to adopt a personal engagement with the world. In this case, the role of religion is therefore seen as that of liberating people from poverty and oppression, rather than teaching them to accept their lot.

Otto Maduro (1982) claims that in modern societies, the role of religion is more complex than suggested by the classical Marxist approach. At different historical periods it is possible to see that religion can have some independence from the infrastructure and can be relatively autonomous, rather than serving to uphold the status quo. Maduro says that religion is not necessarily a functional, reproductive or conservative factor in society. In fact, it is often one of the main (and sometimes the only) available channels to bring about a social revolution. In his view, the clergy can act as Gramsci's 'proletarian intellectuals', providing guidance for the oppressed in their struggle against the dominant group in society.

Bryan Turner (1983, 1991) also claims that the ideological impact of religion is more subtle than that suggested by the classical Marxist approach, and challenges the assumption of the universal role of religion as a legitimating agent for the ruling classes. Rather than as a simple form of social control, Turner says that religious behaviour should be understood more in terms of a force for social cohesion among the dominant class. In feudal Britain, he argues, religious beliefs served to unify the ruling class rather than acting as a justification for the oppression of the peasantry. He points out that evidence suggests that, far from using religious ideas to explain and legitimate their subservient role, the peasants were largely indifferent to the views of the church. Similarly, the historical evidence suggests that rather than appealing to the industrial working class, Methodism was mainly lower middle class in origin and practice, with the workers remaining largely indifferent. This would support Gramsci's suggestion that it is rare for the ruling class to achieve complete hegemony in society.

With regard to modern capitalist societies, Turner points out that property has become depersonalised into unit trusts, pension funds etc. rather than being held by specific individuals or families. Religion, therefore, ceases to unify the whole of capitalist society, but it can be appropriated by different classes for different needs.

NEO-FUNCTIONALISM

These views take a broadly functionalist approach to the role of religion, but apply functionalist ideas on religion to the contemporary world. Functionalist views on religion began to be challenged by the social changes of the 1960s and 1970s, and this coincided with a period of fairly rapid decline in the popularity and influence of the Christian establishment and the equally rapid growth of sectarianism, especially in America, but also in the Third World. Explanations for this new religious 'diversity' made reference to the new social pressures that arose from the economic sphere, notably specialisation, bureaucratisation and professionalisation. So the taken-for-granted functionalist assumptions about the role of religion were questioned, but not rejected, because, according to Beckford, it was assumed that 'the diversification of experiences and consciousness was believed to reinforce the need for a clearer sense of the underlying social mechanisms for producing and reproducing order in society. The concepts of meaning and identity figured prominently in this theoretical enterprise' (Beckford, 1989, p. 11).

Bellah (1970), for example, believes that, despite the evidence pointing towards increasing secularisation, religion still performs essential social functions. In his view, a process of *individuation* has occurred, which means that people seek religious meanings on an individual basis, rather than through a collective entity such as a church. However, religion still provides important meanings for people's lives, and therefore continues to be of social importance.

Parsons, too, believed that religion has gained, rather than lost, social significance. As societies have evolved, religion has become 'split off' from other social institutions; in other words, it has become 'differentiated'. However, this loss of certain social functions (for example, education and welfare), far from causing religion to decline, has liberated it. Religion can now focus on its primary function, namely that of helping people to find meaning in life. As Parsons (1960) says, 'The cognitive meaning of existence, the meaning of happiness and suffering, of goodness and evil, are the central problems of religion' (p. 303). In the face of evil and suffering, religion helps people to recognise goodness and ultimate meanings.

O'Dea (1966) also believes that the function of religion is still to provide answers to fundamental questions such as the meaning of death and the reason for suffering. Religion can put such questions and individual experiences in context, enabling people to focus on the 'larger picture' rather than dwelling on their own individual misfortunes. According to O'Dea, human existence is characterised by three things – contingency, powerlessness and scarcity. 'Contingency' refers to the fact that nothing in this life is certain, and that we live with risks to our lives and well-being; 'powerlessness' refers to our inability to control such risks and uncertainties; and 'scarcity' reminds us that valued things, both material and psychological, are distributed unequally in society.

It is the role of religion to help people adjust to and cope with the uncertainties and deprivations of life. O'Dea accepts, however, that religion is not the only mechanism that can help people to cope, and that therefore religion is not necessarily an inevitable part of society, even though it is found in some form in virtually all societies. O'Dea acknowledges that the functionalist approach to religion is partial and incomplete, and has an undue emphasis on its role as a conservative force in society.

RELIGION AND MEANING:
A PHENOMENOLOGICAL APPROACH

Phenomenologists are interested in the ways in which we make sense of our world – the meanings that people attach to their actions. Meaning is arrived at through the use of concepts and categories of thought, and shared meanings link individuals to the wider social group and thus can be a source of social stability. Religion, then, can help to create order through a shared world view, including that of the place of humans in the cosmic universe and an understanding of what Aldridge (2000) calls 'the existential problems of life, joy, suffering and death' (p. 7). The phenomenological approach is particularly associated with the work of Berger and Luckmann.

> Religion is the human enterprise by which a sacred cosmos is established. By sacred is meant here a quality of mysterious and awesome power, other than man [sic] and yet related to him, which is believed to reside in certain objects of experience. (Berger, 1990, p. 25)

Religion can play an important part in our cultural identities as it affirms our place within a community. It also gives meaning to our life. For Berger and Luckmann, the sociology of religion is closely aligned to the sociology of knowledge. Although science has provided much knowledge of the world around us, it cannot answer questions of ultimate meaning, such as:

- Where have I come from?
- Why am I here?
- Where am I going?
- What is the purpose of life?

For Berger (1973) as with Durkheim, the world can be divided into the 'sacred' and the 'profane'. However, the sacred stands in opposition not only to the profane but to chaos. The opposite of chaos is 'nomos', which refers to a meaningful order. The nomos, which is a social product, provides what Berger refers to as 'a shield against terror'. We would experience this kind of terror if we believed that the world was without order and meaning. Religion gives the nomos a sacred character, whence it becomes the 'cosmos', sacred because it is seen as mysterious and extremely powerful. Religion also gives meaning to 'marginal situations and experiences', such as dreams, social upheaval, suffering, evil and death.

Luckmann also emphasises the importance of 'meaning' in religion. He believes that the trend towards secularisation reflects a decline in traditional religious forms and institutions, rather than in religion itself. For Luckmann, an important function of religion is that it helps us to acquire a sense of 'self', of knowing who we are, and where we fit in, a world view that endows everyday life with ultimate significance. In the past, this acquisition of the sense of self was gained through traditional religious beliefs and practices, but in the present it tends to be achieved through ideas such as self-realisation, self-expression and the importance of individual autonomy. Luckmann refers to this as 'invisible religion'.

Berger and Luckmann (1969) argue that religious belief contributes in greater or smaller part to a society's 'universe of meaning'. This universe of meaning is a repository of all the kinds of knowledge existing in any given society, so it might include ideas about Einsteinian physics as well as astrology. Individuals are socialised into the universe of meaning and it has to be legitimated as 'truth'. What part does religion play in this universe of meaning? According to Berger, it helps both to create and legitimate it: 'Viewed historically, most of man's [sic] worlds have been sacred worlds ... it can thus be said that religion has played a strategic part in the human enterprise of world-building' (Berger, 1990, p. 27).

Each universe of meaning has a 'plausibility structure', which supports what creates its meaningfulness. If this plausibility structure is challenged, then the universe of meaning might be destroyed. Religion helps to prevent challenge by asserting that its doctrines are truthful or even divinely inspired. Only when a society is conquered by another, might this be defeated. So our reality is always fragile, always precarious.

Support for the work of Berger and Luckmann comes from Robert N. Bellah, who argues that religion still plays an important part in the sense-making process. Individuals use religion to work out their own ultimate meaning. Although religion might have withdrawn from the public sphere, it remains central to the personal sphere of meaning. It is important to note that Bellah uses an inclusivist definition so that the term 'religion' can be stretched to cover many different types of belief systems.

However, the phenomenological view has been criticised on a number of counts. One view is that it is guilty of 'cognitive reductionism', and places too great an emphasis on subjective meanings of culture, a well as assuming that there is a common culture shared by all members of society. Also challenged is the assumption that religion is, in fact, a universal human need, when some people appear to live fulfilling lives without religious beliefs. A further criticism is that, in common with many functionalists, this approach neglects to examine the conflict that sometimes rages between and within religious faiths.

EXCHANGE THEORY

Also known as 'rational choice theory', this view of religion is particularly associated with the work of Stark and Bainbridge (1987). It starts from the premise that seeking to understand 'the meaning of life' and a desire for immortality is a universal human need. To meet this need, people will therefore adopt some form of supernatural belief system. In their view of the role and nature of religion, Stark and Bainbridge make great use of the concepts of 'rewards' and 'compensators'. 'Rewards' refer to those things that people desire. 'Compensators' are substitutes that people are prepared to accept when the rewards are scarce or even unattainable. Some rewards that people desire are so great or so difficult to achieve (such as being in a 'state of grace', receiving divine messages, understanding the meaning of life or achieving immortality) that only religion can provide suitable compensators. Religions are therefore 'systems of general compensators based on supernaturalist assumptions'.

The views of Stark and Bainbridge present a radical challenge to the secularisation thesis, as they believe that it is inevitable that people will continue to need supernatural belief systems in their search for immortality and the meaning of life. They claim that religious organisations which water down or abandon beliefs in the supernatural will therefore cease to provide suitable compensators for desired rewards, and will therefore inevitably decline. However, as they do so, their place will be taken by new organisations. The 'supply' of religion therefore remains fairly constant, as there is a stable demand for it. Another concept used in rational choice theory is that of 'resource mobilisation'. This refers to the energetic and successful efforts of 'religious suppliers' both to stimulate and to satisfy demand for their product. For example, some groups persuade believers of the need for particular types of meditation or exercise, and then sell the books, tapes and videos to help them practise these. Stark and Bainbridge also claim that the competitive religious environment of modern pluralist societies is actually more religious than Europe's so-called 'age of faith', which they claim was more of an 'age of apathy'. The modern era is the true age of faith, as people participate in religion freely and because they choose to do so.

FEMINIST PERSPECTIVES

There are, of course, several feminist perspectives, but they share a view of the world through what Abbott and Wallace have called 'the female prism' (1990). From feminist viewpoints, most modern religions are characterised as patriarchal institutions, that is, they serve to assert the power of males over females, as do other patriarchal institutions in society. This claim is made on the basis of examining religious beliefs and texts, and also looking at the roles permitted to women within religious organisations.

Many feminists take as their starting point the ancient religions, many of which celebrated what was seen as the mystical power of women, and in which there were female goddesses and priestesses. The feminist view is that the male-oriented religions, such as Islam, Judaism and Christianity, suppressed the older, female religions and relegated women to a subservient and inferior role. While the Roman Catholic Church has 'the cult of Mary', it is important to note that it is Mary, 'alone of all her sex', who is venerated, rather than all females. Mary is essentially different from all other women, as only she was chosen to be the mother of God through the immaculate conception and a virgin birth.

Many religious ceremonies are forbidden to women altogether, or women, if present, have to stand apart from men, emphasising their separate and inferior status. In most religions women are forbidden to hold priestly office and even where this is the case, such as following the ordination of women priests within the Church of England, it has not been achieved without bitter controversy and some adherents leaving the Church altogether in protest at the change. For feminists, then, one of the major roles of religion is to support patriarchy and the subordination and control of women in society.

Feminist sociologists also draw our attention to the connection between knowledge and power. Much of what we know about religious belief and practice comes to us from the writing of male clerics and male sociologists, and the claim is that women's role in religion has been marginalised and labelled as inferior to, and less important than, that of men. Alan Aldridge (2000) also points out how few religions or religious movements treat women and men equally. He argues that those who might be able to make such a claim include The Religious Society of Friends (Quakers), the Unitarians, the Baha'is and Christian Scientists.

Aldridge also draws attention to the fact that where challenges or conflicts arise over practices which act to place women in a lesser, subservient role to men, these practices will almost always be justified in terms of charismatic and/or traditional authority (to use Weberian concepts). This is largely because legal-rational arguments are rarely sufficient, as they are essentially secular in nature. Thus, the argument that men and women have a right to equal treatment would, in a religious dispute, be regarded as of lesser importance than the argument that the practices in question are justified and legitimated by the sacred texts.

Bruce (2000) argues that it is not simply misogyny that explains the problems that religious conservatives have with accepting and adapting to the changes in the role of women. Or at least, if we call it misogyny, then we must also acknowledge that it is a form of misogyny that has religious roots. He points out that all religions have at the heart of their social teachings a deep, even obsessive, interest in sexuality and the family. His argument is that, after centuries of explaining and defending particular patterns of gender relations, religions find it particularly hard to change their stance on this issue. Bruce finds the importance given to issues of gender in religious considerations unsurprising. He says that while, at least in most societies, the categories of race and class are shifting and ambiguous, and are of concern to only some, gender relations are important to everyone. He points out that, given that it is usually within the household that faith is passed from one generation to the next, it is easy to see why fundamentalists in particular are so opposed to changes in gender roles.

Gender is also important in the practice of religion by minority groups within a culture. The survival of their culture and religion relies on the continuity of the socialisation process, a process historically dependent on women. Women in such minority cultures are therefore typically subject to excessive (and occasionally brutal) subordination to group norms.

It is perhaps because of the generally unequal treatment meted out to women by established religions that many New Religious Movements (NRMs) appear to have a particular appeal to women. The evidence for this needs to be treated with some caution, as women tend to be over-represented compared to males in the membership of most religious groups. However, many NRMs and 'New Age' movements provide women with more powerful and liberating roles than the established religions, and their beliefs and practices offer and celebrate positive images of womanhood. Susan Palmer's exploration (1994) of the roles played by and open to women in seven NRMs shows how they offer women new interpretations of gender and sexuality. Equally, some movements encourage men to explore and become in tune with the more 'feminine' side of their nature.

Despite these exceptions, a common feminist view of at least the established religions is that they serve the interests of patriarchy by keeping women in inferior positions to men, and have a number of ways of justifying such differential treatment.

POSTMODERNISM

One of the features of postmodernity is the alleged end of 'metanarratives', or the collapse of belief in the power of the 'big ideas' of science, rationality and secularisation. The debate within sociology is whether, and to what degree, religions in the West have been significantly affected by postmodernity.

Perhaps surprisingly, there have been few sociological accounts of the links between postmodernity and religion. According to David Lyon (1996), 'In general, sociologists of religion have not exhibited much enthusiasm for postmodernity. Theorists of postmodernity often seem equally lukewarm about religion, an issue that does not figure prominently in their accounts.' Where religion is discussed within postmodernity, it tends to be in the context of a further example of the collapse of 'grand narratives' – overarching accounts of how society is structured and organised. However, one of the problems for those who argued that a feature of modernity would be increasing secularisation is that both religious beliefs and, in some cases, religious institutions, are not only failing to fade away, but are thriving. Those who claim, therefore, that we live in a postmodern society have to offer a social analysis which incorporates and explains the continued existence of forms of religiosity.

One sociologist who has explored what postmodernists have said about religion is James A. Beckford (2004). He looks in particular at the work of Bauman, Giddens and Beck. Bauman (1990) believes that postmodernity has three significant characteristics. These are:

- the displacement of wage labour as the central feature of identity and social existence;
- the emergence of consumer freedom as the driving force in society, with individuals being both driven and motivated by consumption;
- the capitalist system being increasingly dependent on consumption (what Baudrillard refers to as 'seduction') rather than production.

According to Bauman, therefore, the socio-cultural characteristics of post-modernity are the decline of certainty, objectivity and authority, together with the rise of 'neo-tribalism'. By this, Bauman means new ways of people 'belonging' to groups, based on often temporary shared interests rather than on the more traditional links based on kinship and neighbourhood. However, Bauman identifies an 'ethical paradox' in the postmodern condition. As society has become less repressed and regulated, so individuals have to take greater responsibility for their choices and actions. This happens, however, at a time when the old certainties and universal guidance associated with the modern period have been undermined or removed. Moral and ethical questions, then, fall to the individuals to resolve. It is in this 'ethical vacuum' that Bauman sees a role for religion, attributing 'the revival of religious and quasi-religious movements' to the 'increased attractiveness of the agencies claiming expertise in moral values' (1990).

Beckford, however, argues that, in offering this explanation, Bauman shows 'a weak understanding of the history of modern religion'. Beckford's claim is that such an understanding would show that religion has continued to remain important throughout history, including the modern period. The appeal to religious authority for guidance over moral issues is not a recent phenomenon, and not therefore a failure of modernity or a postmodern innovation. In Beckford's view, therefore, Bauman has failed to show a link between religion and postmodernity.

Beckford himself suggests that, while debates about postmodernity are varied and complicated, most postmodern ideas can be compressed into the following four points:

- a refusal to regard scientific and rational ideas as the only basis for worthwhile knowledge;
- a willingness to combine symbols from varied codes or frameworks of meaning;
- a celebration of spontaneity, fragmentation and playfulness;
- a willingness to abandon the search for overarching myths, narratives or frameworks of knowledge.

With regard to Giddens, Beckford draws our attention to the fact that, rather than talking about postmodernity, Giddens prefers the terms 'late modernity' or 'high modernity'. Like Bauman, Giddens identifies three characteristics which in his view typify high modernity and differentiate it from earlier phases of modernity. These are:

- the reorganisation of time and place;
- the 'disembedding' of institutions;
- reflexivity.

Giddens sees the reorganisation of time and place exemplified by the coordination of events taking place in different locations and/or at different times, such as global stock markets, the Women's World Day of Prayer and so on. By 'disembedding', Giddens is referring to the ways in which cultural practices and social relationships can be taken from their original context and combined with other practices and relationships at different times and in different places. Examples would be particular 'ethnic' dishes such as curries and pizzas becoming standard meals found all over the world, or elements of

Eastern medicine or philosophy such as yoga, acupuncture or meditation being incorporated into 'New Age' practices. 'Reflexivity' is found in the way in which we constantly adjust our ideas and behaviour as a result of newly acquired information. An example would be changes in childrearing practices or purchasing habits of food in the light of changing 'expert' information. This continuous process of adjustment, argues Giddens, leads to uncertainty and even instability.

It is Giddens' belief that, taken together, these three characteristics lead to problems of self-identity. The result is that entire aspects of our lives which prove resistant to the ideas of high modernity are 'sequestered', or put aside. This applies to issues which raise existential or strongly moral questions, such as madness, sexuality, criminality, incurable disease and death. Such issues, however, become disturbing because they challenge the view that life can be transformed by 'reflexivity'. Thus high modernity carries with it doubt and uncertainty, which favour a resurgence of religion. This is particularly likely at 'fateful moments' such as birth, marriage and death, because religion connects 'action' to moral frameworks and to fundamental questions about human existence. There is therefore pressure for what Giddens calls a 'remoralising of daily life'. Beckford points out that both Bauman and Giddens view religion in narrow terms of individual responses to moral issues and dilemmas, rather than as a societal force, such as Durkheim's 'conscience collective'.

Another sociologist associated with postmodern ideas is Ulrich Beck (1992). While Beck says very little about religion directly, Beckford argues that his insights support the view that there is a spiritual dimension to what Beck has termed the 'new culture of politics', found, for example, in alternatives to mainstream medicine, politics and technology. It is Beck's view that the processes of scientific and political modernisation that produced the industrial society in the 19th century are now 'dissolving' industrial society and producing a new modernity. This process is 'reflexive', in that it challenges faith in progress and also undermines many features of industrial society, such as the traditional nuclear family structure, the gendered division of labour, class-based conflict and paid employment as a central life feature. These changes result in new forms of society and culture which include 'risks' as well as a self-reflexive critical outlook replacing faith in science, economic growth and progress. It is important to note the way in which Beck uses the term 'risk'. In his usage, 'risk' does not refer to 'chance' or 'danger', but the systematically produced threats which accompany technological modernisation. Although to scientists these risks are side-effects, or the result of mistakes, Beck argues that they are inseparable from scientific and technological development and are potentially catastrophic for the whole of humanity. A growing number of people are now beginning to recognise these risks for what they are, and, as a result, what Beck refers to as a 'new type of community of the endangered' comes into being. This cuts across divides based on social class, gender, generation, ethnicity and nationality. This in turn leads to a (quasi-religious) 'solidarity of living things', a concept which resembles Durkheim's collective consciousness.

However, as Beckford points out, this new solidarity is based on fear. The need for religion, then, stems from a desire for what Beckford terms 'psychological security or moral assurance'. Beck's theoretical framework can thus be interpreted as an invitation or a challenge to explore religious or spiritual group responses to a risk society.

In his exploration of the links between religion and postmodernism, Beckford also looks at the ideas of Ernest Gellner. This is perhaps unusual, as Gellner is a critic of the very idea of postmodernity. For Gellner, postmodernism and postmodernity are simply a form of 'cultural fashion' which leads to 'the abandonment of any serious attempt to give a reasonably precise, documented and testable account of anything' (1992). In Gellner's memorable phrase, this all adds up to 'metatwaddle'. Nevertheless, Gellner does see a place for religion in contemporary society, and introduces the concept of 'constitutional religion'. This is developed from the UK model of constitutional monarchy, in which the symbols and rituals of 'real' monarchy have been retained, but where the actual running of society has been passed to others. With regard to religion, an example would be the adoption of the Christian hymn 'Abide with me' sung in the non-religious context of the Cup Final to produce a sense of shared tradition and solidarity among the spectators.

For Gellner, the importance of ritual is its contribution to social stability, in this case by maintaining what he sees as the 'fantasy or fiction' of past glories. Gellner's case for religion is thus similar to Durkheim's argument about the functional necessity of symbols of national identity. However, Beckford argues that in one striking respect Gellner's idea of 'constitutional religion' is a departure from Durkheim's views, and as such has a major flaw. While Gellner sees the new constitutional religion as providing social stability, its role in society is limited. When a society needs to deal with 'serious matters', such as when human lives or welfare are at stake, or when there is a need for the committal of major resources, then decisions should be made on the basis of 'rational knowledge'. Religion, then, is kept firmly away from matters of state.

However, Beckford points out that this distinction between 'symbolic meaning' and 'serious matters' ignores the fact that many of the world's most serious problems are *at the same time* disputes about symbolic meaning or

Table 3.1 The possible effects of postmodernity on religions

Feature	Evidence for:	Evidence against:
Combinations	Postmodern playfulness and pastiche are apparent in some New Age practices that combine different religious elements.	The number of people involved in such practices is very small.
Religious consumerism	People can choose a religion that suits their taste and lifestyle at the time. Some (mainly young) people in Western societies do partake of this very individualistic form of religion or spirituality.	People's choices are limited by what is on offer in 'the spiritual marketplace'. Given the marketing methods employed, religious consumerism is part of a long-established tradition of reaching out for converts.
Traditions	Some religious traditions are in decline, and there is evidence of a decline in support for some of the central beliefs of Christianity.	Very large numbers of Christians, Muslims and Jews remain strongly committed to traditional beliefs and practices. Some religious traditions have been 'reworked', either within religious traditions or by individuals.

identity and material power. As examples, Beckford suggests conflicts in the former USSR, Yugoslavia, Central Africa, Sudan and the Indian subcontinent.

Beckford also examines the evidence to see whether religions in the Western world have been significantly affected by postmodernity, pointing out that there are various patterns instead of a single one. He looks at the areas shown in Table 3.1.

In his article 'Religion and Postmodernity', Beckford (2004) also reminds us that the range of sociologists' responses to ideas about postmodernism extends from enthusiastic acceptance to outright rejection. For example, in his book *Jesus in Disneyland: Religion in Postmodern Times*, David Lyon (2000) states that 'secularisation as a metanarrative is dead'. He believes that the evidence shows a 're-enchantment of the world', demonstrating that postmodern conditions can enhance religion. At the other extreme, Steve Bruce (1996) does not consider that the term 'postmodern' is necessary, and argues that current trends in religion can be understood within the conventional concepts of the sociology of religion such as church, sect, cult and denomination.

Andrew Holden (2002) raises the interesting question of how, if postmodern ideas are flourishing, we can understand the growing appeal of religious millenarian groups such as Jehovah's Witnesses. At first glance there is indeed a contradiction. The 21st century appears to show a significant decline in religious participation in Western countries, and an acceptance of multiple lifestyle options, flexibility and choice, the constant questioning of knowledge, belief in the freedom and autonomy of the individual, the erosion of fixed boundaries and the increase of risk. How then are we to understand the appeal of a movement that demands unquestioning loyalty, and comes across as puritanical, authoritarian and conservative? Holden's argument is that one of the consequences of the acceptance of postmodern ideas is a continuous self-questioning, leading to widespread feelings of insecurity and confusion. For many people, modern Western lifestyles are characterised by hedonism (pleasure-seeking), a loss of community and shared meanings and a host of social evils such as drug abuse, alcoholism and sexual promiscuity. Critics see postmodernity as resulting in a loss of identity as a consequence of a lack of the old certainties. Holden thus argues that groups such as the Witnesses are flourishing not despite, but *because* of, the ambiguities of the postmodern world. He claims that: 'Joining the Watchtower community [i.e. Jehovah's Witnesses] enables Witness converts to reject those secular institutions that weaken identity: they seek refuge in a movement that offers certainty' (p. 30). Holden concludes his arguments by pointing out that the nature of life in Western societies today poses uncertainties for everyone. However, while most people get on with their life and deal with the uncertainties in various ways, those who embrace millenarian beliefs retreat from the uncertainties and ambiguities into their own 'safe' world. He suggests that the freedoms offered by the postmodern world are, paradoxically, exactly the freedoms that the Witnesses fear.

Beckford (2004) makes the important point that though there is evidence of increasing individualisation, hybridity and scepticism about universal truth, this is against a background of extensive continuity in religious belief and practice from generation to generation. He concludes that, if the term 'postmodern' has any value in the context of the sociology of religion, it is best understood as a way of highlighting the many and diverse tendencies in religion rather than as a particular form of religion.

CONCLUSION

We can see, then, that there are differing views on the role played by religion in modern societies. Sometimes these differences are based on differing views on the nature of society and how it is organised, sometimes they arise because of differing interpretations of the evidence, and sometimes they are a mixture of both. Looking at the world as a whole, however, few would be able to argue that religion plays only a minor role. To a greater or lesser extent, religious beliefs and practices, or the lack of them, exert an influence on many areas of life – family, education, politics, gender, health, relations with other societies and with people within one's own society and so on.

Important concepts

hegemony • liberation theology • individuation • differentiation • 'invisible' religion • rewards and compensators • postmodernity • constitutional religion

Summary points

- Both the neo-functionalists and the neo-Marxists have developed and built on the ideas developed by the classical sociologists, but both groups see religion as continuing to play an important role in society. Feminists focus on the role played by religion in supporting and promoting patriarchal ideas and structures in society. They view the traditional religions largely in terms of their patriarchal structures and beliefs, and suggest that one of the attractions of some New Religious Movements for women is the greater role they give to females and 'feminine' characteristics.
- While relatively little has been written about religion by the postmodernists, they seem to see it as a source of reassurance and moral guidance in societies increasingly characterised by the insecurities brought about by the loosening of community ties and the increase in individual freedom and choice, together with the threats posed by aspects of modern technology.
- On examining the evidence regarding the effects of postmodernity on traditional religions, Beckford concludes that the effects are relatively minor, and affect relatively small numbers of people.

Critical thinking

Points to consider

- Think of **two** reasons why a group might find it impossible to achieve complete hegemonic control in society.
- Taking examples from at least **two** different religions, think of evidence which might be put forward to support the feminist view that religious beliefs and institutions support patriarchy.
- Look again at Gellner's views on constitutional religion (p. 48) and think of two further examples where the symbols and/or rituals of 'real' religion are used in non-religious circumstances or contexts.

Activity

Giddens' three concepts of the reorganisation of time and place, the disembedding of institutions and relfexivity are quite complex, but are important to this discussion. Look again at the examples for each one given earlier in the chapter, and complete the table by writing down another example which could be used for each of them.

Concept	Example
Reorganisation of time and place	
Disembedding of institutions	
Reflexivity	

Essay guidance

The following is an example of a full-length essay question. The list of prompts will again help you to 'unpack' the question to enable you to see clearly what it is that you are being asked to do. The outline is intended to be a guide only – remember that there is never just one single 'right' way of answering a question. However, the outline will help you to become used to working out a logical and coherent way of structuring your response.

> Compare and contrast different sociological accounts of the functions of religion in contemporary societies

1 Note that you are asked to 'compare' *and* 'contrast' different (therefore obviously more than one) sociological accounts – in practice, this means that you should try to find points of similarity and difference between them.
2 Reference is made to 'functions' in the plural – therefore your answer should refer to more than one. If you are looking at different accounts, this will not be difficult. Remember that 'functions' of religion can apply both to societies and to individuals. Your answer could make clear whether each account you examine sees the functions applying to society as a whole, to individuals, or to both.
3 'Contemporary societies' (note the plural) can be treated in different ways, sometimes depending on the question and topic area. It is equally acceptable either to take at least two different societies, and examine each in reasonable detail, or to focus on the aspects that 'contemporary societies' have in common (but be careful to make it clear what kind of societies you mean, e.g. modern industrial societies) and make generalised points.
4 Obviously, how much information you have and are able to include will depend on the stage you have reached in the study of this topic. Don't be tempted to include material about which you are not sure – whoever would mark your essay would know the extent of your knowledge and thus what might be expected to be included.

Suggested outline

Each point below should cover at least one paragraph. Remember that in taking each different account, you will need to summarise and pick out the main points, or focus on just one writer, otherwise your essay will become far too unwieldy. If you are writing your essay under timed conditions, it would also be acceptable to miss out one perspective (perhaps the phenomenological approach, or exchange theory, or feminism), and simply make reference to the omitted ones at the end, showing that you are aware of them, but time and space prevents you from providing a detailed discussion. Point 6 below invites you to choose one approach to discuss at this point. Remember that no question is really inviting you to 'write all you know' about something, so the process of selection is an important one.

1 **Introduction**. Brief reference should be made to the fact that the classical sociologists were writing about religion mainly in the context of societies undergoing industrialisation, and that the huge changes since then have led more recent sociologists to reflect on the role of religion today.

2 **Neo-Marxists**. How have the ideas of Marx been interpreted (or reinterpreted) to fit the modern world?

3 **Neo-functionalism**. To what extent are Durkheim's ideas of religion promoting social solidarity still applicable?

4 **Phenomenological approach**. What aspects of religious beliefs can be argued to give 'meaning' to people to make sense of their life?

5 **Exchange theory**. What evidence is there that some people use religion as a 'compensator' in their life?

6 **Postmodernism**. You have a great deal of material to choose from here, so you will have to decide what seem to be the more significant points.

7 **Conclusion**. If you have been able to identify any strong points of similarity of difference, then this is the place to point them out. Perhaps your different approaches could be divided into two main groups, based on either similarities or differences between them. Always avoid a conclusion that just says something along the lines of 'So, as we can see, there are different sociological accounts of the functions of religion in contemporary societies.'

Chapter 4

Religious Organisations

By the end of this chapter you should:

- be able to examine the different classifications of religious organisations as they relate to each other and wider society;
- understand the appeal of different religious organisations;
- understand why some are more popular than others;
- be able to examine the changes which affect different organisations;
- have practised writing an essay on religious organisations.

INTRODUCTION

Sociologists frequently try to understand their subject matter by the use of classifications, and sociologists of religion are no exception to this. Max Weber and his colleague, Ernst Troeltsch, were the first sociologists to attempt a classification of religious organisations. They distinguished between churches and sects, and although other sociologists have further developed their framework, it is still relevant to religious organisations today. We must be aware, however, that many of the earlier classifications relate only to Christianity and are therefore difficult if not impossible to apply to the other world religions.

A question we might ask is why we need to distinguish between different religious organisations. There are some reasons that are very important to the sociological study of religion.

■   Religious organisations have different functions for society as well as a range of meanings for the individuals who belong to them.

■   They stand in different relationships to the state.

- They show how religious institutions have developed over time.
- They have different implications for the debate about secularisation.

The two major types of religious organisation examined by sociologists are the church and the sect. Although there are others which we will look at, these two are central to an understanding of the role of the religious organisation in society.

THE CHURCH

When we use the term 'church' we take it to mean not simply the actual building in which people attend religious services and worship, but also the beliefs, rituals, the community of believers and the way in which the organisation is structured.

Weber's definition of a church was of a large, well-established religious body, 'a sort of trust foundation for supernatural ends' which includes both the 'just and the unjust'. This is an interesting definition and worth unpacking. We normally associate a trust fund with some form of financial investment for the future, but here we have an investment for supernatural ends or, perhaps, heavenly rewards. In theory at least, a church is open to everyone whatever their background, history and character.

Characteristics of churches include the following:

- a formal organisational structure with a hierarchy of salaried officials;
- membership which is usually ascribed – that is, members are born into the church, rather than coming to it as converts;
- a close link between the church and affairs of state;
- a tendency to adjust to, and make compromises with, the values and institutions of the wider society.

THE SECT

In comparison to the church, the sect is a small, informal organisation which often attracts those individuals who are not particularly satisfied with what the church has to offer. Indeed, the early sects were set up as challengers to the established church, as schismatic or splinter movements protesting about and disagreeing with some doctrine(s) of the established faith.

Characteristics of sects include the following:

- they are often led by charismatic leaders who have gathered a committed group of followers;

- membership often involves a personal spiritual experience which admits the individual as a sect member;
- members often have to maintain a strict moral code;
- there is a separateness from wider society – sometimes a withdrawal from, or defiance of, the rest of the world.

THE DENOMINATION

A denomination is another type of religious organisation, and often develops from a sect that has grown in numbers. It is usually smaller than a church. It has managed to cope with the problem of succession (usually experienced by sects when the original leader dies) by becoming 'routinised', to use Weber's term. This means that it develops a more formal set of rules and regulations and a hierarchy of officials, and also becomes more tolerant of the wider society. It usually expects a lower level of commitment from its followers than a sect, and is tolerant of other faiths. An example of a Christian denomination is Methodism. 'Methodists' was originally a nickname applied to members of a revival movement in 18th-century Britain, and led mainly by the brothers John and Charles Wesley. Charles is principally famous for the huge number of hymns he wrote (more than 6000), while John was the organiser who turned a spontaneous movement into the structured body which became the origin of today's worldwide Methodist church. Although Wesley declared, 'I live and die a member of the Church of England', the strength and impact of the movement made a separate Methodist body almost inevitable. The Methodists grew to be a large, respectable and influential section of society which was particularly attractive, at least in the early days, to some working-class people, who often felt excluded from the churches. Many of John Wesley's sermons were delivered to large crowds in the open air, a practice known as 'field preaching'. In 1784, John Wesley made provision for the continuance of the Methodist organisation after his death by nominating 100 people as Members of a Conference, and laid down the method by which their successors were to be appointed.

THE CULT

The terms 'cult' and 'sect' are sometimes used interchangeably. However, there are differences between them. The cult is the least formally organised religious body. It focuses explicitly on personal experience and it is not always necessary for individuals to commit themselves actively to joining the cult. The cultists may simply accept the ideas, philosophies and theories of the cult leader and might even belong to other religious groups at the same time. Cults tend not to have a prior tie with an established religious organisation; they are often innovative and 'deviant' bodies.

An example of a cult is Rosicrucianism (the followers of the Rosy Cross). This body claims heritage from pre-Christian times and maintains that many of the great world leaders were among its members. There is no necessity to attend meetings, as an individual may receive the teachings by post.

Stark and Bainbridge (1985) identify three different types of cult:

- audience cults;
- client cults;
- cult movements.

Audience cults are the least formally organised. It may be that the cult audience does not in fact attend any cult gatherings, but merely consumes the doctrines via magazines, books, television etc. An example would be UFO believers who might attend conventions on space travel, but also may simply read the literature at home.

Client cults are usually service and therapy based. Cultists in these groups are more participatory, but their membership remains partial and it is possible to be involved with different cults at the same time. Examples of client cults are Spiritualism, Scientology and Transcendental Meditation.

Cult movements are religious organisations that demand much more commitment from their members. Such movements are the closest to the sect in that tension with the outside world is high and some cult movements demand complete submission from members. Examples of cults include the Children of God, and Heaven's Gate.

Table 4.1 should help you to see the main differences between the church, denomination and sect. Note that each type of religious organisation is described as an 'ideal type'.

The concepts of church, denomination, sect and cult are useful classificatory tools. However, we must treat them with caution for the following reasons:

- they refer mainly to Christian organisations;
- they are ideal types and, therefore, useful simply as devices against which we can measure reality;
- not all sects and cults are world-rejecting – some accept and even embrace the values of wider society.

Table 4.1 Characteristics of different religious organisations

Characteristic	Church	Denomination	Sect
Attitude towards wider society	Domination: wants worldwide control	Compromise: no attempt at domination	Rejection of values and way of life of wider society
Attitude of wider society towards the organisation	Fashionable: accepted and often represented at state ceremonies such as Royal weddings and national memorial days	Fashionable or neglected	Ostracised and often seen as a threat
Attitude towards other religious groups	Intolerant – wants complete sovereignty (though the ecumenical movement is bringing some churches and denominations closer together)	Tolerant – accepts coexistence with other faiths	Intolerant – only one path to salvation
Attitude towards members	Concentration on global domination not individuals	Ideological influence	Ideological and social influence over members – sometimes total
Type of membership	Obligatory (often ascribed), therefore large	Voluntary, but also often ascribed	Voluntary – usually in adulthood
Basis of membership	No membership requirements other than ritualistic ones (though the medieval Christian Church required 'tithing')	Loose formal membership requirements	Experiential – as a deeply felt personal experience
Social background of members	All-inclusive, but leaders are wealthy and powerful	Mainly middle class	Typically deprived, but exceptions like cults of success
Scope	Inter/national	Inter/national	Local
Internal organisation	Bureaucratic	Bureaucratic	Often charismatic – often problem over succession

SECT, CULT OR NEW RELIGIOUS MOVEMENT?

It is important to note that the terms we use for religious organisations other than church or denomination can often be seen as interchangeable. Certainly, many sociologists treat them as such. There is a further problem of what is considered to be 'new' for these movements, as Wilson (1992) explains:

New movements have been a recurrent phenomenon in the context of Christian cultures in the West. Most of them – ridiculed, persecuted or suppressed – were destined, in a relatively short time to disappear: some, however, persisted until they ceased to be 'new'. Thus in England, the early divisions of Protestantism – the Congregationalists, Presbyterians and Baptists, the new movements of their day – gradually came to be known as 'historical dissenters'. In Japan, some of what are today referred to as 'new religions' began as long ago as the mid-nineteenth century. The paradox of the idea of 'old new religions' makes abundantly apparent the difficulty of using chronology as the point of departure for a sociology of religious movements.

Wilson attempts a categorisation of the typical characteristics of what he refers to as New Religious Movements (NRMs). He sees the following features as significant:

- *Salvation*: the newness of these movements relies on a 'surer, shorter, swifter or clearer way to salvation'.
- *Elitism and scepticism*: these are characteristics of the old, established faiths. They have tended to encourage spiritual hierarchies whereby priests become remote from the lay public; they may also display a certain scepticism about the actual teachings of the faith, even challenging long-held beliefs. (This aspect has also been shown within the Anglican church, with some clergy discussing the actual existence of Hell, or the reality of the Virgin Birth.)
- *Mobility and therapy*: NRMs have challenged the distinction between priesthood and laity and have offered a more egalitarian faith. They frequently use therapies borrowed from other faiths for mental and physical distress and offer a syncretism or mixture of parts of different belief systems. Examples of this mixing of beliefs can be seen in Christian Science, Krishna Consciousness and Scientology.
- *From scarcity to abundance*: these movements clearly offer more opportunity for salvation to their followers and more immediacy to meet the changing needs of a rapidly changing society.
- *Fervour, discipline and rational organisation*: rather than mere ritualistic or regulated religious observance, members of these movements must show total allegiance to the organisation. However, the organisation needs to retain the initial religious enthusiasm to sustain membership as there is always the danger that what seems spontaneous and emotional will quickly become routine and mundane. Enthusiasm is often maintained by discipline and organisation.

In order to explain the differences between the many varieties of NRMs, we can also use Wilson's earlier (1985) classificatory work on sects that still remains very useful. He based his classification on the deviant responses of sects to the rest of society and the various paths to salvation offered to their members. He outlined seven different kinds of response:

- **Conversionist (Evangelical)**   Salvation is to be gained through a 'heart-experience' or rebirth. This conversion is the result of a visitation from God and hence the individual is saved. These sects are usually fundamentalist, emphasising guilt and redemption.
- **Revolutionist (Adventists)**   These use biblical prophecy to show the path to salvation. They emphasise the coming of another world and/or the Saviour. Only members of this faith will be saved after some millenarian Armageddon.
- **Introversionist**   These withdraw from secular society into a life of inner holiness. Often members live in closed communities isolated both socially and geographically from the rest of society.
- **Reformist**   These have some elements in common with Introversionist and utopian sects. They wish to change the world, but in a piecemeal fashion rather than by revolution. They do not necessarily live in religious communities.
- **Utopian**   These are similar to Introversionists in that they withdraw from society, but not to reject it, rather to create a better community as a model for living.
- **Manipulationist (Cults of Success)**   These sects have turned full circle and instead of rejecting the world, they accommodate it and wish to find success within it. What the sect provides is an alternative path to finding that success. Members are given access to special, arcane knowledge which allows them to progress without having to experience the usual avenues of education and work which make for worldly success. Mainly appealing to middle-class believers, this type of sect is individualistic, impersonal, non-community based and syncretistic (the body of knowledge is an accumulation of different kinds of knowledge, especially Eastern mysticism).
- **Thaumaturgical**   Close to the manipulationist sects, these seek spiritual guidance for success in this world. They often hold beliefs in the existence and power of the supernatural or occult.

Wilson produced the typology below, based on the central characteristics of the sect, particularly with regard to the relationship between the sect and its membership.

1 *Voluntariness*: In the beginning membership was voluntary, although in many cases children of sect members are born into membership.
2 *Exclusivity*: Based on membership being exclusive. Some sects require considerable individual allegiance and personal commitment, often demonstrated by the donation of material wealth.
3 *Merit*: Some sects want evidence of commitment or spiritual experience in order for membership to be allowed to continue. Failure might mean expulsion, especially in the more strict sects. Commitment is more than just attendance at services.
4 *Self-identification*: This is particularly important for sectarian membership as an individual is a sect member before anything else. Thus the sect member is exhorted to live according to the rules of the sect and their individual conscience. Some sects restrict contact with non-members, even relatives.
5 *Elite status*: This means being one of the Elect or one of the Chosen. This gives enhanced personal status to individuals.
6 *Legitimation*: There are sets of ideological values which serve to legitimate and so maintain the life of the sect for its followers.

Wallis (1984) has provided one of the most frequently used typologies of New Religious Movements. He based the categories on the relationship between the sect and wider society. For him the 1960s and 1970s were particularly significant decades for the introduction of these 'new' movements. They appeared most frequently in the United States, but also appeared in Western Europe. Although some were new variants of more traditional faiths, especially of Eastern philosophies, the new movements were more vital, zealous and demanding than these; and also appeared in areas where the earlier religious traditions had no prior base. Examples of these new religious movements include the following:

■ **The Jesus People** was the name of a religious movement that expanded in the 1960s especially in America. It was an evangelical Christian movement offering elements of fundamentalism, a highly moral lifestyle (no premarital sex, no drugs, alcohol or gambling) and with an emphasis on conversion.
■ **ISKCON** (or the International Society for Krishna Consciousness), whose members were better known as followers of Hare Krishna, was a movement that incorporated Eastern traditions. It was essentially a branch of Hinduism which attracted white Westerners who followed an ascetic regime of early rising, chanting and vegetarianism.

■ **Transcendental meditation** (or TM) was a movement that offered the opportunity to enhance one's success in this life. Adherents were attracted to the movement by evidence that TM could reduce tension and stress in individuals, and the belief that as more and more joined the movement, society-wide results would ensue, such as a declining crime rate and a lessening of aggression. Individuals bought a mantra (a personal word which they were given to use for meditation) and were taught meditation exercises.

Wallis examined several of these new religious movements and classified them on the basis of their relationship with the rest of society. He produced a threefold typology:

1 *World-rejecting*
   These groups profoundly reject the world around them, seeing it as corrupt and evil. They look forward to a new world or rebirth and until that time feel the need to separate themselves from the world. Some groups demand more of their adherents than others, some even expecting the followers to give up all previous relationships with families and friends to devote themselves to the new movement. Some of these movements are millenarian. For example, the Muslim Black Power Movement predicted that in the year AD 2000 the non-Muslim world would be destroyed.

   Other examples of world-rejecting movements are the Unification Church or Moonies, the Branch Davidians and the People's Temple. If we incorporated Wilson's classification into Wallis's typology, then the sects which are world-rejecting would be the revolutionist, introversionist and utopian ones.

2 *World-affirming*
   In contrast, these movements accept the goals and values of the world, but provide members with new means of achieving worldly or personal success. They are less like most religious movements in that members are unlikely to attend particular gatherings. There is often no theology or ritual as such. Followers carry on their normal lives and, when necessary, attend meetings at weekends.

   Examples include the TM movement as stated above; and the Sunyasin or followers of (the late) Bhagwan Shree Rajneesh. This was a movement based on individual liberation, mainly psychological and sexual. Members were typically middle class and it was unnecessary to give up a secular life to belong to the group. The movement dissolved in the early 1990s when the Bhagwan died leaving a considerable tax debt in the USA. World-affirming movements have generally evoked less severe criticism from the rest of society than world-rejecting ones because of their acceptance of mainstream norms and values, but their survival depends upon many factors, especially economic. Many of their 'therapies' are expensive. Wilson's manipulationist sects would fit here.

3   *World-accommodating*

This type of movement is usually an offshoot of an established church or denomination. Typically, such groups neither reject nor affirm the world, but seek to restore to traditional religion the spiritual purity that they believe the churches have failed to maintain. Believers will normally continue their everyday lives, as their new religious faith and practice equip them for an increasingly degenerating world.

Examples of such groups include the Neo-Pentecostalists and the New Charismatics. Already committed Christians, members feel the need for a more personal spiritual experience from their religion. Neo-Pentecostalism offers 'gifts of the spirit' which include glossolalia (the ability to speak in tongues) and prophecy. These are mainly evangelical sects, but thaumaturgical sects would also fit here.

POPULARITY OF SECTS AND CULTS

We need to address the question of why it is that sects have appealed to so many people. Weber argued that the appeal of sects was originally and principally to the lower classes. The sect offered a new 'theodicy of disprivilege' to those who were poor, marginalised and oppressed. This theodicy of disprivilege gave them an understanding that, despite (or even because of) their oppressed position, they were chosen to be saved for eternal life and were being offered a path to salvation. Perhaps we could say that, even today, one of the major appeals of the sect is the answer to the question, 'What must I do to be saved?' A follower of Weber's work, Niebuhr, applied this idea of disprivilege to religion and maintained that sects appealed to the economically deprived.

The marginalised groups in Western societies include those in poverty, some ethnic minorities, and those who are unable to enjoy the material successes of the rest of society. They often turn to small religious movements in order to help them make sense of their disprivileged position, but sometimes they may use religion as part of a political and revolutionary movement against oppression. For example, the Black Power Movement in the USA in the 1960s sought salvation through a release from white oppression.

However, there are other forms of deprivation that may be linked to a religious solution. Glock and Stark (1965) referred to forms of deprivation such as ethical, organismic, social and moral. This classification allows us to understand the appeal of the manipulative sects, or the 'cults of success', to middle-class groups. This is hardly evidence of social marginality, but rather a need for a greater ethical meaning in life or a need for a greater sense of communality, as shown by those sects that withdraw from society into small, self-maintaining communities.

The emergence of various sects in the late 19th century, especially, but not exclusively, in the United States, can be seen as a response to the anomic conditions brought about by rapid industrialisation and immigration. However, during the 1960s, cults and sects tended to develop as splinter movements from the major religions. We shall see later the emergence of New Age movements linked to paganism and the occult, as well as some environmental and ecological movements which emerged in the 1990s.

Bruce (1985) has examined the role of these new religious movements in society. He sees four key roles:

- *Integrative*: They enable alienated young people to belong to the dominant social institutions, possibly by bringing them out of the drug culture or off the streets. This has been especially true of the Jesus Army, whose members trawl cities for homeless young people who are invited to join the movement.
- *Disintegrative*: They may help to break down the norms of existing societies and promote social change. Some of the new movements such as the Moonies and Scientology have been perceived as 'dangerous' by governments, and some young people have been abducted from them.
- *Socio-cultural transformation*. Some sociologists viewed with optimism the hippie culture of the 1960s with its 'make love, not war' slogan. It was assumed that this new set of values would spread to the rest of society and transform it. This type of culture has been continued with those New Age faiths promoting environmental issues.
- *Irrelevance*: Other sociologists are more pessimistic and refer to cults and sects as highly marginal movements with no major effect or influence on the rest of society. This view has been expressed by several sociologists of religion, who argue that the most significant movement is secularisation and that the growth of sects is evidence that the secularisation process is well under way.

We do not seem to be able to make safe generalisations about the emergence and appeal of sectarianism. What seems necessary in examining new religious movements is to:

- locate them historically;
- identify their relationship to the wider society;
- explain their appeal to members;
- show how they help to make sense of some of the complexities of modern life.

SECTS AND PUBLIC CONCERN

Some sects and cults have given rise to considerable public concern. In July 2000, a 16-year-old boy was made a ward of court after supposedly being kidnapped in Surrey by a group belonging to the Jesus Christians. Concern that he had been 'brainwashed' by the group was expressed by the media. In the 1970s there was considerable press interest in the possible 'brainwashing' of young people enticed into the Moonies or the Church of Scientology. There were horror stories of parents paying large fees to get their children abducted from these groups and then 'deprogrammed' to allow them to live back in society. There is no doubt that the media help to sensationalise the representation of these groups, but nevertheless there are causes for concern.

The original idea of deprogramming young people who had been attracted to sects against their relatives' wishes was advanced by an American 'born-again' Christian, Ted Patrick. In the late 1960s, he became interested in the appeal of the Children of God to young Californians, believing that they must have been 'brainwashed' before joining the sect. He therefore developed an antidote to the brainwashing process – a deprogramming method. He started a crusade, which turned into a moral panic, against specific sects and cults, and this gave rise to the first anti-cult movement, Freecog.

However, other theorists are more sceptical that mind control has ever been practised by these sects. This was partly the objective of Eileen Barker's research into the Moonies in 1984. She wanted to discover the recruitment processes of the movement in encouraging young people into the organisation.

The Moonies – an update

On a Saturday in November 1997, 30,000 couples were married in a mass wedding ceremony in Washington, DC, in front of the Revd Sun Myung Moon, the Korean founder of the Unification Church, otherwise known as the Moonies. Many of the new couples had not met before the ceremony, but had been matched up from their photographs and by the use of 'deep spiritual insight'. Although his figures must be viewed with a certain scepticism, Sun

Myung Moon maintained that the November blessing in Washington involved over three and a half million people.

The success of the Moonies as a sect seems extraordinary. It is a Christian movement based around the charismatic leadership of Moon himself and espouses family values – hence the mega-wedding ceremonies he arranges. Moon desires to unite the world's Christians under his leadership. He claims that, with his wife and 13 children, his is the 'True Family' which acts as an example to all his followers. Despite claims to a much larger membership, it is estimated that worldwide membership of the group is around 250,000. It is strongest in the USA, Korea and Japan. Moon's latest mission is said to be Uruguay. He is involved in a building project that includes a hotel/conference centre, a bank and a New Hope Farm that so far has cost $20 million. Moon is an extremely wealthy businessman, whose assets were valued in 2005 as worth $10 billion, though he was convicted of tax evasion in 1982. Among other things, he owns the *Washington Post*, a newspaper committed to supporting the Republican Party, a small-arms factory in New York and also the UPI wire service. In September 2005, aged 85, he embarked on a 120-city world speaking tour, delivering the same speech each time. The speech was entitled 'God's Ideal Family – the Model for World Peace'. There has been speculation regarding what would become of the movement when Moon was no longer able to lead, as many sects fail to survive the death or departure of their charismatic leader. However, in April 2008, Moon handed over the control of the movement to the youngest of his seven sons, Hyung Jin Moon. The new leader is a Harvard-educated philosophy and theology graduate, regarded as the most spiritual of Moon's sons. It now falls to him to secure the important donations from members that enable the movement to continue.

SECTS AND SUICIDE

There has been a great deal of public concern about sect membership and suicides of members. A particularly tragic case was that of the Restoration of the Ten Commandments in Uganda, where more than 900 bodies were discovered in April 2000. Although this was initially seen as mass suicide, later forensic evidence pointed to mass murder.

Heaven's Gate

In March 1997, 39 people took part in a mass suicide having left a farewell video for posterity. They were all followers of Marshall Applewhite, a long-term cultist who had set up several different cults in America from the 1970s onwards. His latest, Heaven's Gate, was a UFO cult – members believed that their suicide was the way of allowing them entry through the gate. The group varied in age and class, but they were linked by a belief that the suffering they had endured in this life was to be replaced by peace in the next world. It is not clear whether Applewhite, who died with them, had informed them that he had a terminal heart disease, and, if he had, whether the news would have had any effect on the outcome.

One of the first explanations of the Heaven's Gate incident came from clinical psychologists who had assumed that the individuals concerned were all young men (because the members were dressed identically in black trousers and new black Nikes and had cropped hair). Their explanations were, therefore, based on the appeal of cults to adolescents, especially to those young people who felt rootless and rejected, with less well-balanced personalities and who were, therefore, more malleable to a strong leader's will. However, it soon became clear that there was a wide age range in the membership, from 26 to 72, with the majority being middle-aged. In addition, 21 of those who died were women.

Mass suicides of members of religious groups like that of Heaven's Gate are not as rare as we might think. In 1978 around 900 members of Jim Jones's People's Temple died after taking a lethal dose of cyanide and fruit juice. There was also evidence that there had been a certain amount of unwilling participation, as some of them had been shot.

The Branch Davidians was a breakaway group from the Seventh Day Adventists. In 1993 at Waco, Texas, David Koresh, the group's charismatic leader, and 86 of his followers held out in a siege against the FBI which lasted 51 days until they died in the fire following a massive explosion, allegedly of their munitions dump. A bereaved father of one of the followers of David Koresh said that death had been part of their belief system. 'They spoke about the end of the world. It was part of their teaching. They were told that they would come back, so they would not fear death.'

The Order of the Solar Temple has also claimed 74 victims in three separate suicide events, between October 1994 and March 1997. Again there seems to be evidence of assisted suicide, as bodies showed signs of having been shot, asphyxiated and poisoned.

These sects are examples of Wilson's Introversionist type. Their leaders were all able to exert such influence over the members that they persuaded them to engage in mass suicides. Another example of a group (usually referred to as a cult) that held enormous sway over its members is the Aum Shinrikyo (Supreme Truth) of Japan.

This group received worldwide attention in the 1990s. It was an apocalyptic movement whose prime concept was Armageddon, which would rid the world of evil in a 'catastrophic discharge' evidenced by wars and extreme natural disasters. The cult leader was the charismatic partially-blind Shoko Asahara, who persuaded his followers that he was both Christ and Lord Buddha, and that belonging to the group would give members supernatural powers. At its peak, the cult claimed 10,000 members in Japan and 30,000 in Russia. Members were subjected to bizarre initiations, starvation and forcible doping with LSD. Many people whom members of the cult believed were their enemies were tortured and murdered. The cult was, however, extremely wealthy, raising money from tithes and from a variety of commercial enterprises.

The group had a siege mentality, believing that outside groups were intent on destroying it. Asahara convinced members that if they were to survive the predicted apocalypse, they needed to arm. Using the talents of some brilliant young scientists who had joined the movement, Asahara built up a terrifying arsenal of biochemical weapons, including nerve agents and killer diseases such as anthrax. In March 1995, in an attempt to halt a police investigation into the cult, some members released the nerve agent sarin into five different locations in the Tokyo subway, killing 12 people and injuring over 5000, some seriously.

In February 2004 Asahara was sentenced to death for his role in the various crimes. The cult, which renamed itself Aleph in 2000, now has few members. In March 2008 a court officially ruled the group bankrupt, after ordering the repayment of 1.5 billion yen to be distributed among the victims of its crimes.

NEW SOCIAL MOVEMENTS

Underlying most sociological interest in religious organisations is a theory about social movements. Niebuhr (1929) maintained that the sect was an unstable form of religious organisation that over time was likely either to disappear or be transformed into a church. However, the church is a largely impersonal organisation that often fails to meet the needs of its members, hence discontent sometimes leads to a schism or separation which promotes the growth of a new sect.

This brings us into the realm of social movements and religious movements. If we see a religious organisation as comprising a relatively stable set of roles, norms, values and activities associated with the performance of specific functions, then we can assume it adapts well to social change. However, the social movement seeks either to cause or to prevent change. 'Religious movements are social movements that wish to cause or prevent change in a system of beliefs, values, symbols, and practices' (Stark and Bainbridge, 1985, p. 23).

According to Hannigan (1993) the origin of the New Social Movement (NSM) can be traced back to the German and French students' and workers' movements of the 1960s, and their subsequent impact on social observers. Until the 1960s it was supposed that it was necessary for a social movement to have mass working-class support. However, the new protest groups went beyond traditional class-based issues to a new range of social, cultural and quality-of-life issues.

Since the 1960s New Social Movements have generated considerable interest among sociologists of religion. Recently, new movements have emerged in response to a new set of challenges to life in modern societies that are faced with diminishing natural resources and new social issues. So what are New Social Movements?

Firstly, according to Hallsworth (1994), they constitute a wide and diverse spectrum of non-institutional socio-political movements which emerged, or rather, re-emerged in the 1960s and 1970s. Presenting new challenges to the established cultural, economic and political orders of advanced capitalist societies, among them are the revived (Second Wave) Feminist movement, Black Power, CND, Greenpeace, Gay Rights–Outrage and Queer Nation. These are socio-political movements, but Hallsworth also places New Religious Movements within the category of New Social Movements. These include the Moonies, Hare Krishna, and fundamentalist groups.

Characteristics

New Social Movements can be divided into two discrete groups – those which are based around a specific social issue and those which focus upon specific values. Those which are *issue-based* can be further subdivided in two:

1 Those which defend the natural and social environment against threat. These have politicised a wide range of issues, including the protection of rain forests and other animal habitats, nuclear power and global warming. New Age Travellers are a group who reject industrialisation in favour of an alternative lifestyle.

2 Those which have been organised for the purpose of 'extending the provision of social rights to constituencies in society where the state is held either to deny, limit or repress them' (Hallsworth, 1994, p. 8). These groups have three distinct objectives:
   i   to expose the institutional basis of discrimination;
   ii to advance the social position of marginalised groups;
   iii to destroy the underlying structures which create the basis for such marginalisation.

The second category consists of groups organised around *value issues*. They usually propose an alternative set of values challenging the dominant cultural order, which is perceived as racist, patriarchal, materialist and technocratic. New values include active participation, personal development, collective responsibility – in fact, what we might call 'post-materialist values'. Some critics, however, see these groups as hedonistic, irresponsible, subversive and repressive, as well as being too 'politically correct'.

Organisational structure of NSMs

NSMs are opposed to hierarchy and bureaucracy. Instead they have low levels of official hierarchy, full membership participation, and many are small scale and fragmentary. Some movements may contain a whole range of completely autonomous bodies within them; an example of this kind of movement would be the feminist movement.

Mode of political action

The types of political activism undertaken by these groups lies along a continuum of legality, ranging from lobbying, leafleting and demonstrations, to direct action such as tree protesters and the freeing of test animals from laboratories, and through to the extremes of consumer terrorism.

Social basis of support

While membership of NSMs is open, in practice members are usually drawn from a relatively small sector of society. The typical characteristics of membership are:

- age – youthful, usually 16–30 year olds;
- social class – the new service class (i.e. teachers, social workers and other similar professionals);
- marginality – over-representation of students and the unemployed, and sometimes including those who have retired from the labour market.

NSMs AND THE SOCIOLOGY OF RELIGION

Until recently, sociologists of religion have been reluctant to adopt New Social Movement theory into the sociology of religion. John Hannigan (1993) sees several reasons for this:

- In the 1970s and 1980s, sociologists of religion tended to develop their own paradigms for the emergence of New Religious Movements; the sociology of religion has traditionally been cut off from European left-wing social thought, having been founded within a functionalist framework inherited from social anthropology.

■ European left-wing theorists themselves have been opposed to the incorporation of religion into the study of social change. From a Marxist viewpoint, religion has been perceived as a conservative social force, and as part of the ideological state apparatus.

Recently, however, barriers between the two traditions have been coming down. NSM theorists have been paying more attention to the cultural and spiritual dimensions of beliefs and actions. Klaus Eder (1990) claimed that 'environmentalism as a belief system can transform religious traditions and become the basis for a new religious underpinning of modern societies'. Eder went as far as saying that modern environmentalism in green politics is possibly replacing socialism as the 'first genuinely modern form of religion'. This is an important point to consider when examining the debate about secularisation (see Chapter 6).

NEW AGE MOVEMENTS (NAMs)

During the 1980s and 1990s there was an emergence or, in some cases a re-emergence, of what may loosely be termed New Age groups. The term 'New Age' encompasses a wide range of groups with diverse beliefs and practices. Bruce (1995b) refers to such groups as characterised by 'eclecticism,' which means that they bring different styles and beliefs together. The beliefs and practices of NAMs run from alchemy and astrology through to visualisation and Zen Buddhism.

Bloom (1991) suggests that they can be grouped into the following types:

■ New Science/New Paradigm;
■ New Ecology;
■ New Psychology/New Spirituality.

(There is a further discussion of New Age Movements in the chapter on Secularisation, Chapter 6.)

New Science/New Paradigm

One of the major features of New Age faiths is the scepticism shown to science and rationality. This is demonstrated by the reluctance to look for testable hypotheses. As Bruce (1995b) argues, many New Agers will accept the testimony of a single individual who professes to be 'channelling' the thoughts of 'spirit masters', rather than looking for scientific evidence. There is also a tendency to accept traditional wisdom rather than contemporary rationality: 'Tradition is also a major legitimator of New Age ideas and therapies. By reasoning backwards from the observation that modern societies have many defects, New Agers conclude that pre-modern cultures must be morally and ethically superior. Tibetans, Eskimos, Native Americans, and Aborigines are then invested not only with superior social mores but also with great insight into the workings of the material world' (Bruce, 1995b, p. 107).

New Ecology

Many New Agers are environmentalists. They are supportive of green politics, but usually only in so far as these can be linked to personal enhancement. An example of an environmentally based group is the Findhorn Community in Scotland. This was set up as a utopian community led by Eileen Caddy and Dorothy McLean, who believed that they were in conversation with plant spirits that guided them to agricultural success. So New Agers are critical of environmental pollution and, more recently, of genetically modified (GM) agriculture. Many also hold a belief that the planet is a living organism, which James Lovelock has named Gaia, after the Greek Goddess of Earth.

New Psychology/New Spirituality

Many of the New Age Movements celebrate the human potential. There is widespread belief in reincarnation, with the emphasis on how this improves the self. Individuals do not need the traditional God figure and hence the traditional submission that goes hand in hand with it. Many believe also that spirit guides can be invoked to provide help with the everyday problems besetting the individual in the modern world.

Who are the New Agers?

What sort of individuals are attracted by the beliefs of the NAMs? Weber used the term 'theodicy of disprivilege' in relation to early sectarians, but it is unlikely that social deprivation would be a defining characteristic of the New Agers. Bruce sees them as affluent and cosmopolitan, although no longer living in major cities but having retreated to areas such as the Lake District or rural Wales. There seem to be few working-class New Agers. Rather they are middle-class individuals whose material needs have been met: 'Unmarried mothers raising children on welfare tend to be too concerned with finding food, heat and light to be overly troubled by their inner lights, and when they do look for release from their troubles they prefer the bright outer lights of bars and discotheques' (Bruce, 1995b, p. 114).

So New Agers tend to be middle class, university educated and working in the expressive professions such as social work, teaching, counselling, acting or writing. There are also more women than men although there are gender dimensions to the types of New Age faiths. Those with an emphasis on parapsychology and the more esoteric knowledge attract men, while the more spiritual, healing faiths attract more women.

CONCLUSION

Sociologists have grappled with the issue of identifying the particular characteristics of religious organisations to enable them to put them into a specific category. While this may make the study of religion and religious organisations more manageable, it is important to remember that the classifications arrived at will be ideal types, and it may be difficult to fit some organisations into the typology. Recent interest has centred on new religious and social movements, on the social characteristics of their members, and on the reasons for the appeal to these members. It is important that a close and thorough examination of the aims, practices and membership of such new movements is carried out, because their emergence and growth has important implications for the debate about the nature and extent of secularisation in contemporary societies.

Important concept

church ● sect ● denomination ● cult ● charismatic ● New religious movements ● theodicy of disprivilege ● anomie ● alienation ● new social movements ● New Age movements

---

Summary points

● It is important to distinguish between different types of religious organisation, particularly church, denomination, cult and sect, in terms of their organisational structure, their membership and their relationship to the wider society. However, the distinctions are not always easy to make, and it should be remembered that at least the early analyses took a Christian framework.

- Some more recent religious groups can be placed under the heading of New Religious Movements, and sociologists have been interested in exploring the reasons for their popularity. Some NRMs have been the source of public concern regarding the degree to which their members may be 'brainwashed' into becoming and remaining members of the group. Sociologists are also interested in whether or not membership of NRMs acts as a counter-balance to increasing secularisation.
- New Social Movements is the name given to relatively recent socio-political groups. These usually seek either to cause or prevent social change, and may have a focus on either specific issues or specific values. The study of NSMs is now more frequently being incorporated into the sociology of religion.
- New Age Movements have also been studied in terms of their impact or otherwise on the secularisation of society. The social composition of NAMs has a bias towards middle-class, older females.

Critical thinking

Points to consider

(E)

- Look again at the table showing the characteristics of religious organisations (p. 58). Take examples of a church, a denomination and a sect and consider the extent to which each of your examples meets the characteristics given in the table. If there are differences, consider the possible reasons for these.

(A)

- It is always useful to be able to include relevant examples to illustrate points made in essays. Take an example of a New Religious Movement, a New Social Movement and a New Age Movement. Note some of the main characteristics of the group, then reread the relevant sections of the text to see whether and to what extent the classifications and characteristics of such groups suggested by various sociologists match those of your chosen groups.

Essay guidance
Using the notes and tasks to help you, plan an answer to the essay question given below. When you write the essay, do so without your notes.

> Assess sociological explanations of the emergence and growth of new religious movements in contemporary societies.

1 Plan a brief paragraph that would act as an introduction to this question. A good way would be to make the point that the term 'New Religious Movements' covers a wide variety of groups. You could make a few general comments about their emergence (when did they start appearing in numbers?) and growth (are there a lot of them?). Note that the question refers to 'contemporary societies' in the plural. This means that in the body of your answer you will need to focus your discussion on a relatively recent period, and should try to include examples from more than one society. Now, for the main body of your answer, start by making a list of the different types of group you would include under 'new religious movements'.

2 Then make a list, with brief explanatory notes, of some of the different sociological explanations that have been given for the *emergence* of NRMs. Against each explanation, note the type of NRM under discussion.

3 Now identify some criticisms that could be made of each of the explanations you have identified. Think carefully about the evidence which could be used (a) to support and (b) to refute each of the explanations, and make brief notes on this aspect of the question.

4 Now find a sociologist or group of sociologists who might question the *significance* of the growth of NRMs by arguing that their impact on religious belief and religiosity is actually quite small. Think carefully about the use of the word 'growth' in the question: does this refer to the number of NRMs or the number of members or both? Raising this as an issue will show your ability to evaluate the question itself. Look through your notes – think about the conclusions that would logically follow from the material you will present in your answer. Is there one single explanation that would suit all cases? If not, why not? The question assumes that there has, in fact, been an 'emergence and growth' of NRMs in contemporary societies – is there anything in your answer which casts doubt on any part of this assumption and to which you would like to draw attention in your conclusion? (Remember, though, that a conclusion should not be too long – one or two paragraphs at the most.)

E

Chapter 5

Religion, Social Order and Social Conflict

By the end of this chapter you will be able to:

- examine the influence of religious bodies and belief on public life;
- understand the arguments for religion as a conservative force;
- understand the arguments for religion as an agent of social change;
- examine religion as a source of social conflict and social control;
- discuss some examples of the influence of religious beliefs and organisations on public life and social structures;
- write an essay on this topic.

INTRODUCTION: THE INFLUENCE OF THE ENGLISH CHURCH AS AN INSTITUTION

In medieval England, the church and the state were closely entwined. Much of the law of the land was influenced by the desires of the church, such as the tithe law which asserted that one-tenth of all goods produced had to go to the church, a system known as tithing. Nowadays, the Anglican Church has no such influence over English law. In fact, apart from a state ceremony such as a royal marriage, an investiture or a coronation, the established church plays a relatively insignificant role in public life. The following extracts demonstrate two differing views on the relationship between church and state:

> I believe politics and religion should be kept separate. The parliamentary system is based on political parties, not on religions. The government is thinking of reforming the House of Lords, and is looking into how different faiths can be represented. I was one of the nominations for Sikh

representatives in the House of Lords. But I think that's wrong. I don't believe in that. It is the confusion between religion and politics that has caused problems in places like Israel and Kashmir.

(Professor Harminder Singh, quoted in the *Observer*, 12 August 2001)

Religion provides a valuable counterweight to the state, nurturing values and sensibilities which it neglects. Just as we need opposition parties to check the government of the day, we need powerful non-state institutions to check the state. Religion should not be left to sulk and scowl in enmity from outside the public realm but welcomed in and subjected to the latter's educational and political discipline.

(Bhikhu Parekh (Lord Parekh), quoted in the *Observer*, 12 August 2001)

So there is a view that the state should be a secular institution, and that introducing aspects of religion is wrong and capable of causing problems. However, some hold a different view, namely that religion can and should provide a valuable and essential check to the power of the state. The histories of many societies bear evidence of the conflicts that can ensue when following one path or the other, whereas trying to find a middle-ground between the two often pleases neither side.

However, the following illustrates how sensitive and controversial the relationship between the church and the state can be. In February 2008, the Archbishop of Canterbury, Dr Rowan Williams, caused a storm of controversy following the reporting of some of his comments during a Radio 4 interview. The Archbishop was using the interview to draw attention to a lecture he was giving on Civil and Religious Law in England, discussing the issue of Islam in English law. In the interview, Dr Williams appeared to support the adoption by the UK of some aspects of Islamic Sharia law. He said that he thought that the adoption of some Sharia law seemed 'unavoidable', and that the UK had to 'face up to the fact' that some citizens did not relate to the UK legal system. Dr Williams said that adopting parts of Sharia law could help social cohesion, with Muslims, for example, choosing to have marital disputes or financial matters dealt with in a Sharia court. He believed that Muslim citizens should not have to choose between 'the stark alternatives of cultural loyalty or state loyalty'. He remarked that an approach to law which said that 'there's one law for everybody and that's all there is', was dangerous. His comments, often taken out of context, were widely reported and widely condemned. Trevor Phillips, Chair of the Equality and Human Rights Commission, said that the 'implication that British courts should treat people differently based on their faith is divisive and dangerous'.

There are, however, two areas in which British law has already acknowledged religious considerations. These include regulations allowing animals to be slaughtered according to both Jewish (kosher) and Islamic (halal) practices. There are also some Sharia-compliant financial products, such as mortgages and investments. Islam forbids interest, as it is regarded as money unjustly earned. In 2005, Canada considered allowing Sharia law to be used there, leading to widespread protests, including from some Muslim women, who felt that in certain instances their interests were better protected by Canadian laws than those of Sharia.

What exactly, then, is Sharia law? It is the legal system of Islam, and is derived from the Hadith, the collection of stories about the prophet Muhammad's life – his actions, sayings, likes and dislikes. Most Muslims believe that the Hadith form an essential addition to, and clarification of, the Qur'an. However, while Western laws are concerned mainly with matters of crime, contract, civil relationships and individual rights, Sharia rulings have been developed to give Muslims guidance on all aspects of their life, to ensure that their actions conform to the requirements of their faith. It is important to note that, just like Western law, Sharia law is very complex. Its interpretation is open to different schools of thought, which can lead to different rulings. Another important point is that Sharia courts already exist in the Western world, giving guidance on matters such as family or business disputes.

ISLAM IN FRANCE

Issues arising from the relationship between the state and religion are found in many societies. In France, for example, a law was passed in 1905 which introduced the system of *laïcité*, the legal and total separation of church and state. Indeed, the idea of secularism in France dates back to the 1789 revolution, and has become a cornerstone of the Republic. However, increasingly, Islam is seen as a significant threat to the secular values of the French state. Such concern was brought to the forefront following a series of serious disturbances in November 2005 in some of the suburbs surrounding many large French cities, including Paris. Since the 1960s, these suburbs have contained large concentrations of immigrants to France – many of whom are now, of course, third-generation immigrants. Some areas of these suburbs are virtually ghettoes, with extremely high concentrations of Muslims originating from the former French colonies in Africa and from Turkey. These areas have high rates of poverty, deprivation and unemployment, and also crime.

A result has been the growth of an underclass that increasingly defines itself by its religion – Islam. Ten years ago, such young French people from the suburbs were described as 'French Arabs'. Increasingly, they are identified, and identify themselves, as Muslims. One problem for the French state is that official statistics on ethnicity or religion are banned, so the number of Muslims in France can only be estimated. Recent estimates put the number at between 5 and 6 million, somewhere in the region of 8–10 per cent of the population – the largest proportion in Western Europe. There are some 1600 places of Muslim worship in mainland France.

Increasingly, the assertiveness of French Muslims is seen as a threat not just to the secular values of the state, but also to its security. However, research among the inhabitants of Muslim areas shows that this alarm may be misplaced. While some young Muslims have become increasingly radical, many others do not share their values. A BBC news item in November 2005 quotes a Muslim youth worker, Nour-eddine Skiker, who said: 'I feel completely French. I will do everything for this country, which is mine' (*http://news. bbc.co.uk/go/pr/fr/-/hi/world/europe/4375910.stm*).

Interestingly, all national Muslim groups in France also profess to support the doctrine of secularism. In the BBC news item quoted above, the President of the Union of Islamic Organisations of France (UOIF), Lhaj Thami Breze, said that those organisations had 'no problem' with secularism: 'Islam must adapt to France, not France to Islam.' Indeed, he argued that by establishing state neutrality in religious matters, the doctrine of secularism allows all religions to blossom. This view was supported by a 2004 poll, which reported that 68 per cent of French Muslims regarded the separation of religion and state as 'important', and 93 per cent felt the same way about Republican values. However, it is widely accepted that jihadism does pose a direct threat to the country. The French expert on Islam Olivier Roy points out that, although many in France do not recognise this, the great majority of Muslims resent the extremists in their midst.

One side-effect of the 1905 law in France has been that many French mosques are financed by foreign powers – notably Saudi Arabia, but also other Muslim countries. This is because when the 1905 law was passed, the French state offered to take over the existing religious buildings – which were, of course, overwhelmingly Roman Catholic. The result is that millions of euros are spent each year maintaining often under-used or even redundant Catholic churches, while Muslims increasingly rely on outsiders to provide and finance their places of worship. Some people in France, including some politicians, now argue that the 1905 law should be amended to make it fairer. The Socialist MP Manuel Valls, who has written a book entitled *La Laïcité en Face* [Looking Secularism in the Face, 2005], argues that a change in the law would prevent mosques being financed by foreign powers, which he sees as a real threat to the

Republic. When he was Minister of Finance, Nicolas Sarkozy also supported reform of the law; now that he is President, it will be interesting to see whether he is prepared to take on the considerable number of traditionalists who oppose any change to the legislation.

Another issue in France between the state and religion was that of the so-called 'hijab affair'. On 2 September 2004, a law came into force that banned the wearing of religious symbols in public (i.e. state-run) schools. While no faith was mentioned by name, the target of the legislation was recognised as the wearing of the headscarf, or hijab, by Muslim girls. As it happens, relatively few actually wore the headscarf to school, but the proposed ban resulted in large demonstrations against it. These died down, partly because two French journalists had been abducted by Islamic militants in Iraq, and many French Muslims did not wish to be associated with this. When the proposal came to the vote, every single party represented in the National Assembly voted in favour, showing the strength of secularism in France.

An interesting counterpoint to the so-called 'hijab affair' in France concerns recent events in Turkey. Although 99 per cent of its inhabitants are Muslim, Turkey is officially a secular state. In 1997, following pressure from the staunchly secular military, who were concerned that the then government was too Islamist, a ban was imposed on women wearing the headscarf in universities. Given that two-thirds of Turkish women cover their heads, the result was that a great many women were missing out on higher education, preferring to continue wearing the scarf if forced to make a choice.

However, in February 2008, the Turkish parliament approved two constitutional amendments which will have the effect of easing this ban. The first amendment, passed by 403 votes to 107, will insert a paragraph into the constitution stating that everyone has the right to equal treatment from state institutions. The second, passed by 403 votes to 108, states that no one can be deprived of the right to higher education. In practice, however, only traditional headscarves, tied loosely under the chin, will be permitted – wearing the chador or the burka remains forbidden in universities. Despite the large majority of votes in favour, opposition parties, the military and many academics are against the changes, regarding the move as a first step towards allowing Islam to feature more prominently in public life, and religious beliefs to exert an influence on the constitution.

RELIGION AND CHANGE

There is an ongoing debate among sociologists of religion regarding whether religion acts to help create social change in society or whether, by acting as a conservative force, it simply serves to maintain the status quo. Among those who argue that religion acts *against* change are the classical Marxists and the functionalists. On the other side of the debate are the Weberians and the neo-Marxists.

It is accepted by many sociologists that religion can act to produce social change. Nelson (1986) demonstrates several situations where this has been the case:

- In Northern Ireland, Roman Catholicism has been associated with Republicanism which has been viewed by some as a revolutionary force in the province.
- The Civil Rights Movement in the USA in the 1960s was closely linked with the leadership of the black preacher Martin Luther King.
- In the 1960s in Latin America, several radical and revolutionary groups emerged as splinter groups within the Roman Catholic Church. This was liberation theology at work, where many priests and nuns fought on the side of the oppressed against right-wing dictatorships. In the late 1970s, Catholic priests supported the Sandinistas against the right-wing Contras in Nicaragua. However, the actions justified by liberation theology were not sanctioned by the Vatican.
- Islamic fundamentalism has been an extraordinary force for change, bringing down the Westernised regime of the Shah of Persia and replacing it with the state of Iran led by the Ayatollahs.
- In Poland the Roman Catholic Church opposed the communist state and supported the trade union Solidarity to achieve social changes.

From examples such as these it can be seen that religion can, in certain circumstances, act with relative autonomy and effect changes within society. However, it could also be argued that these are minority instances and that, generally, the established churches act in the interests of the most powerful.

McGuire (1981) is interested in those situations in which religion does play a significant role in promoting social change. She argues that there are four main factors which are significant:

1 *Beliefs*: Where there is an emphasis on a strong moral code, members are more likely to be critical of their society and look for change.
2 *Culture*: Where religion is seen as important in the society and to the culture of that society it can be used to justify action for change. In a more secularised society this is much less likely.

3 *Social location*: This relates to culture and structure. Where religion is firmly embedded in the structure of a society it has greater potential to play a role in change.
4 *Internal organisation*: Those religions with a strong and centralised source of authority have more chance of becoming agents for change.

These factors will affect the role of religion in any given society and, therefore, we would have to examine each specific situation as it presents itself.

RELIGION AND SOCIAL CONFLICT

In its role as an agent for social change, religion has also been associated with social conflict. While the functionalist view of religion has a focus on its importance for achieving social cohesion and consensus, religious beliefs and practices have often been associated with sometimes violent and bloody conflict. This is because religions are used not only to legitimise but sometimes to challenge the exercise of power.

From the 1970s onwards the considerable social upheaval in the shape of capitalist crises, military involvements, political protests and the rise of fundamentalism, especially in the Middle East, has necessarily called into question the role of religion in maintaining social order and stability. Religion came to be viewed increasingly as a vehicle of social unrest – a source of social disorder in itself.

> Late nineteenth-century sociologists found religion interesting and impor-
> tant for its presumed capacity to supply order and continuity in the emerg-
> ing industrial society. Mid-twentieth century theorists attributed to religion
> the capacity to supply meaning and identity at the level of individuals and
> groups at a time when the basic orderliness of industrial society seemed to
> be assured. But the unrest which is characteristic of the world system of
> states under the domination of advanced industrial societies is beginning
> to alert social theorists to religion's capacity to threaten or challenge our
> prevailing order.   (Beckford, 1989, p. 12)

As Beckford shows, it is usually far too simplistic to say that religion 'causes' war – there are other factors operating within and sometimes outside a society that contribute to conflict. For example, Beckford (2003) points out that the risk of serious conflict is highest in parts of the world where deep religious divisions coincide with strong political and social divisions. In many cases, the social basis for the divisions is ethnicity, tribalism or 'race'. As examples, he shows that outright warfare has occurred between Muslims in the north of Sudan and Christians in the south, and that Nigeria has also suffered a split between the Muslim north and the Christian south. The tensions between the Orthodox Christians of Serbia and religious minorities contributed to the collapse of the former Yugoslavian state. Similarly, argues Beckford, the virtual war between the state of Israel and the Palestinians owes much, though not everything, to conflicts between Jews and Muslims. The hostility that has been simmering between Hindus and Muslims in India since 1947 has erupted into violent conflict in recent years. Finally, Beckford reminds us that the long history of conflict between Protestants and Catholics in Northern Ireland has its roots in ethnic and political divisions as well as in religious differences. Some aspects of all these conflicts confirm Weber's ideas about the capacity of religion to legitimate and to challenge political, social and economic power structures.

RELIGION AND SOCIAL CONFLICT – FUNDAMENTALISM

The issue of fundamentalism is discussed in more detail in Chapter 8 (pp. 157–67), but it is worth mentioning it briefly here. The term 'fundamentalist' is applied to any religious group that has as one of its aims a desire to return to what is regarded as the original, 'true' religious beliefs and practices of the group. These beliefs and observances are usually enshrined in a sacred text, which is regarded as containing the literal truths concerning the origins of the religion, together with the rules of how believers should demonstrate their faith and live their life. The notion that not only 'unbelievers' are outside the faith but that some within the faith have allowed the original beliefs and practices to become 'corrupted' in some way means that fundamentalists can be as opposed to some nominally within their faith as to those outside it.

Bruce (2000) suggests that the following are features common to many fundamentalisms:

- the claim that a particular source of ideas, usually a text, is complete and without error;
- a belief in the past existence of some perfect social embodiment of the 'true religion';
- sufficient elements of the 'old religion' need to have survived to provide the inspiration and symbolism for those wishing to assert its predominance;
- a creative reworking of the past for present purposes;
- as with all movements, the appeal is greater to some social strata than others;

■ fundamentalists often occupy an ambivalent social status, either recently excluded from power, or recently upwardly mobile but unable to fulfil their newly raised aspirations.

While fundamentalist groups can be found within all faiths, the events of 9/11 in the United States have led to Islamic fundamentalists being regarded as posing a particular threat to Western societies. Islamic fundamentalism has become synonymous with modern terrorism, al-Qaeda, the Taleban and militant Muslim groups in Europe, East Africa, the Middle East and Southeast Asia. The term 'fundamentalist' is widely rejected by those Muslims so labelled, not least because of its Christian origins (see Chapter 8). They prefer to be called simply 'Muslims', while many Westerners now prefer to use the term 'Islamist'. While fundamentalism is obviously a religious movement, Siddiq Wahid, former Professor of Central Asian Studies at Harvard University, says that it is actually a reaction to *political* circumstances, such as imperialism or the inability to face modernity (Wahid 2007).

The link to political circumstances seems particularly strong. Indeed, one could argue that what is termed Islamic fundamentalism is often much more about politics than religion. For example, the Muslims ruled Hindu India for centuries before the arrival of the British, with Babur founding the great Mughal Muslim empire in 1526 after the capture of Delhi. Many scholars claim that the British policy of dividing Hindus and Muslims in India contributed to the rise of Islamic fundamentalism. In August 1947 India was divided by the act of partition into Hindu India and Muslim Pakistan. Over 7 million Muslims left India for Pakistan, and an approximately equal number of Hindus went to India. It is estimated that in the ensuing clashes between Hindus and Muslims over a million people lost their lives, and the results of partition are felt in the region to this day. In Gujarat in 2002, for example, hundreds of Muslims were killed by Hindus. Similarly, in 1949 the disputed territory of Kashmir was divided in a UN-sponsored settlement, with one-third being given to Pakistan and two-thirds to India. The resulting clashes have meant that UN peacekeeping forces have served in Kashmir for longer than in any other place in the world.

Southeast Asia is a region of great strategic importance which, despite its huge population and multi-racial and multi-religious character, has been, until recently, a predominantly peaceful region. The two major Muslim countries are Malaysia and Indonesia, but the form of Islam practised was liberal and tolerant. The area has now witnessed the emergence of a strong Islamic fundamentalist movement. In the last 10–15 years there has been a large number of young people from the region attending madrassas in Pakistan and Saudi Arabia, where many of the teachings are radical and fundamentalist.

RELIGION AND SOCIAL CONTROL – THE TALEBAN

Another region whose Islamic fundamentalism has primarily political origins is Afghanistan. It is an interesting example of how a religious group can use its power to exert great social control over a population, backed up by force if necessary.

The Taleban (translated as 'students of Islamic knowledge') is an Islamic group from Afghanistan. They emerged as one of the groups of 'mujahideen' (holy warriors) formed during the war against the Soviet occupation of Afghanistan between 1979 and 1989. Following the withdrawal of Soviet troops, the mujahideen became a group of feuding warlords, with the various factions fighting each other. These often corrupt groups became the target of the Taleban, who promised to restore peace and security to Afghans and, importantly, to enforce Islamic Sharia law.

Afghanistan is a devoutly Muslim country, with 90 per cent Sunni Muslims and the remainder Sufi or Shiites. Many members of the Taleban were educated in madrassas, or religious schools, in Pakistan, where many Afghans fled during the Soviet occupation. The Taleban first came to power in Afghanistan in the autumn of 1994 and in effect ruled the country from 1996. By 1998 they controlled about 90 per cent of the country. They were defeated in 2001 by an American-led military coalition following their refusal to hand over Osama bin Laden to face trial for organising the 9/11 attacks on American soil.

Initially, the Taleban were very popular among Afghans, largely due to their success in rooting out corruption, dealing with crime, improving the safety of the roads and restoring peace to allow better trade and commerce. However, their administration, led by Mullah Omar, was extremely authoritarian, and resulted in considerable international condemnation. Their interpretation of Islamic law was very harsh. There were public executions and floggings, and those convicted of theft had limbs amputated. In order to root out what were seen as 'non-Islamic' influences, television, music, the internet and so-called 'frivolous activities' such as kite flying were banned. Men were required to grow beards and women had to wear the all-enveloping burka. When the Taleban took control of Kabul in 1996, girls aged 10 and over were forbidden to go to school and women were barred from working outside the home, which led to an immediate crisis in education and health care. A section of the Taleban worked as the 'religious police', enforcing these rules.

In 1999, following the Taleban's refusal to expel Osama bin Laden, the UN Security Council imposed sanctions on Afghanistan. In 2001 the sanctions became more severe and the Taleban were denied their seat in the United Nations. However, the result was that the Taleban began to pursue a more isolationist and fundamentalist agenda. Despite the outrage of the international community, they carried out their threat to destroy the 2000-year-old Buddhist statues carved out of a mountain cliff in central Afghanistan.

Both Osama bin Laden and the Taleban leader Mullah Omar evaded capture during the 2001 offensive and, from 2005, the Taleban have re-emerged as a fighting force in Afghanistan. Despite its religious views, the Taleban funds its insurgency through the drug trade. A report by the United Nations in August 2007 claimed that Afghanistan's opium production had doubled in two years, and that the country supplies 93 per cent of the world's heroin.

RELIGION AND SOCIAL CONTROL – POLITICS

Another arena in which religious groups and organisations can attempt to exert social control over individuals and social structures is that of politics. America provides several interesting examples. The Pew Forum on Religion and Public Life was set up in 2001 as a non-partisan, non-advocacy organisation seeking to promote a deeper understanding of issues at the intersection of religion and public affairs. In December 2007 it published the following statement:

> The United States has a long tradition of separating church from state, yet a powerful inclination to mix religion and politics. Throughout our nation's history, great political and social movements – from abolition [of slavery] to women's suffrage to civil rights to today's struggles over abortion and gay marriage – have drawn on religious institutions for moral authority, inspirational leadership and organisational muscle. In recent years, religion has been woven more deeply into the fabric of partisan politics than ever before. (*http://pewforum.org/religion-politics*)

A poll by the Pew Forum and Pew Research Center in August 2007 found that fully 69 per cent of Americans agree that it is important for a president to have strong religious beliefs. The 2004 American Presidential election saw churches becoming increasingly active in political mobilisation. Interestingly, voters could be sorted not only according to their policy preferences, but also by the depth of their religious commitment. In fact, regular attendance at religious services was a more powerful predictor of a person's vote than the standard demographics of gender, age, income and region.

The Twelve Tribes of American Politics

A simplistic analysis of the relationship between religion and party preference in the USA might suggest that the religious right would support the Republicans and the religious left would give their vote to the Democrats. However, this would be misguided. Just before the 2004 American Presidential election, which was a battle between George Bush (Republican) and John Kerry (Democrat), the American website Beliefnet (*http://www.beliefnet.com*) introduced what they termed the 'Twelve Tribes of American Politics'. They wanted to demonstrate that the religious groups that are a significant factor in American political decision making are more complicated than a simple division between the religious right and the religious left. The Twelve Tribes identified by Beliefnet are briefly described below, and Table 5.1 shows how they voted in the 2004 election.

Table 5.1 2004 US Presidential election – voting by religious group

Group	% of voting-age population	% of 2004 voters	% voting for Bush	% of total Bush vote	% voting for Kerry	% of total Kerry vote
Religious right	12.6	15	88	26	12.0	4
Heartland culture warriors	11.4	14	72	20	28	8
Moderate evangelicals	10.8	9	64	11	36	7
White-bread Protestants	8.0	7	58	9	42	7
Convertible Catholics	8.1	7	55	7	45	6
Religious left	12.6	14	30	9	70	21
Spiritual but not religious	5.3	3	37	2	63	4
Seculars	10.7	11	26	5	74	16
Latinos	7.3	5	45	5	55	6
Jews	1.9	3	27	1	73	4
Muslims and other faiths	2.7	3	23	1	77	4
Black Protestants	9.6	8	17	3	83	13

Source: (http://beliefnet.com/story/153/story_15355.html)

The religious right

These are highly orthodox white evangelical Protestants: 88 per cent believe that the Bible is literally true ('Bible literalists'), 87 per cent report attending worship once a week or more, and 44 per cent live in the South. They are more likely to care about social and cultural issues than the nation as a whole; 84 per cent are pro-life and 89 per cent oppose gay marriage or civil unions. They are also strong supporters of Israel, and strongly believe in the political involvement of religious organisations. Four-fifths claim that religion is important to their political thinking.

Heartland culture warriors

This group comprises conservative Catholics and conservative mainline Protestants, Latter-Day Saints and other smaller groups. They are more theologically diverse and slightly less orthodox than the religious right; 54 per cent of the Protestants are Bible literalists, and 60 per cent of the Catholics agree with papal infallibility. However, they are regular churchgoers, with three-quarters attending a service weekly or more often. They are conservative on social issues – 73 per cent support traditional marriage – and they support churches being active in policies.

Moderate evangelicals

These are white evangelical Protestants who hold less orthodox beliefs than the religious right: 54 per cent are Bible literalists, and 35 per cent attend worship weekly or more often. However, they belong to evangelical churches, and regard themselves as born-again Christians. Although pro-life, pro-war (in Iraq) and anti-gay rights, they place a greater emphasis on economic issues, where they tend to be moderate. While only 40 per cent said that their faith was important to their political thinking, they still support the political involvement of religious organisations.

White-bread Protestants

These are the core members of the Protestant 'mainline' churches, e.g. the United Methodist Church, the American Episcopal Church, the Presbyterian Church. Just 19 per cent are Bible literalists, and about a quarter go regularly to church. Almost half (47 per cent) agree with the statement that 'all the world's great religions are equally true and good'. They said that foreign policy and the economy were the most important issues.

Convertible Catholics

These are the core of the white Catholic community, outnumbering con-servative Catholics by almost two to one. They are moderate in both practice and belief – 42 per cent claim to attend church weekly; less than a half agree with papal infallibility; 53 per cent agree with the statement about all the world's great religions being equally true and good. Small majorities are pro-choice (in abortion) and support stem cell research. Only about one-fifth say that their faith is important to their political thinking. They were divided between the economy and foreign policy as the most important issues.

The religious left

This group comprises Catholics, mainline and evangelical Protestants who are theologically liberal. Less than one-quarter report weekly attendance at worship, and two-thirds agree with the statement about the world's great religions being equally true and good. The main factor in their overall vote was foreign policy.

Spiritual but not religious

This group is not particularly fond of places of worship or organised religion, but 85 per cent believe in God and more than half believe that there is some kind of life after death. A majority report seldom or never attending services of worship; 47 per cent of this group are aged under 35. While liberal on economics, abortion and foreign policy, 58 per cent favour traditional marriage. Only about one-fifth say that their faith is important to their political thinking. Members of this group gave the economy as the most important factor in determining their vote.

Seculars

These are the non-religious, atheists and agnostics; 54 per cent are 'uncomfort-able' when candidates talk about their personal faith. Members of this group are very liberal on social issues – 83 per cent are pro-choice, and 59 per cent agree with same-sex marriage; 47 per cent are aged under 35. Their main concern in the 2004 election was foreign policy.

Latinos

The majority of this group are Catholic, though there is a large Protestant minority. They are fairly orthodox in both practice and belief – 53 per cent attend worship once a week or more often, 60 per cent of the Catholics agree with papal infallibility and 58 per cent of the Protestants are Bible literalists. On social issues, 59 per cent oppose abortion or gay marriage, but they care twice as much about economics as social issues. A majority says that their faith is very important to their political thinking, and they are strongly in favour of the political involvement of religious organisations.

Jews

While members of this group share a common cultural identity, it contains diverse religious beliefs. This was the only group that put foreign policy first regarding their voting decision: 75 per cent say that the USA should support Israel over the Palestinians. They are liberal on social and economic issues, and are uncomfortable with politicians discussing their faith in public. This group was especially troubled by the political involvement of religious organisations.

Muslims and other faiths

This group consists of Muslims, Buddhists, Hindus, Wiccans and other smaller groups. They are concerned about, and have a liberal view of, economics, but some (particularly Muslims) are conservative on issues such as gay marriage. They are opposed to the political involvement of religious organisations.

Black Protestants

This group is fairly orthodox in both practice and belief – 59 per cent report attending worship weekly or more often, and 56 per cent are Bible literalists. However, their history of slavery and segregation has given them a distinctive theology. They are most concerned with economic and social welfare issues, with two-thirds putting these first. They are fairly conservative on social issues – 72 per cent support traditional marriage and 54 per cent are pro-life. Members of this group are highly politicised, and are quite comfortable with the political involvement of religious organisations.

Looking at Table 5.1, note, for example, that 28 per cent of the so-called heartland culture warriors voted Democrat, while 30 per cent of the religious left voted Republican. Similarly, while 58 per cent of white-bread Protestants voted Republican, only 17 per cent of black Protestants did so.

ABORTION AND GAY MARRIAGE

As indicated above, two social issues in particular are of great importance to religious voters in the United States. These are gay marriage and abortion.

Recently, a third issue has emerged, namely the use of human stem cells for research. An article in the *Economist* (23 June 2005) pointed out that for the fourth year in a row, President George W. Bush broke from affairs of state to address the Southern Baptist Convention. This powerful evangelical group, estimated to have 16 million members, is capable of exercising significant influence on American politics. In his address, the President assured delegates that their 'family values' were his values too, and that he would work hard to ban gay marriage and abortion.

The issue of gay marriage is one that ignites particularly heated debate. In November 2003 the Massachusetts Supreme Judicial Court declared that the state's ban on gay marriage was unconstitutional. The consequences of this have included battles in Congress over a federal marriage amendment that would define marriage as the union of a man and a woman, a spate of same-sex wedding ceremonies (in some cases in violation of state laws), and the passage of numerous state constitutional amendments banning gay marriage. The American religious community is itself divided over the issue. The Catholic Church and evangelical Christian groups have played a leading role in the public opposition to gay marriage, while some other religious groups debate whether they should permit the ordination of gay clergy and the performing of same-sex marriage ceremonies.

A 2007 survey by the Pew Forum showed that religiosity was an important factor in the opposition to gay marriage. Americans at large oppose gay marriage by 55 per cent to 36 per cent, but those with a high level of religious commitment oppose it by 73 per cent to 21 per cent. It is opposed by 81 per cent of white evangelicals; 64 per cent of black Protestants are also against gay marriage, as are 48 per cent of Catholics and 47 per cent of white main line Protestants. Only among the religiously unaffiliated is a majority (60 per cent) in favour. (See Chapter 7, pp. 151–3 for a discussion of gay clergy in the USA.)

With regard to abortion, religious groups, particularly Catholics and evangelicals, play a prominent part in the so-called 'pro-life movement'. This term is applied to those that oppose abortion, many because they believe that life starts at the moment of conception. At the heart of American abortion laws is the landmark case of Roe v. Wade. Roe, the pseudonym of a pregnant single woman, brought a class action challenging the constitutionality of the abortion laws in Texas, which proscribed abortion except on the grounds of medical opinion that it was necessary to save a woman's life. The case went to the Supreme Court, which on 22 January 1973 ruled that a woman has a constitutional right to an abortion during the first six months of pregnancy. The pro-life movement started almost immediately, and public opinion on the issue has been divided ever since. What has emerged is a state-by-state battle to restrict abortion. In some states, unmarried women under 18 need to obtain parental consent before an abortion (though they cannot legally be denied one if consent is withheld), while 34 states have a law which requires parents to be notified when a minor applies for an abortion.

In March 2006 the law makers in the state of South Dakota proposed a law to make abortion illegal, which was passed by the state Senate by 23 votes to 12. Under the proposed law, doctors who performed an abortion – even in cases of rape or incest – unless it was necessary to save the woman's life, faced up to five years in prison. The proposed law was, however, overturned by voters in November 2006.

While there seems to have been a slight gain in support for the pro-life movement, polls of the American public suggest that a quarter favour abortion on demand, a quarter would like an outright ban, and half would like abortion to remain legal, but with restrictions regarding the length of gestation. The pro-life lobby, however, has friends in high places. A rally of thousands of anti-abortionists in Washington on 22 January 2008, to mark the 35th anniversary of the Roe v. Wade ruling, received a broadcast message of support from President Bush. Fears have been expressed by liberals that the President will use his remaining months in office to continue to use his power to appoint judges to the Supreme Court who are openly against abortion. In 2008, of the 12 Supreme Court judges, five were openly against abortion, one was keeping an 'open mind' (but was widely regarded as being very conservative on the matter) and six supported a woman's right to choose. On the issues of gay marriage and abortion, there is little doubt that religious groups in America play a prominent role.

Another country in which religious groups actively oppose the passing of abortion laws is Northern Ireland. When the 1967 Act that legalised abortion in England and Wales went through the Westminster Parliament, Northern Ireland had its own parliament, which was left to decide the issue. It did nothing about it, leaving the law as it was before 1967 in England, essentially banning all abortions except to save the mother's life. It is estimated that about 1500 women a year travel to England to obtain abortions. In 2001, the Family Planning Association was given leave for a judicial review of abortion in the province, but has come up against strong opposition from the Catholic Church and four pro-life organisations, including Christian Action Research and Education. The calls for a change to the law were rejected.

In Ireland the law is that no abortions may be carried out unless the life of the mother is threatened. It is, however, legal for information to be displayed about gaining an abortion overseas. It is not lawful to promote or advocate abortion in individual cases. It is estimated that as many as 6000 Irish women a year travel to England for the procedure.

Sweden provides another interesting example of the relationship between religion and social policy. In 2000, Sweden formally separated the state from the Lutheran Church, and it is one of the most secular countries in the world. Only one person in ten of the 9 million people thinks that religion is important in everyday life and fewer than 5 per cent regularly attends church. Despite this, eight out of ten Swedes are members of the Church of Sweden (the Lutheran Church) and seven out of ten children are baptised. Half of marriages in Sweden take place in church. However, in matters of policy secular ideals are strongly supported and take prominence. In April 2007 Swedish doctors were given the right to discontinue life-extending treatment if so requested by a patient – so-called 'voluntary euthanasia'.

CONCLUSION

As we have seen, religion can be, is and has been used both as a conservative force in society, helping to maintain the status quo, and also as a force for social change. The same religion can sometimes be used for both these purposes, as with the 1979 Islamic revolution in Iran. Ayatollah Khomeini, for example, is quoted as saying: 'Islam is the religion of militant individuals who are committed to truth and justice. It is the religion of those who desire independence.' Once in power, the Ayatollahs were committed to the creation of a state based on the principles of high Islam, with the emphasis on preserving the new order. However, it is important to remember Beckford's point that we should consider the political and social divisions, as well as the religious ones, in societies in which religion appears to be the basis of social conflict.

Important concepts
Sharia law • secularism • fundamentalism • social policy

Summary points
• Different societies have different views regarding the relationship between religious organisations and the state.
• A secular state is one in which religious organisations play little or no part in public life and policy making.
• Under certain circumstances, religious ideas, groups and organisations can be a powerful force for change.
• Religious beliefs and organisations can be a source of conflict in society.

- Religious fundamentalism can have a political, as well as religious, dimension.
- In certain societies, e.g. the United States, religious groups have a significant influence on social policies.

Critical thinking

Points to consider:

- What is the extent of the influence of the Anglican Church in England – and is it growing or declining?
- How far can, and should, politics and religion be kept separate? Think in particular of the debates on abortion and gay marriage.
- What problems can be posed for political and legal institutions when some citizens/inhabitants have different religious beliefs and come from different political cultures from the indigenous population?
- To what extent are religious beliefs responsible for some of the current world conflicts?

Activity
The following item was published on the BBC News website in 2004, just before the first anniversary of the war in Iraq and the fall of Saddam Hussein. Read it and then try to answer the questions that follow it.

Can religion be blamed for war?
Are religion and religious differences to blame for war and conflict? Many war leaders claim to have God on their side, but should religion get the blame? A 'War Audit' commissioned for the BBC programme *What the World Thinks of God* investigated the links between war and religion through the ages. The audit was carried out by researchers at the Department of Peace Studies at Bradford University. The authors of the audit conclude that the Iraq conflict was arguably a war driven by religion. However, they point out that the Pope and the US Catholic Bishops, the Archbishop of Canterbury and many theologians around the world argued that it fell well short of the rigorous criteria for a 'just' war.

President Bush and Saddam Hussein were only the most recent of a long line of political leaders who have drawn on religion to help them in battle or to justify a military campaign. But the War Audit set out to identify conflicts that were more closely linked to religious belief than to political causes – that could most properly be called religious wars. And that, it concluded, means going back to the wars of Islamic expansion beginning in the 7th century, the Crusades starting in the 11th century and the Reformation wars beginning in the 16th century. Here the wars were fought primarily because of religious differences. Most are much more complex.

Osama bin Laden portrays the campaign being waged by his terror network as a religious duty. But the authors of the War Audit say it is much more about his opposition to the political order in Arab countries and the presence of US forces in Muslim nations.

Source: adapted from Mike Wooldridge, BBC World Affairs Correspondent, 24 February 2004.

1 Search the internet for occasions when President George W. Bush used religion or religious ideas to justify the war on Iraq.
2 Now search the internet (online archives from a quality newspaper would be a good source) to find examples of religious leaders such as those mentioned in the article who argued that the war was not a 'just war' and make a note of these.
3 Briefly state whether you consider that the arguments put forward by the religious leaders are convincing, giving reasons for your answer.

Essay guidance
Using the notes and tasks to help you, plan an answer to the following question.

'Religion is inevitably a conservative force in society.' Assess the extent to which this statement is supported by sociological arguments and evidence.

1 Look carefully at the statement in quotation marks. The question obviously has a focus on religion as a *conservative* force, so you will need to be able to show relevant knowledge and understanding of this aspect of the role of religion. However, note too that the statement says that religion *inevitably* performs this role – in other words, it must *always* do this. In looking at examples in which this is *not* the case, you will be able to display the skill of evaluation.
2 Now look at the instruction which follows the statement. The command word is *'assess'*, so you will have to attempt to weigh up the arguments and evidence you present. Note that you will have to present *arguments* and *evidence* – failure to discuss both will keep you from gaining the highest marks. Remember that 'arguments' refer to theories, perspectives and claims, while 'evidence' refers to empirical data.
3 Make notes for the main body of your essay by jotting down appropriate names, words and phrases in the boxes below. In your 'evidence' column, try to include material from different societies. Remember that by presenting material based on your notes in the lower boxes, on religion as a radical force, or a force for social change, you will be displaying further evaluative skills.

Role of religion	Arguments	Evidence
Religion as a conservative force		
Religion as a force for social change		

4   Write a brief introduction in which you show that you understand what is meant by religion as 'a conservative force'. Expand the definition so that it takes up at least two or three lines. You might also indicate here that this position on the role of religion is not universally accepted – but don't go on at any length about this, or you will be making points that properly belong in the main body of your essay.

5   Now write a series of linked paragraphs, drawing on the notes in your upper set of boxes, presenting the arguments and evidence which has been, or which could be, presented to show religion as a conservative force. As some of your arguments and evidence are likely to be historical, remember to indicate that you are aware of (roughly) when these views were expressed and this evidence collected.

6   Now present the counter-arguments, namely those from your lower boxes showing religion as a force for social change. Again, if there is a historical perspective, show your awareness of this.

7   Write the conclusion. This is where you must draw your arguments together to make an attempt to 'assess' the view in the question. Remember that you do not have to come down firmly on one side or the other. It is perfectly acceptable – indeed, often necessary – to show that there is no clear-cut answer. However, avoid the overly simplistic 'sometimes it is, sometimes it isn't' type of conclusion. Try to tease out some of the complexities of the question – does it depend on the period, religion or society under consideration; does the theoretical position of the sociologist make a difference, are there problems regarding the interpretation of the evidence? Drawing attention to these demonstrates a high level of skill in both analysis and evaluation.

(A)

(E)

Chapter 6

The Secularisation Debate

By the end of this chapter you should:

- be able to examine the factors suggesting that secularisation is taking place;
- be able to examine the factors suggesting that secularisation is not taking place;
- understand the relationship between 'New Age' spirituality and secularisation;
- compare levels of religiosity in the UK with some other countries;
- come to a conclusion on whether religion is declining or simply changing;
- be able to answer an essay question on secularisation.

Secularisation ranks as one of the most complex of all the sociological concepts, not simply because it has been defined by sociological theorists and researchers in so many different ways, but also because considerable moral significance has been attached to it. Evidence of secularisation is seen by many as an indicator of a society which is losing its moral standards and values. However, some sociologists argue that we should look at the changing nature of religion in different societies rather than seeing secularisation as a single process.

It is extremely important for sociologists not to be ethnocentric or Eurocentric when it comes to discussing the decline of religion. In general, what European and American sociologists have been exploring is the decline of the *Christian* faith in Europe and the West. The major world faiths remain strong in many parts of the world and even Christianity remains a vital social force in many developing countries.

So what is secularisation? To try to make sense of this we should look at the different ways that sociologists have used the concept. Shiner's early overview of the concept of secularisation (1967) remains a useful classification. He demonstrated six major definitions of the secularisation process used by sociologists in their research. He produced this categorisation from many other definitions in use. There was some obvious overlap between the categories:

1 **Decline of religion.** This is where religious symbols, doctrines and institutions lose their social significance. This is the type of definition most frequently used in survey research, and is commonly associated with the work of Bryan Wilson.
2 **Conformity with this world.** This is where religious movements become oriented to the goals of 'this world' rather than the life hereafter. We can see this happening with those world-affirming cults and sects which emphasise ways of enhancing one's own individual fulfilment in this world rather than in the afterlife. Religious concerns become indistinguishable from social concerns.
3 **Disengagement.** This is where the established religion begins to lose its prominence in society, where the church or other religious organisations lose functions to other institutions such as schools, social services and the mass media. If the established church also becomes less significant in moral and political terms, then we might argue that this is a sign of secularisation.
4 **Transposition of religious beliefs and institutions.** This is where things that were previously regarded as grounded in divine power become seen as the creations of individuals. Although it is difficult to find examples of 'pure' transposition, we could use the idea that the Calvinist ethic of hard work in a calling has become the pursuit of greed. In another example, Troeltsch (1958) spoke of the 'complete severance of sexual feelings from the thought of "original sin"'.
5 **Desacralization of the world.** This is where scientific and rational explanations take precedence over religious faith. Wilson argues that there are four factors which have encouraged a decline in religious belief:

   - ascetic Protestantism and the development of an anti-emotional, logical ethic;
   - the rational organisation of society in terms of bureaucracy and organisation;
   - an increased body of scientific knowledge giving more satisfactory explanations of life;
   - the development of rational ideologies to solve problems practically, rather than relying on God.

6 **From a sacred to a secular society.** This is a general concept of social change where a society moves from reliance on religion to promote social solidarity

towards a more complex situation where religion takes its place in a 'market' of other possible philosophies. A society which had reached this type of secularisation would have all its decisions based on rational, instrumental considerations and be a society in which social change would become an accepted part of life. This is a more difficult definition to put into practice because it depends on the pinpointing of a time when a particular society was deeply religious or 'sacred'.

Although all of these definitions have been used by sociologists of religion at some time, it might be useful for us to start with the first type of definition. Bryan Wilson (1966) defined secularisation as the process whereby religious thinking, practice and institutions lose their social significance. If we were to accept this definition, our analysis could be relatively straightforward. The factors that we would need to examine would be:

- evidence to show that people search less and less for religious explanations to make sense of their world;
- evidence regarding the time taken up in religious rather than secular activities in people's everyday lives;
- evidence for the decreased significance of the church in state affairs;
- evidence for the decline of participation in religious ceremonies;
- evidence of a decrease in the numbers of churches and clergy.

Taking each of these elements in turn, we might have to rethink our ideas. For instance, do people look for scientific explanations rather than religious ones? Which groups of people are we referring to? Does non-participation in religious services and ceremonies necessarily mean lack of belief?

However, we must be aware that how we come to assess whether secularisation has taken place will also be dependent on our definition of religion. Look back to Chapter 1 for the differences between inclusivist and exclusivist definitions of religion.

RELIGION AND MODERNITY

The concept of secularisation was first associated with the 'founding fathers' of sociology because each of them predicted that the future would bring long-term social changes, including that of the role of religion. Comte (1798–1857), Marx (1818–83), Durkheim (1858–1917) and Weber (1864–1920) all argued that increasing secularisation was an inevitable outcome of modernity.

What is modernity?

'The fundamental promise of modernity is that human beings – potentially all human beings – can be in command of their own future and free to shape it for the better' (Bilton et al. 1996). In order for this to happen two things are necessary:

1   We must be freed from the restraints of the past.
2   We must gain real, effective powers and abilities.

James Beckford (2004) identifies the following features as central to most models of modernity:

■   the declining force of tradition and the pursuit of happiness;
■   the rising influence of science, rationality, education and the professions;
■   the growing strength of sovereign states and rational bureaucracies;
■   the improvement of communications technologies;
■   the rapid rate of social change and upward social mobility;
■   the sharp increase in economic productivity and urbanisation;
■   the importance of values associated with liberty, democracy, justice and equality;
■   the significance of individualism.

Both Comte and Marx believed that religious knowledge and belief, with their reference to supernatural power, were incompatible with scientific knowledge. Comte's Law of Three Stages placed traditional religions in the theological stage of thought. They would decline when society entered the third stage of thought, namely the positivist stage. Science would dominate and direct social behaviour. It is interesting to note that Comte believed that this final positivist stage would be led by sociologists, who, by understanding society, would be able to control developments in the interests of everyone. They would be able to recreate a new moral order on a scientific basis through a new secular religion – sociology.

Marx believed that religion would no longer be necessary after the proletarian revolution. As there would be no need for the dominant bourgeois ideology to be legitimated, so the people would no longer need a 'veil' to hide the oppressive society around them. When they were liberated from oppression, they would no longer need to look for comfort in the promise of heavenly reward. Marx predicted an end to religious practices under communism. However, the persistence of religious beliefs and practices in the countries of the former Soviet Union and other Eastern bloc countries has challenged the Marxist assumptions of secularisation after a proletarian revolution.

Durkheim claimed that in pre-industrial societies religion was the normative system which held the society together. Religion was 'the system of symbols by means of which society becomes conscious of itself; it is the way of thinking characteristic of collective existence'. He believed that in a modern society religion would give way to contractual arrangements between individuals as the mechanical solidarity would be replaced by organic solidarity formed through the laws of contract. Mechanical solidarity is a form of social cohesion based on shared norms and values in simple societies which are relatively undifferentiated in structure. Organic solidarity, on the other hand, refers to social cohesion in highly complex, industrialised societies based on laws of contract.

Weber was fairly pessimistic about the future. He believed that increased rationalisation would bring about bureaucratic societies in which individuals' lives would become impersonal and dominated by capitalist materialism and where control would be increasingly centralised. Weber also argued that religion would have little significance in an industrialised society where the world becomes disenchanted and desacralized and no longer seen as being controlled by supernatural forces. The rationality of the early Puritans had led to the disenchantment of the world. Protestantism rejected the magical elements of Catholicism in favour of rationality and intellectualisation. These would characterise industrialised societies of the future.

These early sociologists therefore assumed that when societies achieved scientific and technological complexity, individuals would cease to rely on religious meanings, and instead would use rational explanations to understand their world. Religion would no longer be the collective social cement producing social solidarity, and if it were to survive at all, it would be confined to the realm of the intensely personal.

We can see that the tremendous social changes which took place in Europe during the 19th and 20th centuries and the start of the 21st century have challenged the orthodoxy of religion, especially Christianity. We may be guilty of exaggerating the impact of science on religion, but it is undoubtedly true that science and technology have given us control in areas that were previously the specific domain of religion. For example, even though some people may attend church to give thanks for a successful harvest, it is likely that the same people would not attribute the success to God alone, but to the impact of fertilisers and insecticides – either chemical or organic.

To explain the gradual process of the decline of religion, Bruce (1992) suggests: 'as our ability to control what were previously precarious areas of life has increased, so the range of things for which we seek religious solutions has narrowed'. However, since the events of 11 September 2001 ('9/11') in the USA, the strength of survival of religion as a motivating force for whole nations and for particular groups within a society seems to have been demonstrated, and, at a personal level, religious or spiritual belief still remains significant.

Possible explanations for a secularisation process to be taking place

Before we examine the different positions in the debate, it would be useful to think about the social changes that may have contributed to the possibility of a secularisation process taking place. The following list of social changes gives those relevant to modern Western societies though not necessarily to the rest of the world:

- the expansion of secondary and higher education, making for a better-informed population;
- the decline of close-knit communities with the rise of urbanisation and rehousing programmes;
- the privatisation and home-centredness of modern families;
- the rise of alternative lifestyles with the increase in cohabitation, separation and divorce, widespread availability of contraception, acceptance of gay lifestyles;
- the rise of the mass media as a challenge to traditional faiths by emphasising consumerism, alternative role models and lifestyles;
- the end of Sunday as a day of rest;
- the acceptance of scientific and rational explanations for events in the modern world.

THE DEBATE ITSELF

There are three major areas of investigation in the debate on whether modern societies have become increasingly secular:

- **Formal religious practice.** This includes the extent of participation in religious services and ceremonies and membership of particular religions.
- **The influence of the Church as an institution.** This includes disengagement, disenchantment, desacralisation, differentiation, pluralism, transposition and ecumenicalism.
- **The status of individual belief.** This is mainly individuation and the idea of religion as helping to provide a sense of personal identity.

Let us look at these in more detail with regard to the UK.

Religious belief and participation in Britain

'Do you believe in God?'

'Yes.'

'Do you believe in a God who can change events on earth?'

'No, just the ordinary one.'   (Abercrombie et al. 1970)

The exchange quoted above illustrates the problems that may be encountered when asking people about their religious or spiritual beliefs. For some, God is omnipotent, and their belief encompasses the knowledge of that power and its influence on their life. For other people, however, belief in God appears to mean belief in the somewhat vague but benevolent figure of childhood Sunday-school lessons – a figure just 'there' in the background of their life. So while two people may each express a belief in God when asked the question in a survey, what this belief actually means to them and how it influences their life can be fundamentally different.

More than 18 million people in Britain who used to attend church now no longer do so. A research study on church leavers (Richter and Francis, 1998) showed that 90 per cent of those who had left the Church (of England) had heard nothing from their church after they had left. The research involved interviews with 800 church leavers and identified key reasons for non-attendance. These included:

- loss of faith (20 per cent approx.);
- frustration at the Church's teachings, worship, pastoral care and leadership (20 per cent approx.);
- lack of authenticity and credibility (the Church was seen as too impersonal, static and not valuing their own personal lifestyles and values) (10 per cent);
- by accident, moving house, changes in domestic circumstances etc. (20 per cent approx.);
- other reasons, such as inability to make necessary commitment, past experiences and a lack of feeling they belonged.

Church statistics are prone to the same kinds of criticism as other types of official statistics and we must use them with caution. However, in some cases they provide the only concrete evidence of the participation and membership of individuals in religious organisations.

Membership itself may be counted differently by different organisations and we cannot compare like with unlike. As Davie (1989) shows, to be a full member of the Baptist community depends on baptism and a public statement of faith, whereas the Anglican church has no set rules over full membership. Comparisons over time also pose problems as the organisations may have vested interests in showing high or low figures. The Church of England's decision to base financial contributions on membership figures was bound to produce a decline in parish statistics.

Even though there may be inaccuracies, the Christian church statistics show a steady decline in attendance over the recent past. The Electoral Roll of the Church of England, which records registered members, shows a decline from 3,693,000 in 1930 to 1,206,000 in 2002 (*www.cofe.anglican.org/info/ statistics/churchstatistics2002*).

According to UK Religious Trends (Brierley 2005), over the past 20 years, the number of adults regularly attending a Christian church has fallen from 7.5 per cent in 1998 to 6.3 per cent in 2005. Christian Research reported in its 2005 Church Census that on 8 May 2005, there were 3,166,200 adults and children at a Christian church service in England. It also reported that 57 per cent of Christian church attenders came from towns and suburbs, 24 per cent from cities and estates, and 19 per cent from rural areas. The Census also found that 10 per cent of Christian churchgoers are now black, and this figure rises to 44 per cent in inner London. Some decline has also taken place in Christian faiths other than Anglican. For example, Methodist membership has dropped from 520,000 to 366,000, but there is a slower decline amongst Baptists.

If we look at trends over time, it is clear that the membership and participation figures for the Christian churches are in decline. However, the rate of this decline appears to be decreasing. The 2005 Church Census showed that among Christian churches in 1998, 21 per cent were growing, 14 per cent were stable and 65 per cent were declining. In 2005, however, the figures showed that 34 per cent were growing, 16 per cent were stable and 50 per cent were declining.

Although, as we have said, there is some increase in the evangelical churches, this is relatively insignificant when we look at the whole picture. While the Muslim community has grown and now outnumbers the Methodists, the Jewish community, having experienced no recent influx of Jewish immigrants, is declining.

As Davie (1944) argues, 'a *limited* pluralism is probably the best way to describe the religious life of Britain' (p. 51). She also points out that there are considerable regional differences in religious membership and participation, with ethnic minority faiths concentrated in the major cities. Other factors such as social class, gender and age affect membership. Middle-class older women are the most regular church-attenders.

Nevertheless, the sheer number and variety of new movements suggests that many people, dissatisfied with mainstream Christianity, are actively seeking supernatural 'enlightenment' of some kind. At first sight the simultaneous decline of traditional faiths and rise of new or unorthodox religious movements may appear sociologically paradoxical. The decline in membership and participation of the Church of England seems to confirm the secularisation thesis. However, the enthusiasm with which sectarian members embrace the new movements seems to undermine a thesis of decline, so how are sociologists to explain what is happening to religion in modern Britain?

Rating Religion

In a survey published by the Policy Studies Institute (Modood et al. 1997), respondents were asked whether religion was important to how they lived their lives. Responses were categorised by the ethnic group of the respondents. The groups seeing religion as being very important were the Bangladeshis and Pakistanis; 76 per cent and 73 per cent respectively responded positively to the question. Only 13 per cent of white respondents and 11 per cent of Chinese rated religion in this way.

When a sample of respondents was questioned on their beliefs in 1995, the following responses were noted. Those believing in the existence of God amounted to 21 per cent of the sample; a further 23 per cent doubted, but still held some belief; 15 per cent of respondents said that they did not know whether God exists, or could not find evidence for God's existence; 11 per cent said that they did not have any belief in God, whereas 12 per cent believed in a higher power of some kind.

FORMAL RELIGIOUS PRACTICE

Participation and membership

This is perhaps the easiest factor to measure, as it involves the number of people participating in religious ceremonies in a church or other place of worship. We might argue that this includes the most objective data we have on secularisation. However, we must also be wary of such 'hard' data, as it may include many problems of reliability and validity. As Davie (1989) says, 'Religious statistics are notoriously hard to handle.' An examination of the statistics on the number of people attending church or an orthodox place of worship on a regular basis suggests quite clearly that we are living in a secular society.

For example, the 1801 Census showed that just under 40 per cent of people attended church each week, whereas results from the 2005 English Church Census showed that only 6.3 per cent of the population (3.17 million people) were regular attenders at a Christian church. While there is one church for every 1340 people in England, the size of the average Sunday congregation in 2005 was 84. However, this figure conceals wide variations. For example, the average congregation size in Anglican churches was 54, in Pentecostal churches 129, in Baptist churches 107 and Roman Catholic churches 244 (see Table 6.1). Statistics also show a small rise in the number of church-based marriages and funerals, but significant drops in the number of baptisms and confirmations.

The English Church Census referred to above was carried out by Christian Research on 8 May 2005 with the participation of 18,270 churches – half of the total of 37,501 known churches in England originally contacted. Statistics and figures are therefore based on information supplied by churches on attendance figures for all services on 8 May 2005. Estimates have been made for those who did not respond, partly on the basis that their figures would on average be similar to those who did respond, but also comparing the results with previous studies and/or published denominational figures.

The 2005 Church Census compared church attendance figures for 2005 with those from 1998, and found the following:

■ Roman Catholic churches showed a 27 per cent decline;
■ Methodists had lost 24 per cent of regular Sunday churchgoers;
■ Anglican churches showed an 11 per cent decline;
■ Baptists and 'new' churches had each lost 8 per cent of regular attenders;
■ Independent churches showed a 1 per cent decline;

Table 6.1 Regular churchgoers at Christian churches by denomination, and average congregation size (2005)

Denomination	% of regular churchgoers	Average congregation size
Anglican	28	54
Roman Catholic	28	244
Methodist	9	48
Pentecostal	9	129
Baptist	8	107
Independent churches	6	84
'New' churches	6	140
United Reformed Churches	2	48
Orthodox	1	81
Other types of church	3	63

Source: Church Census, 2005.

- Orthodox churches showed a 2 per cent rise;
- Pentecostal church attendances showed a 34 per cent rise – 40 per cent of regular churchgoers now attend evangelical services.

However, the validity of many statistics on church attendance has been questioned. It has been suggested that due to taxes enforced by the Vatican, Roman Catholic churches may have consistently underestimated their figures in order to reduce capitation fees. Similarly, the Anglican Church may have overestimated their attendance figures in order to avoid closure of many of their less frequented churches.

It could also be claimed that the *meaning* of church attendance has changed. During the 19th century attending church was a sign of middle-class respectability, and may have had no direct relationship with the strength of a belief in God. We are always going to encounter problems when we try to compare modern times with the past, not only with regard to the reliability of the statistics, but to the meanings behind church attendance, because if Sunday was the appointed day of rest, many working-class people might have used church attendance as a cover for other activities, such as meeting up with loved ones or engaging in political dissent (Martin, 1969).

Attendance at many Christian ceremonies is also on the decline. If we take baptisms and christenings, those rituals where young members are entered into the church, we find that in 1900, 67 per cent of infants were baptised. This had dropped to 47 per cent by 1970 and in 1993 it had fallen to 27 per cent. It was reported on the 'Babyworld' website (*www.babyworld.co.uk*) that Michael Saward, former Canon of St Paul's Cathedral, said that in 2001, fewer than 8 per cent of babies were baptised into the Church of England in the London diocese, while in other areas the percentage was under 25 per cent.

The overall trend for marriages in church is also one of decline. This is in part owing to the decline in first marriages generally, but according to Bruce (1996) around 70 per cent of couples were married in church at the beginning of the 20th century, and by 1990 this figure had fallen to 53 per cent. Figures for marriages in England and Wales taken from Population Trends 115 show that in 2002, only 33.8 per cent of marrying couples opted for a religious ceremony, down from 50.7 per cent in 1991.

The closure of Christian churches in the UK also points to serious problems for the faith. In 1989 there were 38,607 Christian denominational churches in England. By 1998, 2667 had closed. However, 1777 new churches had been started since 1989 so the overall loss was only 890 in total (Williams 2000). It is important, of course, to remember that places of worship for other faiths were being built or opening during this time.

How does the UK compare with other countries?

In February 2004 the BBC ran a series of programmes under the title *What the World Thinks of God*. In preparation for these programmes, the BBC commissioned a survey of people's religious beliefs in ten different countries. Ten thousand people were questioned in the poll, which was carried out by the research company ICM and conducted in January 2004. The countries surveyed were the UK, the USA, Israel, India, South Korea, Indonesia, Nigeria, Russia, Mexico and the Lebanon. The results showed that the UK was one of the most secular nations.

Tables 6.2 and 6.3 are extracted from the data that were reproduced on the BBC 'What the World Thinks of God' website. They show the question asked, and the results from selected countries. There are two important points to note. Firstly, the totals for a particular country will often not add up to 100 per cent, as not all the choices given to respondents are reproduced here (a dash means that the percentage was too small to be significant). Secondly, the figure in the 'total' column refers to all ten countries taking part in the survey, and not just those selected here.

The programme producers concluded that, overall, the results of the poll showed that levels of belief and religious activity in the UK are consistently lower than in most of the other countries polled. Respondents were also given a list of statements about religion, with which they were asked to agree or disagree, or say that they didn't know. The results from these showed that those

Table 6.2   'Belief in God' survey

Q1: Which of the following comes closest to your own view?

Statement	UK %	USA %	Israel %	India %	Nigeria %	Russia %	Total %
I have always believed in God.	46	79	71	92	98	42	73
I used to believe in God but no longer do so.	6	1	4	–	–	1	2
I have never believed in God.	10	1	6	1	–	7	5
I do not believe in God but I do believe in a higher power.	11	5	9	2	–	12	6
I do not believe in God but I am a spiritual person.	12	3	4	–	–	12	4

Source: ICM Research Ltd.

Table 6.3 Responses to selected statements on religion

Statement	UK %	USA %	Israel %	India %	Nigeria %	Russia %	Total %
I regularly attend an organised religious service:							
Agree	21	54	38	52	91	7	46
Disagree	78	45	61	48	8	93	52
Don't know	4	1	1	–	1	1	2
I would die for my God/beliefs:							
Agree	19	71	37	46	95	20	52
Disagree	76	25	63	50	3	57	40
Don't know	5	5	11	4	2	23	7
My God/beliefs is the only true God/beliefs:							
Agree	31	51	70	60	94	55	67
Disagree	65	45	25	38	5	29	29
Don't know	4	3	5	2	1	16	4
The world would be a more peaceful place if people didn't believe in God/Higher Power:							
Agree	29	6	11	8	6	8	10
Disagree	67	91	84	89	92	82	85
Don't know	4	2	5	3	2	10	5
I blame people of other religions for much of the trouble in this world:							
Agree	37	15	33	17	23	23	22
Disagree	61	83	62	81	55	65	71
Don't know	2	2	5	2	22	11	7

Source: ICM Research Ltd.

willing to die for their God or their beliefs included more than 90 per cent of respondents in Indonesia and Nigeria, and 71 per cent in the Lebanon and the USA. Among Britons polled, 29 per cent said that the world would be more peaceful without beliefs in God. Very few people in other countries agreed with this. Table 6.3 gives a selection of some of the statements given to respondents. Again, the figure in the 'total' column refers to all respondents, not just those in the countries shown in the table.

This survey was not the first to reveal significant differences between the UK and the USA with regard to religion. A Gallup Poll released in November 2003 found that 60 per cent of Americans said that religion was 'very important' in their life. By contrast, in Canada and the UK, often perceived as being in many respects similar to the USA, the proportions were 28 per cent and 17 per cent respectively.

Unlike some countries, the United States does not include a question about religious affiliation in its census, so statistics about religious adherence are obtained mainly from surveys. One of the largest was the American Religious Identification Survey (ARIS) carried out between February–June 2001 (Kosmin et al., 2001). This was a telephone survey of 50,281 adults, and to a large extent replicated an earlier survey, the National Survey of Religious Identification, carried out in 1990, thus making possible some comparisons between the two sets of data. The ARIS survey question 'What is your religion, if any?' generated more than one hundred different categories. The survey results showed that whereas in 1990 more than 90 per cent of the adult population identified with a religious group of some kind, by 2001 such identification had fallen to 81 per cent – still, by Western standards, a very high figure. The proportion of the population that could be classified as Christian fell from 86 per cent in 1990 to 77 per cent in 2001. However, the proportion of people belonging to non-Christian religious groups had increased by only a small amount, from 3.3 per cent in 1990 to 3.7 per cent in 2001. The greatest increase, in both absolute and percentage terms, was among those adults who said that they did not subscribe to any religious identification. Their proportion rose from 8 per cent in 1990 to over 14 per cent in 2001. The ARIS survey also found an increase in the number of adults who refused to reply to the question about religious preference, from 2 per cent in 1990 to over 5 per cent in 2001. These findings might suggest a tentative conclusion that, while still a strongly religious society, the United States is also showing possible signs of an increase in secularisation.

Another survey into American religious affiliation was published in 2002 by the Pew Research Council (*http://pewforum.org/publications/reports/*

Table 6.4 US religious affiliation, 1996–2002

Religious Preference	% June 1996	% March 2001	% March 2002
Christian	84	82	82
Jewish	1	1	1
Muslim	*	1	*
Other non-Christian	3	2	1
Athiest	*	1	1
Agnostic	*	2	2
Something else (specified)	*	1	2
No preference	11	8	10
Don't know/refused	1	2	1
Total	100	100	100

Source: www.adherents.com/rel_USA.html

poll2002.pdf). This survey was of 2002 adults, again the researchers were able to compare findings with earlier research in June 1996 (see Table 6.4).

Religious beliefs in Australia

As well as the indigenous religions existing in Australia (see Chapter 2, pp. 22–5) there are, of course, other religious faiths. The English and European settlers that colonised Australia brought their religions with them, which were overwhelmingly Christian. The first permanent clergy of Anglicans was established in 1788. These were followed by ministries of Methodists (1815), Roman Catholics (1820), Presbyterians (1822), Congregationalists (1830) and Baptists (1834).

In 1901, 74 per cent of the population identified themselves as Protestant and 23 per cent Roman Catholic. After World War II there was a rapid growth in Eastern Orthodox migrants, while more recent migrants often come from non-Christian backgrounds. The first Muslims in Australia were Afghan camel drivers, who arrived in the 19th century. However, their numbers declined following the Immigration Restriction Act of 1901, widely known as the White Australia Policy. The 1911 Census recorded just under 4000 Muslims, which represented 0.09 per cent of the population. By 1947, the number of Muslims had fallen to less than 1000. However, from the 1960s, when the White Australia Policy was abandoned, numbers began to rise, firstly with migrants from Turkey and the Lebanon. By the time of the 1971 Census, there were more than 22,000 Muslims, representing 0.17 per cent of the population, and between 1971 and 1981, another 55,000 Muslims arrived to settle in Australia. By 1996 their numbers had grown to more than 200,000, or 1.3 per cent of the total population. At the time of the 2001 Census, there were 281,578 Muslims, representing 1.5 per cent of the population. This made Islam the third fastest growing religion in Australia, after Buddhism and Hinduism.

The 2001 Australian Census showed the religious identification of its population as demonstrated in Table 6.5. The 5 per cent of 'other religions' was made up of Buddhists (1.94 per cent of the total population), Muslims (1.53 per

Table 6.5   Religious identification in Australia, 2001

Faith in Australia (%)	
Christian	69
Other religions	5
No religion	16
Not stated	10

Source: 2001 Australian Census.

cent), Hindus (0.52 per cent), Jews (0.46 per cent) and Traditional Australian Aboriginal Religion (0.3 per cent).

As in many other countries, there is a gap between what people profess to believe, and the number attending acts of worship. In 1998, the Australian Community Survey questioned 8500 Australians from diverse regions of Australia. The survey data showed the following:

66 per cent claimed that a spiritual life was important to them;
74 per cent believed in a God or spirit, higher power or life force;
35 per cent believed in a personal God;
42 per cent believed that Jesus was divine;
53 per cent believed in heaven;
32 per cent believed in hell;
33 per cent claimed to pray or meditate at least once weekly.

A 2003 survey revealed that about 19 per cent of Australians claimed to attend church at least once a month. In a typical weekend, about 1.7 million people (9 per cent) attend a Catholic, Anglican or Protestant church, with an average congregation size of between 60 and 70 people (National Church Life Survey 2001). As in many other countries, church attenders have an older age profile than the wider community. The Anglican and Catholic churches have only 11 per cent and 12 per cent respectively of their members between the ages of 15–29. Other demographic characteristics of Australian Christian church attenders are gender (61 per cent are female), ethnicity (75 per cent are Australian-born), education (23 per cent have university degrees compared to 13 per cent of the adult population) and marital status (62 per cent are in their first marriage). Approximately half are employed and 30 per cent are retired.

In terms of the gap between professed religious belief and attendance at services of worship, Australia therefore appears to show a similar profile to that of Britain.

New Religious Movements

Some sociologists have argued that although the established churches are in decline, the New Religious Movements and New Age Movements have made up for this shortfall. Heelas (2000) has argued that individuals in the USA and in Britain are increasingly looking for New Age forms of spirituality and ways of exploring their identities. However, in statistical terms, taking old and new movements as a whole, there is still an overall decline of almost half a million established church members.

The Kendal Project

Between October 2000 and June 2002, Paul Heelas and his team conducted a study of religion and spirituality in the town of Kendal, in the Lake District. The research (known as the Kendal Project) collected data on all the religious congregations, New Age groups and one-to-one activities through which people came together to 'engage with the sacred'. Heelas et al. were testing the claim that a 'spiritual revolution' was taking place in Britain. The alleged spiritual revolution has two components. Firstly, certain forms of 'the sacred' are declining (secularisation), while at the same time other, alternative forms of 'the sacred' are growing (sacralisation). In Kendal, Heelas and his colleagues were keen to examine participation in traditional forms of religious participation – what they referred to as the congregational domain – and participation in groups or one-to-one encounters exploring forms of body–mind spirituality – referred to as the holistic milieu. Taking attendance at church or chapel on one particular Sunday in November 2000, the Kendal team found that there were 2175 active worshippers in Kendal – 7.9 per cent of the town's population. Heelas acknowledges that measuring the number of people in the holistic milieu was more difficult, not only in terms of finding those involved, but also in ascertaining whether certain practices (e.g. yoga, aromatherapy) were undertaken for their 'spiritual' content or for more secular reasons, such as health and well-being. To this end, participants were asked about the reasons for their involvement. Taking a typical week in November 2001, Heelas et al. found that 650 individuals took part in a holistic activity with a spiritual dimension – 1.7 per cent of Kendal's population. On this basis, it could be questioned whether the evidence showed that a spiritual revolution was taking place. However, when the Kendal team looked at what had been happening in the town over time, they found that, relative to the growth of the town, all the congregations in Kendal were in decline. By contrast, the holistic milieu had gone from being almost non-existent in 1970 to 128 different provisions being offered in 2001. The Kendal team therefore concluded that, 'if the congregational domain continues to decline at the same rate as it has done since the 1960s and if the holistic milieu continues to grow as it has been doing since the 1970s, the holistic milieu will overtake the congregational domain during the third decade of the third millennium' (Heelas and Woodhead, 2003).

However, the Kendal Project has not been without its critics. David Voas and Steve Bruce (2006), while acknowledging that the research of Heelas and Woodhead is 'a rare and admirable attempt to quantify the reach of "New Age" practices and compare them with traditional churchgoing', nevertheless have reservations concerning their conclusions. For example, Voas and Bruce estimate that almost two-thirds of the New Age activities counted in the research cannot be considered indisputably 'spiritual' – rather they are what most people would view as leisure, recreation or pampering. Similarly, the descriptions given by the Kendal respondents seldom mention the supernatural or the sacred – they are more likely to talk of good feelings. Taking the wider view of the impact of New Ageism, Voas and Bruce point out that the holistic milieu is populated mainly by women of a particular generation – women mainly in middle age, educated and in people-orientated professions. Voas and Bruce claim that: 'The evidence shows that the holistic milieu is doing no better than the congregational domain (i.e. conventional religion) in transmitting the "faith" to children.' As certain New Age-type practices such as meditation, yoga and aromatherapy 'go mainstream', any spiritual content will be drained off, and such practices are becoming less, rather than more, like religious activity. Voas and Bruce view the increasing individualism of the 'spiritual' as a sign that New Age practices represent the consequences of secularisation rather than an alternative to it.

New Age spiritualities

What exactly are the main characteristics of New Age spiritualities? Steve Bruce (2002) suggests that the essence of New Age religion and its appeal to modern societies can be encapsulated in the following five themes:

1 *The self is divine*
   Unlike Christianity, which has the assumption that humans are essentially evil and need the grace of God to become good, New Age beliefs start from the premise that people are basically good. In order to free our 'inner self', we need to strip away the bad effects of our environment and circumstances. Some New Agers believe that this 'inner self' is divine.
2 *Everything is connected*
   New Ageism is holistic, believing that people, the environment and the supernatural world are one single essence.
3 *The self is the final authority*
   The New Age belief is that there is no single truth, no authority higher than the individual. The only 'truth' that matters is personal belief and experience.
4 *The 'global cafeteria'*
   New Agers can 'pick and mix' from a wide range of belief systems and practices to find their own path to 'enlightenment'.

5 *Therapy*
Most New Age practices and rituals emphasise self-improvement and self-gratification, and are intended to make believers more successful, happier and healthier.

It is interesting to reflect on why New Age beliefs have grown in popularity. Bruce (2002) argues that New Age spirituality has grown in popularity because it fits in with certain aspects of contemporary society:

- Its relativism helps to solve the problem of cultural diversity. There is no problem and no conflict if it is quite acceptable for people to believe different things.
- It mirrors the modern emphasis on the right of the individual to choose. Such individualism is also now finding its way into mainstream Christian churches, where followers increasingly can choose which doctrines they will accept and follow.
- It empowers the consumer. New Agers decide for themselves how much time and effort they will commit to which beliefs and practices.
- It mirrors the modern obsession with self-improvement and pampering.

With regard to the impact of New Ageism on secularisation, Bruce goes on to argue that the superficial popularity of New Age spirituality makes little difference to the overall secularisation of the Western world. Firstly, he says, the numbers of those involved come nowhere near to compensating for the loss of people from mainstream churches in the last half-century, and secondly, unlike previous religious innovations such as Methodism, whose followers brought about wide-reaching social changes, New Ageism affects only the lives of those involved and has little, if any, impact on the rest of the world.

However, the picture with regard to secularisation in Britain is quite complex. Despite the overall falling attendances in the major Christian churches, there is an example that seems to go against the trend. This is the Alpha course, originally started by clergyman Nicky Gumbel as a means of presenting the basic principles of the Christian faith to new Christians at Holy Trinity Church, Brompton, London. The course proved so attractive that Gumbel decided to try to attract non-churchgoers as well as committed Christians. The method of welcoming people, the atmosphere and the material of the talks is all designed to make them as attractive as possible to the person who walks in 'off the street'. Each session is relaxed and informal, involving a meal, a talk and then a discussion exploring questions such as 'Who is Jesus?', 'How and why do we pray?' and 'How does God guide us?'. The Alpha courses have now been running for more than 20 years, and have proved extremely successful. More than 1.6 million Britons have taken part, and Alpha courses are now running in more than 7200 churches of all denominations around the UK, and by 28,000 churches worldwide. In the UK, the vast majority of participants are in the 18–35 age group.

Further evidence regarding attendance at church services comes from the 2005 English Church Census, undertaken by the organisation Christian Research and published in February 2006 (*www.christian-research.org.uk/pr180906.htm*). This research shows many churches in England to be in a healthier state than they were seven years earlier with regard to the number of people attending services. The author of the Census, Dr Peter Brierley, said that the two major reasons for the improved figures were the number of churches that were growing in membership, and a considerable increase in the number of ethnic minority churchgoers. For instance, black people now account for 10 per cent of all churchgoers in England (up from 7 per cent in 1998), with a further 7 per cent (previously 5 per cent) from other non-white ethnic groups. However, the Census also showed that it is the *rate* of decline that has slowed, and that the declining churches are still losing more people than the growing churches are gaining. A major factor in the overall decline is that churchgoers tend to be significantly older than the average population – 29 per cent of churchgoers are 65 or over, compared with 16 per cent of the general population.

Participation rates in different parts of the world vary enormously. A study conducted by the University of Michigan (www.ns.umich.edu/htdocs/releases/story.php?id=1835) showed that weekly church attendance is higher in the USA than any other developed country. Around 44 per cent of Americans said that they attended church once a week, not including funerals, baptisms and christenings. This figure compared with 27 per cent of British, 21 per cent of French, 4 per cent of Swedes and 3 per cent of Japanese. However, almost 50 years ago, Herberg (1960) argued that Christian and Judaic religions in the USA had themselves become internally secularised. The major faiths, Catholic, Protestant and Jewish, increasingly emphasised a this-worldly orientation and had compromised their traditional doctrines. Herberg argued that religious participation in the USA was more a demonstration of being an American citizen than of being a believer.

Herberg's work is dated and we would be ill-advised to apply it without considerable modification to the USA half a century later, but there are some religious groups in the USA which demand more than just lip service to belief. The New Christian Right is estimated to involve 15 million Americans. Many are associated with right-wing causes such as anti-abortion, anti-divorce, anti-gay rights. Some are opposed to women's rights and black rights. Some are 'soldiers for Christ', being very well armed in preparation for a fight to restore traditional values. (You can find more references to the New Christian Right in Chapter 8.)

THE INFLUENCE OF THE CHURCH AS AN INSTITUTION

Disengagement

This refers to the withdrawal of the established church from wider society. It could be measured by the amount of political influence the church has over politicians as well as over the population as a whole. Although over 20 bishops have the right to sit in the House of Lords, they seem to exert little major political influence. An example of this is the way some churches will allow divorcees to remarry in a church. This 'fitting in' is a turnaround from previous years where society tended to fit in with the wishes of the Church, rather than the other way around.

Yet it can be argued that the church continues to involve itself in some areas of the wider society. The Salvation Army is a very active organisation involving itself in charitable works and other welfare services, as do a number of other religious groups.

The process of disengagement has been refuted by using evidence of the Christian Coalition that supports political parties in America. The financial contributions its members make to parties gives them some influence in the way the party shapes its policies. It is argued that the politicians are in 'debt' to the religious organisations and therefore their policies will reflect the interests of the religious organisations in order to receive continued financial support.

However, we are again guilty of taking a predominantly Christian focus here. Casanova (1994) challenges the existence of disengagement. He argues that religion still maintains an important political role in conflicts across the world: Jews and Palestinians in the Middle East; Protestants and Catholics in Northern Ireland, Muslims, Serbs and Croats in the former Yugoslavia; Sunni and Shi'ite Muslims in Iraq. Religious leaders were involved in the struggles for liberation in Latin America and we must also include the conflict between the West and Islamic terrorism since 9/11 in the USA. Casanova goes as far as to argue that we have experienced a 'deprivatisation' of religion. Unlike other sociologists, who argue that religion is withdrawing into the realm of the private and personal, Casanova claims that it has become more public. However, he still supports the general theory of secularisation as being a process of differentiation.

Differentiation

Parsons (1966) according to his theory of structural differentiation, believes that the church, as an institution, has lost several of its functions to other institutions such as education, the family, the workplace etc. This is not to argue that religion has lost out, but rather it has become a more specialised organisation. Religion for many people is the most important arena for morality, values, comfort and succour in times of crisis and in giving meaning to everyday life. For some, it is an inextricable part of their identity. Parsons argues that religious values and ethics have become *generalised* as the basis of societal values often enshrined in law.

Transposition

This is linked to generalisation in the sense that there has been a transformation of what was once seen as religious knowledge and beliefs into more secular forms. Dominant ideologies of egalitarianism, self-responsibility and justice become secular ideologies standing independently of faith. We can see this with the Protestant ethic and its emphasis on work as a calling. Although in Britain we work more hours than most other European countries, it is not seen as work for the greater glory of God, but rather work for increased salary and promotional chances.

Desacralisation

This is the idea that the 'sacred' has little place in modern Western societies. Supernatural explanations for accidents, fate and destiny tend to be disavowed in favour of scientific and/or rational explanations. For example, Britons today are unlikely to believe that the outbreak of foot and mouth disease in 2001 was a direct result of the 'evil eye' or witchcraft curses.

However, as recently as the 1980s some commentators were referring to AIDS as if it were a curse from God. As Pattman (1988) explained, 'The social reaction towards AIDS which seeks scapegoats has historical precedents in the social reaction to diseases such as the Black Death or last century's cholera pandemics for which Jews and the "great unwashed" were respectively blamed.' We can see from the comments of John Junor, the then editor of the *Sunday Express*, that ideas about the causes of illnesses were not completely scientific or rational. As he said, 'If AIDS is not an act of God with consequences just as frightful as fire and brimstone, then just what the hell is it?' (quoted by Pattman).

The concept of desacralisation is attributed to Weber and linked to his ideas of disenchantment of the world. He maintained that disenchantment was the first indicator of secularisation. As the Puritan was faced with an 'unprecedented inner loneliness' before God, he lost his reliance on magical solutions to salvation.

Against this argument of a decline of magical thinking we have to interpret the rise of New Age faiths which themselves might have elements of magic about them. For example, many would argue that a belief that wearing certain crystals or reorganising a living room according to the doctrines of Feng Shui will have beneficial effects is an indicator of irrational rather than rational ways of behaving. Large numbers of people still read their horoscopes regularly, although we do not really know how strong their beliefs in astrology actually are.

Pluralism

The emergence of New Religious Movements (NRMs) may be used as evidence to suggest that society is becoming more secular because such movements represent a move away from the more conventional religious wisdom. The short-lived nature of most of these NRMs suggests that they are unlikely to become the churches of the future. (For further discussion of NRMs, see Chapter 3.)

NRMs and New Age Movements help to make up the rich variety of faiths on offer in the West. This pluralism itself may be a manifestation of secularisation because religion becomes a commodity on offer like other products and lifestyle choices. As individuals are free to make choices, then religion has no greater significance than any other choice. The large number of denominations and sects means that religion can reflect the beliefs of only a section of the population. Wilson argues that religious values have ceased to be community values. The church no longer provides a single universe of meanings for all members of society.

Although NRMs can be used as evidence for secularisation, they also show that religion is still needed by some members of society. The incidents in Waco and the sacrifices of the members of the Order of the Solar Temple show how some people are willing to sacrifice everything for their beliefs. This is of course a characteristic of many fundamentalist groups who fight to assert what they believe in.

Ecumenicalism

Over the past 50 years, there has been a movement which has tried to bring about a unity of Christian churches. This is known as the ecumenical movement and it encourages religious denominations to unite together.

Ecumenicalism may be viewed as evidence to refute secularisation. The joining of denominations has been seen as a move to strengthen the church and bring people together in worship. However, this could also be used as evidence to support the secularisation debate since organisations tend only to unite in situations of weakness rather than when each is in a position of strength.

THE STATUS OF INDIVIDUAL BELIEF

Individuation: the retreat to the personal sphere

Individuation is a concept which poses a challenges to the secularisation debate. It refers to the withdrawal of religion into the most personal sphere – that of the consciousness of the individual. As such it cannot be measured or compared, nor can predictions be made from it. Interpretivists still maintain that religion contributes to the universe of meaning of individuals, and even though they may not publicly practise their faith, religion continues to provide personal meaning for individuals. It is what Davie (1994) calls, 'believing without belonging'. The decrease in church attendance does not mean that people have necessarily stopped holding religious beliefs. Religion becomes a highly personalised experience independent of religious ceremonies and ceremonials. Surveys have shown that around two-thirds to three-quarters of people in the UK believe in something greater than themselves. For example, in 1987, 79 per cent of a UK sample said that they believed in the existence of a personal God or in some 'sort of spirit or vital force which controls life' (Svennevig et al. 1988). If we include the occasional believers with those who say they really believe in God or a supernatural power, then 68 per cent of the sample had some faith. This illustrates the idea of individuation – people seem to be making some choice about what they actually want to believe.

We could argue that this is an indication that religion has become commodified. Individuals make selections from the various faiths on offer and produce some kind of belief system that might incorporate Eastern philosophies alongside more Western belief systems. Many commentators see the move from collective to individual worship as further refutation of the secularisation process. This, together with our increased material standard of living, has guaranteed a present-day focus rather than an investment in the life hereafter. The areas for which we seek religious explanations or solutions have, therefore, narrowed.

Stark and Bainbridge (1985) also challenge the secularisation thesis. They argue that although there has been a decline in established churches, it has not produced individuals who are irreligious, merely non-church attenders. For them, the increase in sects and cults indicates that individuals are searching for meaning in their lives. Stark and Bainbridge use a form of exchange theory or rational choice theory to explain the individual's relationship to religion. Their work, which is based in the USA, introduces the term 'compensators'. These compensators can include anything which is accepted as a compensation when the desired rewards which individuals seek are not forthcoming. 'A compensator is the belief that a reward will be obtained in the distant future or in some other context which cannot be immediately verified' (p. 6).

Compensators are not exclusively religious, but Stark and Bainbridge maintain that religion is necessary because 'only by assuming the existence of an active supernatural can credible compensators be created'. They believe that there are essential human needs, one of which is to understand the meaning of life. Individuals have always asked questions about ultimate meaning and they still ask those questions in a scientific world in which science is not equipped to answer them. Only a belief in a god allows individuals access to the answers to those ultimate questions. If we accept this proposition of Stark and Bainbridge, then there can be no inevitability about secularisation because individuals will seek other 'religious' compensators when one type of faith ceases to be meaningful to them.

The rational choice approach is an interesting model to apply to religious belief, because belief tends to defy rational explanation and argument. American researchers who have applied this model to religious belief in the USA explain the continued popularity of religion there by the greater diversity of faiths available in the 'marketplace'. In the USA there is no established state church, so the situation of decline in an established church and a lack of adequate alternatives does not apply to that society.

However, there are several critics of the views of Stark and Bainbridge:

- Wallis sees their theory as a significant one in the development of the sociology of religion. However, he is critical of it. He and Bruce (Wallis and Bruce, 1984) criticise it on three fronts: the vagueness of the term 'compensators', the methodology, and the lack of sound empirical evidence.
- Beckford's critique focuses on the membership of the new sects. Stark and Bainbridge maintain that as the established churches decline, their place is taken by new religious movements. However, Beckford challenges this point by saying that cult members are not all simply disillusioned ex-church members. Certainly in Britain, the numerical decline in the established church is in no way compensated for by the increase in sectarian membership.

■   It is also claimed that Stark and Bainbridge fail to examine the ways in which religion functions to sustain powerful groups, especially men. They are neglecting to see that religion is often maintained by social rather than essentialist factors.

THE EVIDENCE REGARDING SECULARISATION

Whether one can argue that secularisation is a feature of modern societies or not will undoubtedly depend upon the definitions of religion, the societies examined and the interpretation of the evidence put forward. Using an exclusivist definition is likely to bring us closer to the conclusion that secularisation is taking place. However, an inclusivist definition leads us to count anything that gives meaning to people's lives as a form of religion or religious substitute.

Another problem is which definition of secularisation we are going to use, and, as we have seen, there is a diversity in the use of the concept by sociologists of religion. So the secularisation debate is fraught with both theoretical and methodological problems.

At its simplest, the debate about whether secularisation has been or is taking place rests between those who maintain that the established religions have declined in function, power and credibility, and those who see religion as becoming more, rather than less, socially significant by having adapted to various social and political changes.

■   Many sociologists have examined the **measurable** or **objective** factors of decline. Statistics have shown an overall decline in religious membership, attendance and rituals, but all statistics have reliability and validity problems and sociologists have differed widely in their interpretations of the figures; low attendance rates in England and Wales, high participation rates in the USA – both have been used to argue in favour of secularisation.

■   Others have documented the decline of **functions** and the **disengagement** process. Sectarianism and the generation of new religions have either been seen as indicators of the decline of religion or the rise of a new religiosity, depending on the standpoint of the sociologist.

■   We have seen how the USA and Britain have been used comparatively. The USA has presented an interesting sociological problem because although it is a highly developed modern society it has consistently shown a higher degree of church involvement and a vigorous evangelical Christian fundamentalism, even though this seems to be regional rather than national.

- However, Bruce (1995a) argues that we may have misinterpreted the evidence for the USA. The relative popularity of religion resulted from two factors: America's late industrialisation compared with Britain and the role of religion in maintaining or emphasising ethnic identity. Though this may be correct, it is still fascinating from the viewpoint of Britain to have observed the tragedy of the Branch Davidian sect at Waco, the gun-toting Christians of the Midwest and, more recently, the all-male 'Promise Keepers' who spend their weekends at sports stadiums promising to become better men under Christ's guidance. Religious belief remains important for many in the USA, but what about Britain?
- In the 1991 British Social Attitudes Survey the results showed that whilst many people claimed a belief in God, few actually attended church services. There was evidence too for the decline of belief in the Bible as the Word of God.
- Religious broadcasting can be used as evidence for continued belief without belonging. Television audiences stay high for programmes such as *Songs of Praise* – higher even than those for *Match of the Day* (Davie, 1994, p. 112).

Overall, 'most people . . . are not connected to the churches, do not subscribe to the core beliefs of the religion that shaped their culture, and are rather suspicious of those who take religion "too seriously" and who have "got God"' (Bruce, 1995b, p. 54).

- This evidence refers mainly to Christian faith but, as we have seen, Britain is a multi-faith society where minority populations have increased their religious participation. As Britain's population has become more ethnically and culturally diverse, the idea of an established church has become somewhat outdated.
- To assume that there is increasing secularisation is to dismiss the importance of other major world faiths. We may be confusing secularisation as a process with that of dechristianisation (Wilson 1982). In Britain some people may be more likely to indulge in an array of new religious movements and new age movements, but many people from the ethnic minority communities, especially Muslims, are demonstrating strong adherence to their faiths. Cultural and religious pluralism clouds the debate about religious decline. On a global level there are forces making religion more important and actually reversing the process of secularisation, for example, the rise of Islam since the reinstatement of Ayatollah Khomeini in Iran in 1979, and 'ethnic cleansing' of Muslims by Bosnian Serbs in the former Yugoslavia since 1991.

In evaluating the role of religion in contemporary societies and its possible decline, the processes of cultural defence and cultural transition become significant as explanations for different developments in different societies (Bruce 1992).

Cultural defence operates when there are at least two competing faiths jostling for prominence and religious loyalty is strengthened, as between Protestants and Catholics in Northern Ireland or, alternatively, when a nation is dominated or oppressed by another with a different belief system; for example, when communism was imposed on Eastern bloc countries, the traditional faith was assimilated.

In addition, **cultural transition** helps to maintain or strengthen faith by offering migrant communities a sense of their cultural identity within a new and often hostile environment. This has been the case for the Asian and Afro-Caribbean communities in Britain. More recently, we have seen increased attendance at Roman Catholic churches in Britain as a result of the number of migrants from Eastern European countries such as Poland.

NEW APPROACHES

Wallis and Bruce (1992) have updated the theory of secularisation. They see three processes which have been responsible for promoting secularisation in modern society. These are social differentiation, societalisation and rationalisation.

- **Social differentiation** is recognisable as the process whereby social institutions lose some of their non-essential functions to other agencies and become more specialised.
- **Societalisation** refers to the process whereby aspects of social life are controlled by the state rather than the local community. Since religion stems from the community 'whose identity it celebrates and legitimates', when the community's influence diminishes, then so does the significance of religion (Hamilton, 1995).
- **Rationalisation** is the process examined by Weber whereby science and rational thought come to challenge magic and religion. As Hamilton (1995) concludes, the evidence for secularisation having taken place is ambivalent. 'We observe at the same time a loss of the supernatural element in traditional religion and, in certain quarters, a re-magicalisation of the world; we see secularisation within some churches while more traditional and conservative churches flourish; new religious movements and sects grow up at a bewildering pace, yet they involve only small numbers and remain marginal.'

The postmodern challenge

The postmodernist argument would be that modern society is based on multiple life choices, relativism (where we question the prevailing knowledge and refuse to accept any single version of the truth), and the rise of risk in our life. New religious movements and New Age beliefs tend to dwell on individual self-actualisation and individual achievement, rather than holding out the promise of life in the hereafter or the solidarity of community. People become consumers of faiths, buying their own mixture of beliefs and practices.

> Faced with so many rival movements, no single religion can ever be the final arbiter of truth and falsity. This religious pluralism enables New Age converts to bypass Christianity, Islam and Judaism, which have for centuries revered a single, all-powerful god. A huge number of new spiritual beliefs and practices now exist alongside theologies that many currently regard as restricting and old-fashioned. The rise of individualism has led to the adoption of beliefs that are as unconventional as they are diverse. (Holden, 2002, p. 30)

'Celebrity' Religion

While it is debateable whether it has had significant impact in terms of converts, there is no doubt that considerable public interest has been raised by a few examples of so-called 'celebrity religion'. By this is meant the overtly expressed religious commitment of a few well known figures. Scientology, for example, claims John Travolta and Tom Cruise among its more famous adherents, while Madonna has done much to publicise the Kabbalah, the mystical side of Judaism. Mel Gibson's controversial 2004 film *The Passion of the Christ* also led many people to become aware of Gibson's fundamentalist/ traditionalist Catholic views, even if they did not share them. It is interesting that the film was turned down by mainstream Hollywood studios and distributors and Gibson ended up financing the project himself. Despite being considered by many as being extremely violent and anti-Semitic, the film was a huge box-office success.

THE SECULARISATION OF RELIGION

It has been argued that in some instances, it is religion itself that becomes secularised, in an attempt to continue to appeal to people in the context of a modern world. The 'televangelism' in the USA and the growth of so-called mega-churches offering a wide range of activities have been used as examples.

While Islam is often viewed in terms of its appeal to fundamentalists, an interesting experiment is currently going on in Turkey. Although Turkey is officially a secular state, 99 per cent of its population are Muslims. The prime minister, Recep Tayyip Erdogan, has asked scholars to establish a form of Islam compatible with the 21st century. Erdogan argues that his AK party is a Turkish Muslim equivalent of a European Christian Democratic party – traditionalist, conservative, based on religious values, but democratic, tolerant and liberal. A team of reformist Islamic scholars at the University of Ankara is therefore working on a 'reinterpretation' of parts of the Hadith which form the basis of Sharia law. They are working under the auspices of the Directorate of Religious Affairs, a government body which oversees Turkey's 8000 mosques and which appoints imams. Mustafa Akyol, an Istanbul-based commentator who reflects the thinking of the liberal camp in Erdogan's governing party, says of the team working on the revisions: 'They have problems with the misogynistic Hadith, the ones against women. They may delete some from the collection, declaring them not authentic. That would be a very bold step. Or they may just add footnotes, saying they should be understood from a different historical context.' Interestingly, working with the Ankara professors is a Roman Catholic Jesuit expert on Turkey and Islam, Felix Koerner. He is reported to be schooling the Turkish team in the history of religious and philosophical change, and how to apply the lessons of Christian reform movements to modern Islam. He says: 'This is really a synthesis of modern European critical thought and Muslim Ottoman Koranic tradition. There is also a political agenda. With this government there is more confidence in these modern theologians.' It is claimed that the Islamic reform project, though unfinished, is already making a difference in Turkey. The death penalty has been abolished, there is a campaign against so-called honour killings, and there is a programme for training and appointing several hundred women imams ('Turkey strives for 21st century form of Islam', *Guardian*, 27 February 2008).

Meanwhile, in Japan, it is claimed that Buddhism is in crisis. About 75 per cent of the 127 million Japanese describe themselves as Buddhists, compared with only 1 per cent who say that they are Christians. However, many self-reported Buddhists only go to a Shinto shrine for the new year celebrations or to a temple for the traditional funeral of a relative. Public donations have fallen, and many of the 75,000 temples are in financial difficulties. Applications to Buddhist universities have seen a dramatic fall. The decline in faith is particularly noticeable among the young.

There has been an interesting response from some Buddhists. In the Bozo (monks') bar in Tokyo, Gugan Taguchi, a Buddhist priest, is a regular visitor, encouraging young people to come and talk to him. He sits and drinks and smokes among the clients, and says that he can understand why younger people are not attracted to Buddhism. He says that most priests are getting on in years, and young people may not want their advice. The owner of the bar, Yoshinobu Fujioka, another Buddhist priest, says that Japan's mainstream sects must shed their conservative image to broaden their appeal. He says: 'There was a time when people would go to their local temple for advice on all sorts of problems, not just spiritual matters. This bar is just the same, a place where people can come and talk freely about their problems.' Other examples of the attempt to bring the Buddhist message to younger people include a temple with an outdoor café and one that operates a beauty salon. The Tsukiji Honganji temple in Tokyo recently staged a fashion show, with dozens of Buddhist monks and nuns on the catwalk in colourful robes. The event, a public relations exercise, opened with the recital of a Buddhist prayer to a hip-hop beat, and ended with a shower of confetti in the shape of lotus petals. One of the organisers, 37-year-old Buddhist priest Kosuke Kikkawa, said: 'We won't change Buddha's teachings, but perhaps we need to present things differently so that they touch the feelings of people today.' ('Buddhism forced to turn trendy to attract a new generation in Japan', *Guardian* 10 January 2008).

CONCLUSION

The debate about the nature and extent of secularisation is inevitably a complex one. It is, of course, important to decide what definition of 'secularisation' is going to be used (and there is no universal agreement among sociologists on this), and then to decide what type of evidence should be used to address the question. As we have seen, there are problems not only with the validity of the statistics used, but also with their interpretation. There are also issues regarding whether religious beliefs and practices are changing, rather than declining, and if this is the case, what this means for the secularisation debate. Recognition also has to be made of the fact that there are significant differences both within and between different religions, and within the same religion in different societies.

Hamilton (1995) made an interesting point. He said: 'We cannot yet answer the question: "Is religion declining or changing?" Changes of the scale we are concerned with are measured not in decades but in hundreds of years.'

Important concepts
disengagement • differentiation • disenchantment • desacralisation • fundamentalism • religiosity • individuation • ecumenicalism • rewards and compensators • cultural defence • cultural transition

---

Summary Points

- Before one can examine the evidence regarding whether the process of secularisation is taking place, it is important to define the concept. Even where sociologists broadly accept the same definition, there are disagreements regarding the reliability and validity of the data, and its interpretation.
- An important aspect of the secularisation debate is the extent to which 'modernity' and the development of rational ways of thinking and investigation has had an impact on religious belief.
- Even within Christianity, the nature and extent of secularisation differs between different churches and sects, and these differences widen when other faiths and other societies are taken into account.
- There is considerable debate regarding the growth of so-called New Age beliefs and practices. While some see this as evidence of the changing nature of religious and spiritual belief, others question both the significance of the number of people involved, and the extent to which their beliefs and practices can be termed as 'religious'.

Critical thinking

Activities

1 The following table shows some aspects of secularisation and some problems with investigating them. Consider each of the problems, and for each aspect, identify others that could be suggested.

(A)

Aspect	Problem
The historical decline of religion	Was there ever a 'golden age of faith'?
Increasing conformity with this world	This is very difficult to measure. From what date does it start and is it now complete?
Disengagement	Has this taken place to the same extent in all social spheres – e.g. education, politics, social welfare?
Transposition of religious beliefs	It is difficult to prove that secular belief systems and thought emerged from religion.
Desacralisation of the world	Individuals may believe without 'belonging'. They also embrace alternative therapies, superstitions, beliefs in alien life forms etc.
From a sacred to a secular society	This is the assumption of the modernists. There is evidence to show that religion and religious beliefs are changing, rather than declining.

2 Look again at what Beckford suggests are characteristics of modernity. For each of the points, think of an example that illustrates it. Then, for as many as you can, think of an example that casts some doubt on it – or at least suggests that it is not yet found in all levels of society or in all 'modern' societies.

3 The following is a list of some of the problems associated with using statistical evidence to assess the extent of secularisation. Divide the problems into those of **reliability** and those of **validity**. In each case, consider the reasons for your answer.

- The statistics are often for attendance at important occasions such as Easter Communion and Christmas Mass. People may attend these special services but few others.
- Membership figures are collected with different criteria being used by different churches.
- Surveys asking people about the nature of their belief are using second-order constructs and therefore do not get at the true meaning held by the individuals themselves.
- There are variations in the kind of statistical evidence from one country to another.
- If participation and membership rates are high, it is assumed that the country is a religious one.
- Comparisons are often made with the past and a supposed 'Golden Age of Faith' that is now over.

Essay guidance

The following task will help you to develop the skill of identifying relevant material for the separate sections of an essay, and to see how these fit together logically to develop a sociological argument focused on the question.

Underneath the essay title given below you will find a series of boxes containing a number of words and phrases, together with a box reminding you of the need for a brief introduction and a suitable conclusion. Each box represents the basis of a section containing a number of paragraphs which should contain all the words and phrases contained within the box, in any order you choose. However, the boxes are not placed in any particular order, so you must decide what is the most logical sequence to place them to develop your argument. Remember that you must try to use all of the words and phrases within each box, but also that there are many other relevant sociological concepts and references to sociological theories and writers that you should also include. There is also a 'wild card' box which contains some questions which should be addressed at whatever points in your answer seem appropriate.

Important point: One of the most common failings of students writing essays on this topic is to present a prepared answer on 'the secularisation debate'. While this debate will form part of your answer, you must remember to keep a clear focus on the main thrust of the question, which is to *assess* the *extent to which* science has *replaced* religion as the *main belief system* in modern societies. Note the italicised words carefully, and be sure that your answer covers them.

Assess the extent to which science has replaced religion as the main belief system in modern societies.

Growth of sects

Postmodernism

Problems of statistics

'Believing without belonging'

'New Age' beliefs and practices

Fundamentalist movements

'Golden Age of Faith'

'Pick 'n' Mix' religious beliefs

The Enlightenment

Rationalisation

Traditional

Legal-rational

Max Weber

Disenchantment

Charismatic

Beliefs based on magic and superstition

Secularisation

Church attendance statistics

Alternative sources of norms
   and values

Decline in religiosity

Membership of major religions

Separation of church and state

Role of religion in society

Belief in the supernatural

The importance of religious ritual

Religion as a source of meaning

Religion as a source of norms and values

Religion as ideology

Postmodernism

Disenchantment with science

Rise of individualism

End of metanarratives

Civil religion

Continuing belief in superstitions

Wild cards
- Are all 'modern societies' the same with regard to the issues raised by the question?
- How reliable is the evidence that religion ever formed 'the main belief system' of what are now termed 'modern societies'?
- What proportion of the population actually has a good understanding of science?
- Is there a single 'belief system' in science?
- Are there examples of scientific and religious beliefs coming into conflict? What are some of the outcomes?

- Is it possible to talk of a 'main belief system' in modern societies, especially where these are multicultural?
- What evidence is there for the process of secularisation in faiths other than Christianity?

Introduction
Remember to use this to 'set the scene' and to show your understanding of what the question is asking you to do, and why this issue is important to the debates within the sociology of religion.

Conclusion
Give a brief summary of your arguments. Do they show that you have addressed the issues raised by the question? Have you reached a conclusion (which arises from your arguments and evidence) regarding 'the extent to which' science has replaced religion?

Chapter 7

Social Factors and Religious Belief

By the end of this chapter you will be able to:

- examine the patterns of religious belief in Britain;
- examine the relationship between ethnicity, faith and religious participation;
- examine the relationship between gender, faith and participation;
- examine the relationship between faith, participation and other social characteristics such as age, social class and sexuality.

ETHNICITY, FAITH AND IDENTITY IN THE UK

Although the established church in Britain is the Anglican Church or the Church of England, Britain is a multicultural and multi-faith society where the major non-Christian faiths are Islam, Judaism and those originating in the Indian subcontinent, namely Hinduism and Sikhism. The ethnic minority communities make up around 8 per cent of the British population, but it is amongst these communities that we find some of the strongest religious commitment and adherence. Data from the 2001 census for ethnic groups in Britain is shown in Table 7.1.

There are, however, problems with the classifications used in the census. Firstly, people are asked to self-classify according to pre-set categories; secondly, ethnic groups do not necessarily relate to distinct cultures or religions; and thirdly, the 'white' category hides many different ethnic groups such as Irish, Welsh, Scottish, East European etc. The term 'ethnic group' does not necessarily refer to ethnic minorities or to communities with a shared sense of origin and identity.

There is, however, little doubt that immigration has altered the religious profile of Britain. Tables 7.2 and 7.3 show membership of different faiths in

Table 7.1   Ethnic groups in Britain, April 2001

Ethnic group	Percentage of total population	Percentage of non-white population
White	92.1	
Mixed	1.2	14.6
Indian	1.8	22.7
Pakistani	1.3	16.1
Bangladeshi	0.5	6.1
Other Asian	0.4	5.3
All Asian or Asian British	4.0	50.3
Black Caribbean	1.0	12.2
Black African	0.8	10.5
Black Other	0.2	2.1
All Black or Black British	2.0	24.8
Chinese	0.4	5.3
Other ethnic groups	0.4	5.0
All minority ethnic population	7.9	100.00

Source: 2001 Census, National Statistics Online.

(i) 1980 and 1990, and then (ii) in 2001, the latter taken from the 2001 census data. Note that Table 7.2 shows data in millions, while Table 7.3 is in thousands. This illustrates the care that has to be taken when comparing statistics.

In 2001 the National Census collected information about religious identity in the UK. This question was new to the census for England, Wales and Scotland, though the topic had been included in previous censuses in Northern Ireland. Although the census question on religion was voluntary, over 92 per cent of people chose to answer it. Just over three-quarters of the UK population reported having a religion. People in Northern Ireland were most likely to say that they identified with a religion (86 per cent) compared with 77 per cent of people in England and Wales and 67 per cent in Scotland. About 16 per cent of the UK population stated that they had no religion.

Table 7.2   UK religious community, 1980 and 1990

	1980 (millions)	1990 (millions)
Christian	39.8	38.6
Non-Trinitarian	0.8	1.1
Hindu	0.4	0.4
Jew	0.3	0.3
Muslim	0.6	1.0
Sikh	0.3	0.5
Total	42.4	42.2

Source: Fact File (1999).

Table 7.3   Religions in Britain, 2001

	Thousands	%
Christian	42,079	71.6
Buddhist	152	0.3
Hindu	559	1.0
Jew	267	0.5
Muslim	1,591	2.7
Sikh	336	0.6
Other religion	179	0.3
All religions	*45,163*	*76.8*
No religion	9,104	15.5
Not stated	4,289	7.3
*All no religion/not stated**	*13,626*	*23.2*
Base	58,789	100.0

* Includes 234,000 cases in Northern Ireland where data is only available as a combined category.
Source: Office for National Statistics, Census, April 2001.

The increasing numbers of ethnic minority groups coming into Britain throughout the 20th century might have been an opportunity for the established churches to embrace those ethnic minorities who were already Christian into their congregations. However, this did not happen and the new Christian immigrants, mainly from the Caribbean islands, tended to form their own churches that were mainly Pentecostal and evangelical. Those who were non-Christian established their own mosques, temples and gurdwaras.

In terms of Christian churches, the 2005 Church Census showed that 83 per cent of regular churchgoers are white, 10 per cent black and 7 per cent from various other non-white ethnic backgrounds. This means that non-white church attendance has increased by 19 per cent since 1998, while the white churchgoing community decreased by 19 per cent. The figures also show that the representation of black churchgoers is around three times their proportion in the population, which is estimated to be about 3.8 per cent.

RELIGION AND IDENTITY

One of the more recent developments in the sociology of religion is the study of the relationship between religious faith and individual identity. This is especially relevant to ethnic minority faiths because for many individuals, their religion is an important definer of their identity. As Modood et al. (1994, p. 5) argue:

> While some groups assert a racial identity based on the experience of having suffered racism, others choose to emphasise their family origins

and homeland (even when they have never visited it or have any plans to do so), others group around a caste or religious sect as do Hindus such as Patels or Lohanas, while yet others promote a trans-ethnic identity like Islam.

It is possible for one individual to have to cope with the competing claims of being, for example, black, Asian, Pakistani and Muslim as well as having to reconcile these demands with those of gender, class and what being 'British' means. We might think that ethnic minority identities were simply products of cultural practices, but there is no straightforward link between the two. Hutnik (1991) found that of young British Asians who thought of themselves as 'Indian', many were not Indian in cultural behaviour, whilst those who were more culturally Indian did not see themselves as such. The study by Modood et al. examined the relationship between, among other factors, religion and identity. They found that a significant factor was whether a person had been brought up in Britain. Nearly all of the first-generation immigrants saw religion as important to the way they led their lives. They mentioned religion as a moral structure, a guideline on food and drink restrictions, and in defining correct patterns of behaviour for the family. However, second-generation Asians were more diverse in their responses and there were differences between the faiths. Some of the Muslim respondents saw the most important everyday manifestations of faith as being dietary – what they could and could not eat. It is interesting that at the time of this study there was little support from the respondents for single faith schools apart from some of the Muslims. Even with some of the Muslim respondents, separate faith schooling was not endorsed: 'I find the whole idea of Muslim schools is wrong. Separating our children from children of other communities will mean that when the child gets to the age of 16, he or she will find it hard to mix with these children because they would only know one culture' (Modood et al., 1994, p. 54).

This point is interesting as the Labour government in 2001 recommended the setting up of more single faith schools. Polly Toynbee, however, thought that it was a policy unlikely to be successful:

A new education minister cast a colder eye on religious schools even before the calamitous riots in Oldham and Bradford. Shocking scenes in Ardoyne with Catholic girls spat at by Protestant parents showed the worst face of apartheid schools. After September 11 [2001] the hot breath of religious passion made that special ethos look more sinister. From many quarters now comes the sound of screeching brakes on a policy that threatens to divide by race and religion. (*Guardian*, 9 November 2001)

However, by 2007, there were about 7000 faith schools in the state sector in England, 600 of them secondary and 6400 primary. This represents approximately one third of all schools. The vast majority of these are Christian, mainly Church of England or Roman Catholic. Together, they take about 1.7 million pupils. Twenty-one per cent of secondary pupils in faith schools are from ethnic minority groups. However, the government wishes to make it easier for independent faith schools to get into the state sector, and has pledged support for religious schools where there is parental demand. It has already given the Association of Muslim Schools £100,000 to make the transition into the state sector smoother for more of the 120 independent Islamic schools. Once in the state sector, schools receive capital funding and their day-to-day running costs are met.

The existence of faith schools remains, however, controversial. A *Guardian/ICM* poll published in August 2005 showed that 64 per cent of those polled agreed that 'the government should not be funding faith schools of any kind'. The poll was of a random sample of 1008 adults carried out by telephone across the country. The results were weighted to the profile of all adults.

One of the main concerns expressed about faith schools, particularly those catering to ethnic minority faiths, is that they have the potential to divide communities. In 2005, David Bell, the chief inspector of schools, said in a speech to the Hansard Society that traditional Islamic education did not entirely fit pupils for their lives as Muslims in modern Britain. The Association of Muslim Schools responded by saying that their faith schools turned out rounded citizens, more tolerant of others and less likely to succumb to extremism.

This optimism is perhaps not unfounded. Between 2005 and 2007, a team of researchers from Lancaster University carried out research in Burnley, the site of so-called 'race riots' in 2001 (Holden, 2008). Part of the research involved trying to ascertain the attitudes to religion of Year 10 pupils. While the research did not look at pupils in faith schools, questionnaires were completed by 435 pupils from three different state schools – a 'majority Asian', a 'majority White' and a mixed school. The research showed that Asian pupils, the overwhelming majority of whom were Muslim, had a far greater level of religious conviction than their white counterparts: 97 per cent of the Asian pupils believed in God, 81 per cent regularly attended a place of worship and 94 per cent lived in accordance with religious rules. The author of the research said that despite popular media representations of British Muslims as insular, intolerant and unwilling to integrate, 86 per cent of Asian pupils showed a willingness to listen to other people's religious views, 76 per cent felt that faith communities should work together in pursuit of harmonious social relations and 87 per cent believed in showing loyalty to the UK. Although the Asian pupils were not being educated in a faith school, the findings suggest a high degree of religious tolerance. The white pupils surveyed in the research showed a different profile. Only about 50 per cent said that they were willing to listen to other people's religious views and only 29 per cent thought that religious unity was a worthy goal. In response to a question about racial equality, almost one-third of white pupils believed in the superiority of their own race and only one-quarter believed that it was important to show tolerance towards people from different religious, cultural and ethnic backgrounds. Although these views represent a minority of those questioned, the research paints a fairly bleak picture for the future of race relationships in areas of ethnic and religious diversity.

In 2005, the European Group for Research on Equity in Educational Systems published a report based on research on 13,000 pupils in five European countries (Gorard, 2008). The pupils were around 14 years old at the time of the study. Among the sample were 732 students who were born in – or at least one of whose parents was born in – a predominantly Muslim country. The report classifies these students as 'recent immigrants' to their host country. As part of the research, all the students involved were presented with a particular situation (adapted to be specific to each of the five countries), and given a choice of two proposed answers. For England, the question was worded as follows: 'Jenny's family has a different religion to most people in Britain, and they want Jenny to be taught in a school based on that different religion. This means that she will not go to her local school.' The students were asked to select one of two proposed answers:

1 This is not fair because school is one place where people who are different should be able to work alongside each other.
2 This is fair because people who are different should have the opportunity to attend different schools.

The authors of the research found that recent immigrants from Muslim countries showed the same responses as other students, with 79 per cent choosing option 1. The authors point out that in general, and in so far as the research reflects the views of at least some Muslims, recent immigrants want the same opportunities and treatment as everyone else.

Religion and Afro-Caribbean identity

Modood et al. (1994) found several features regarding religion and ethnic identity which differentiated first-generation Afro-Caribbean settlers from Asians:

■ First-generation migrants from the Caribbean were Christian and so religion was less significant as part of their ethnic difference, whereas the Asian groups had to set up religious structures in order to practise their faiths, and religion became an important aspect of identity.

■ Religion seemed to play a different role for the people from the Caribbean. It was a support in coping with everyday problems and it was celebratory and joyful. For the Asian respondents, religion was more related to duty, routine and the patterning of everyday life.

■ The Afro-Caribbean respondents said that their children could make their own decisions about faith in adulthood, but the Asians held expectations that their children would follow the family faith.

■ Asians saw religion as having a significant influence on the rules of everyday life concerning food, drink, dress and marriage partners. This was strongest among Muslims.

Modood et al. argued that to second-generation Asian respondents, religion became much more an issue of ethnic identity, but this was not the case for second-generation Afro-Caribbeans. As Christianity is the majority faith for white British people, it was not part of the minority identity of Afro-Caribbeans – not something that only they could keep alive.

By far the largest religious movement amongst Afro-Caribbeans in Britain is Pentecostalism. This is a Christian movement which was very common in the West Indies and which was exported to the USA and to Britain. An evangelical movement, it emphasises participation from the congregation, the importance of personal spiritual experience and the importance of 'gifts of the spirit', especially glossolalia or speaking in tongues. As Pryce (1979, p. 199) explains, 'Glossolalia is a form of repetitive unintelligible vocalisation uttered by the believer in a state of ecstasy and euphoria. Almost always, glossolalia is accompanied by uninhibited dancing, shouting, stomping, whirling, twitching ... and cries. Possession by the Spirit is a sign that the individual is in direct contact with God.'

This would fit with Weber's analysis of the appeal of particular religious groups to those who are socially and/or economically disprivileged. In fact his term 'the theodicy of disprivilege' seems to be significant here.

Rastafarianism

Hall (1985) has argued that religion can be seen as an act of rebellion or resistance to colonial rule and oppression. This is the case with the Rastafarian movement, which he sees as a mixture of religious, political and nationalist ideas. The ideas of Rastafarianism were those of the evangelical preacher

Marcus Garvey who, in the 1920s, promised to deliver the followers of Ras Tafari – the Emperor Haile Selassie of Ethiopia – back to their promised land and away from the oppression of white 'Babylon'. Babylon stood for anything that involved racist oppression. Rastafarianism became popularised in the 1970s and 1980s through the music of Bob Marley and the Wailers.

Many second- and third-generation Afro-Caribbean men in Britain adopted the Rastafarian faith and their distinctive appearance and cultural behaviours often brought them into conflict with the forces of law and order. The wore their hair in 'dreadlocks' which represented the lion's mane after Haile Selassie, the Lion Emperor, and they smoked 'ganja' (marihuana), which remains illegal in Great Britain. Not all men who adopted the style necessarily accepted the faith and the idea of return. Today there seems to be a reduced emphasis on Ethiopia as the Promised Land and a stronger one on style and transformation of their present situation.

Bruce (1998) maintains that religion can serve different functions for members of ethnic minority groups. He uses the terms 'cultural transition' and 'cultural defence' to illustrate these.

Cultural transition, according to Bruce, is a means whereby religion gains an enhanced importance because of the assistance it can give in helping people cope with the shift from one world to another. It might be that the people in question have migrated; it might be that they remain in the same place while that place changes under their feet. For Irish Catholics in Boston, USA in the 19th century and for Muslims settling in Bradford in the 20th, religion provided practical and ideological help and support in the transition from old to new societies. We can see how this can be applied to many Asian and Afro-Caribbean communities in Britain, where their places of worship become concrete evidence of their various faiths and the faiths themselves make up an important part of their cultural and individual identities.

The other concept, **cultural defence**, occurs when two or more communities find themselves in conflict and they are of different religions. Then the religious identity of each can call forth a new loyalty in which their religious identity becomes a way of asserting ethnic pride. Religion becomes involved in the generation of ethnic identity because it identifies a people or community and, thus, distinguishes them from their neighbours. As well as this, the content of the various belief systems can provide legitimation – often by claiming divine support for their actions. (There is a further discussion of religion and identity in this chapter, pp. 134–7.)

An example of what Weber called 'ethnic honour' is shown in the early migrations into the USA. The WASPs (White Anglo-Saxon Protestants) considered themselves to be superior to the more working-class settlers from

Ireland and southern Europe. The WASPs saw themselves as uniquely possessing civic virtues because of their Protestant faith, in contrast to the less desirable social characteristics displayed by Catholics.

GENDER AND FAITH

'Religion has been a major institution for the social control of women' (Neitz, 1993). Feminist writers have criticised the invisibility of women in most of the mainstream works in the sociology of religion. In 1895, Elizabeth Cady Stanton commented upon the maleness of the Christian faith in *The Woman's Bible*. She even challenged the assumption that God was male. Her argument was that although God had created men and women equal, the men responsible for writing the Bible had imbued it with their own, male, viewpoint: 'The canon and civil law; church and state; priests and legislators; all political parties and religious denominations have alike taught that woman was made after man, of man, and for man, an inferior being, subject to man. The fashions, forms, ceremonies and customs of society, church ordinances and discipline all grow out of this idea' (Stanton, 1895).

Several feminist researchers have studied the way in which religions and religious ideologies have fostered sexism. They have identified a strong relationship between religious ideology, familism and the control over female sexuality. This is somewhat paradoxical as, with the Christian faith, at least, there has always been a higher attendance figure for women than for men. In 1991, for example, women constituted 61 per cent of frequent church attenders and 65 per cent of regular attenders. Table 7.4 shows the frequency of attending religious services by gender.

Table 7.4   Frequency of attending religious services by gender, Great Britain, 1999

Frequency	Males (%)	Females (%)	All (%)
Once a week or more	10	13	12
Less often but at least once in two weeks	1	2	2
Less often but at least once a month	4	6	5
Less often but at least twice a year	8	10	9
Less often but at least once a year	6	7	7
Less often	5	5	5
Never or practically never	53	44	49
Varies too much to say	–	1	1
Not answered	1	2	1
No religion	11	10	10
All	100	100	100

Source: British Social Attitudes Survey, *Social Trends* 31 (2001).

In 1985 part of a large-scale international study on beliefs and values was undertaken in Britain by Abrams et al. for the European Values Systems Study Group. In this study, 1231 respondents answered questions on their religious affiliation, participation and beliefs. Of this group, 76 per cent reported a belief in God; 56 per cent defined themselves as religious, and only 4 per cent defined themselves as atheists. The study demonstrated the importance of gender as a factor affecting religious belief and practice. Women were more likely than men to see themselves as religious, but there were differences in economic position within the female sample. Working women were more likely than non-working women to have a religious commitment and this continued into middle age.

Table 7.5 shows the differences between religious commitment between working and non-working women. It can be seen that commitment increases with age, but economic status runs counter to Berger's argument that the most secular are those closest to the economic process.

YouGov, in conjunction with the *Daily Telegraph*, carried out an online poll of 2015 adults aged 18+ throughout Britain on 7th and 8th December 2004. The results by gender, shown in Table 7.6, have been weighted to the profile of all adults. The zero shown for Hindus and Sikhs indicates that the number of responses was too small to result in a whole number.

The ordination of women into the priesthood of the established Christian church was only accepted after lengthy and often acrimonious debate. In 1992, the General Synod, the ruling body of the Church of England, finally decided to allow the ordination of women. Its decision was met with considerable antagonism and several high-ranking officials of the church defected to Roman Catholicism as a result. Many opponents cited a passage from St Paul in the New Testament: 'Women should remain silent in the churches. They are not allowed to speak but must be in submission as the law says.' (1 Corinthians

Table 7.5 Religious commitment of women, by age and working status, 1985

Religious commitment	Working women %			Non-working women %			
	Under 24	25–44	45–64	Under 24	25–44	45–64	65+
Low	32	18	13	54	20	8	9
Low–medium	28	25	13	29	32	26	10
Medium	16	17	19	11	16	12	14
Medium–high	19	25	21	4	11	25	33
High	14	15	32	0	22	29	35

Source: Adapted from Abrams et al. (1985).

Table 7.6   Results of YouGov survey, 7 and 8 December 2004, by gender

Which of these statements applies to you?	Male (%)	Female (%)	Total (%)
I am a Christian and go to church services regularly.	7	8	8
I am a Christian and go to church services from time to time	6	11	8
I am a Christian but go to church only for special services (e.g. weddings, funerals, Christmas)	31	33	32
I am a Christian but never go to church services	11	11	11
I am Jewish	1	1	1
I am a Muslim	1	1	1
I am a Hindu	0	0	0
I am a Sikh	0	0	0
I belong to another faith	3	4	4
I am not religious at all	39	31	35

Source: www.yougov.com/archives/pdf/STI040101003_2.pdf

14:34). In 1987, the Anglican Bishop of London cited a more contemporary reason. When asked whether he thought the Christian notion of God would be affected by seeing a woman regularly up at the altar, he said, 'I think it would. My instinct would be to take her in my arms' (quoted by Giddens, 1997, p. 452).

The Church of England is part of the wider Anglican Communion which has already ordained some women in other parts of the world (e.g. Canada, the United States, Australia, Ireland and South Africa). Although the measure to ordain women was passed, women are still unable to become bishops and it will need a new law to allow this. The Church of England was not alone in its rejection of women as priests. No woman can be ordained into the Roman Catholic priesthood, and the same is true for Russian, Greek and Other Orthodox Churches. There are, of course, women's orders whose nuns have been influential in teaching and nursing establishments, but not as prime movers in the policy making of either the Anglican or Roman Catholic Church.

However, church leadership is open to women in many of the non-conformist Christian faiths, notably Baptists and Methodists. It is also interesting to note that several of the charismatic leaders of sects and cults have been women. The Spiritualist movement was started by the Fox sisters in the USA in the late 19th century. Mary Baker Eddy was the originator of the Christian Science movement and Ann Lee founded the Shaker movement.

New Age Faiths and Women

Bruce (1995b) argues that the New Age faiths attract more women than men. These faiths include:

- *New Science*, which challenges conventional science and medicine and includes diverse beliefs ranging from an emphasis on herbal and homeopathic remedies for illness to ideas about witchcraft and the occult.
- *New Ecology* (often linked with eco-feminism), which is concerned with environmentally 'green' issues such as pollution and conservation, and animal rights issues such as those concerning the testing of cosmetics and medicines on animals.
- *New Spirituality* (and New Psychology), which ranges from ideas about reincarnation to the new therapies such as aromatherapy and massage.

These New Age movements typically attract largely middle-class followers. In Britain followers are mainly from the south-east and other predominantly affluent areas. However, more women than men find their ideas appealing. Bruce sees several factors at work here. Firstly, women have traditionally been involved with 'deviant' religious movements such as those stressing charisma and spirit possession. There are many examples, including Madame Blavatsky and Annie Besant, founders of the Theosophical movement in the late 19th century. In the New Age movement there is a gender split between parapsychology and esoteric knowledge elements, which attract mainly male followers, and the healing, channelling and spirituality elements, which are mainly female.

Why should women be more interested in the spiritual aspects? Bruce sees two possible reasons:

- The focus of religious activity – religion has become increasingly personal or concerned with the domestic world, but Bruce also believes that there is a resonance between femininity and spirituality. As women are socialised to be more expressive than men, this conforms more easily to the spiritual elements of New Age faiths.
- The challenge to patriarchy inherent in New Age faiths – this encourages women since they have more to gain from the demolishing of traditional gender roles in society.

Women and Islam

Men have authority over women because Allah has made the one superior to the other, and because they spend their wealth to maintain them. Good women are obedient. They guard their unseen parts because Allah has guarded them. As for those from whom you fear disobedience, admonish them and send them to beds apart and beat them. Then if they obey you, take no further action against them.   (The Qur'an 4.34)

It is from passages such as this that the rest of the world takes its stereotypical views of the position of Muslim women. Indeed, one of the areas that can cause controversy between Muslims and some non-Muslims concerns the treatment of women. The most common references to Muslim girls and women in the British press are those relating to arranged or forced marriages, and even so-called 'honour killings'. However, Charlotte Butler's research (1995) presents a very different picture of Muslim women in Britain:

Islam's not to blame for women being kept in the house, covered up 24 hours a day, it's the menfolk that do this. It's not Islam, Islam doesn't impose and say you've got to do this. And covering your hair, it's not important, or covering your legs and so forth, it's not that important as obeying Islam and following Islam. To follow is more important than to wear clothes and so forth, and dress in a certain manner. If your heart follows Islam then you follow Islam, and clothing's got nothing to do with it, or culture. Cultures are man's invention I suppose.   (One of the female interviewees)

For her research, Butler undertook 30 semi-structured interviews in Coventry and Bradford with both men and women, aged between 18 and 30 years. She recruited her interviewees from youth centres, community centres and various other contacts. Results from the interviews with the women showed a continuing commitment to their faith which was cultivated by their families and the Muslim community at large. Many saw faith as a defining aspect of their personal identity, and, along with faith, gender and ethnicity were seen as important in the creation of an identity.

Many of the women believed that it was their culture rather than their faith which affected the position of women in Muslim society and that gender inequality was a legacy of the traditional Asian community. All believed that life was changing for Muslim women in this country and there were significant differences between the experiences of the different generations. Overall, Butler found considerable optimism in their views of their chances of adopting lifestyles consonant with changing times.

In Britain in 2006 a national 'listening exercise' was undertaken, run by the Muslim Women's Network and the Women's National Commission. The exercise, which lasted for five months, included five 'road shows' which enabled Muslim women to speak freely on a variety of issues. The published report was entitled *She Who Disputes* (2006), and contains the direct words of over 200 women who took part. The title of the report refers to the story of a woman who complained to the Prophet Muhammad after she was divorced by her husband according to an old Arab pagan custom that freed husbands from any responsibilities or duties to their former wife. She argued with the Prophet about this form of injustice to women, and subsequently verses of Surah 58 of the Qur'an were revealed to him, and the custom was abolished.

The report shows that Muslim women felt that their views are being ignored, because community leaders and male-dominated national Muslim organisations are failing to represent them. The women agreed that the media are guilty of stereotyping Muslim women as oppressed and submissive, which can fuel Islamophobia, but they considered that the Muslim community itself silences women at local and national level. The women accused men within their communities of using Islam 'as a way to control women', even though such control is based on cultural practices rather than true Islam. The women also criticised the government for consulting the Muslim community through groups such as the Muslim Council of Britain, in which women's voices are 'either absent or extremely marginalised'. (*www.thenwc.org.uk/wnc_work/ muslim_women.html*)

In June 2006 the Pew Research Center in Washington USA published the results of a survey which collated the opinions of 14,000 people in 13 countries (Pew Global Attitudes Project, *http://pewglobal.org/reports/display.php? ReportID=253*). One of the findings was that Westerners, by a large margin, did not regard Muslims as 'respectful of women'. (Interestingly, majorities in four out of the five Muslim countries surveyed said the same about the West.)

Women and Judaism

The first survey of Jewish women's opinions was commissioned by the Chief Rabbi in 1994 (Goodkin and Citron, 1994). The report revealed that women from all walks of life experience an overwhelming dissatisfaction with their marginal position in Judaism. Of the sample, 58 per cent said that they found it difficult to express themselves spiritually in the synagogue. The problem is that Halakhah (Jewish religious law) forbids the involvement of women in the synagogue.

RELIGION AND SOCIAL CLASS

There is very little written systematically linking social class to religious beliefs and participation. However, there is a great deal that we can infer from what we already know about appeal and participation. Certainly, in past centuries there was a closer fit between social class and religious membership and participation. In our more postmodern world, the relationship has fragmented and the picture is less clear cut.

Religion and the working classes

In Weber's analysis of religion we can see a direct link to class when he wrote about the appeal of religious organisations such as sects. He emphasised the marginality and relative deprivation of those individuals who joined sects as a response to their feelings of social and economic deprivation. The sect offered a theodicy of disprivilege; this was an explanation as to why individuals might be suffering poverty or low social status on earth and how their rewards were to come in the next life or heaven. It is not surprising then that the evangelical sects that offered gifts of the spirit would be embraced by the economically deprived.

It is also possible to link some denominations to social class position. Early Methodism is an example of a working-class denomination, which provided considerable political opportunities for workers who were unable to combine together in trades unions.

Religion and the middle classes

We can again make reference to Weber's work here because his analysis of the Protestant ethic looks at the new middle-class entrepreneurs of the 17th century. He explains the link between economic success and religious faith by using the methodology of *verstehen*. From his work we can see the how development of the Protestant Ethic has affected work in modern capitalism.

Today the middle classes are slightly more likely to attend church services than the working classes. Members of the Church of England are generally middle class and more likely to be conservative in terms of their politics. The Roman Catholic Church is less class-based and has a broader appeal. It is difficult to generalise about the denominations; the Quakers, for example are likely to be middle class, whereas the Pentecostals are more socially mixed.

Using Wilson's categorisation of sects (see pp. 59–60) it is possible to link the middle classes to the manipulationist sects or the sects of success. These sects offer a means of achieving success and status in this world and the appeal has been mainly to the lower middle class. However, sects such as Scientology and, more recently, the Alpha Course have attracted wealthy celebrities. Hollywood stars such as Tom Cruise and John Travolta have been attracted by the appeal of Scientology, and former Spice Girls member Geri Halliwell found support in Alpha courses. Wallis's typology (see pp. 62–3) could also be used to examine the world-affirming sects and their essentially middle-class appeal.

It has been said that the Church of England is 'the Tory Party at prayer'. The assumption underlying this saying is that the Church attracted the largely Conservative-voting middle classes rather than people from the working class or poorer groups. The upper classes in Britain have always been associated with the established church and the Sovereign remains the Head of the Church of England.

New Religious Movements also pose problems in terms of generalisations. As we have seen, the cults of success are more likely to attract the middle classes, as are New Age Movements, because they tend to depend on the affluence of their members. The Kabbalah (a sect of which the pop-star Madonna is a member) expects its members to sign up for expensive seminars and residential conferences and to buy the various artefacts and water that they sell. Other therapeutic sects demand high subscriptions from their members to pay for the various therapies they offer. However, in the USA the black Muslims are mainly working-class. One reason for their appeal to working-class members is that middle-class black Americans are not hostile to the capitalist structure of the USA. The Moonies and Scientologists still target younger, middle-class individuals, often in their first days at university. The appeal is obvious; they offer friendship and welcome to young people who are away from home and in need of support and companionship.

RELIGION AND AGE

It is interesting to see the general age pattern as it relates to religious membership and participation in Britain. Those most susceptible to religious belief and practice are the young (under 15) and the elderly (over 65). We might argue that young people under 15 are more likely to be influenced by their parents and family. It is also possible that the social activities attached to churches might be attractive to them. The 2005 Church Census carried out by the Christian Research Association showed that the largest group likely to attend Christian worship was the 45–64 age group, of whom 24 per cent were regular attenders. The average age of regular churchgoers was 45, but there was variation between denominations (see Table 7.7). The lowest rate of attendance was found among 15–19-year-olds, of whom only 5 per cent were regular churchgoers. However, we must be aware of possible Eurocentrism here as this is true mainly for white Christian families. For children from ethnic minority families, religious commitment may be long-lasting. Religious practice tends to diminish after 65, probably because of increased physical

Table 7.7 Average age of regular churchgoers at Christian churches, by denomination

Denomination	Average age
Anglican	49
Roman Catholic	44
Methodist	55
Baptist	43
United Reformed Church	55
Pentecostals	33
'New' churches	34
Independent churches	42
Other smaller denominations	44

Source: 2005 Church Census

disabilities, but this does not mean that belief also diminishes. In fact, the age group over 65 is probably the most highly committed to faith. Adherence to sects and cults tends to show a younger age profile and this may be because some sects are seen as esoteric and related to a drugs or counter-culture, and the 'cults of success' have more appeal for younger adults still trying to gain economic and psychological success. However, those cults associated with alternative therapies may be more attractive to an older group of followers, those who grew up in the 1960s. These groups may be 'catering for people in the mainstream, with an emphasis on the body and healing' (Heelas, quoted by Ward, 2001).

Table 7.8 Results of YouGov survey, 7 and 8 December 2004, by age

Which of these statements applies to you?	18–29 (%)	30–50 (%)	Over 50 (%)
I am a Christian and go to church services regularly.	4	7	10
I am a Christian and go to church services from time to time	9	6	10
I am a Christian but go to church only for special services (e.g. weddings, funerals, Christmas)	23	29	39
I am a Christian but never go to church services	9	12	11
I am Jewish	0	1	1
I am a Muslim	1	1	0
I am a Hindu	1	0	0
I am a Sikh	0	0	0
I belong to another faith	5	5	2
I am not religious at all	48	40	26

The YouGov Survey referred to above also broke down the responses by age. These are shown in Table 7.8.

Children and religious belief

Relatively little sociological research has been carried out on the topic of children's religious beliefs. However, in July 2005 a report was published by the National Children's Bureau for the Joseph Rowntree Foundation, which detailed research on children's perspectives on 'believing and belonging'. The study, which was carried out by Greg Smith and a team from the University of East London (Smith, 2005), examined the views of more than a hundred children aged between 9 and 11 years.

The researchers found that school is often one of the few places where children from different religious and ethnic backgrounds meet on a regular basis. In school, friendships developed across and between religious and ethnic groups, whereas friendships outside school were more likely to be shaped by family circumstances and religious affiliation. Out-of-school friendships were often influenced by the unequal power relationships between adults and children, with some adults actively discouraging children from mixing with those from a different religious background. This was particularly evident where there were significant levels of racism and intolerance in the wider society.

The children described their beliefs in terms of both social practice and teachings about morality and ethics. The researchers therefore developed a threefold typology to organise the children's accounts of their experiences. This covered the areas of:

1 **Religious identity.** This included identification with a particular religious tradition and the rituals and activities associated with it.
2 **Social practice.** This included formal learning about the religion and the public rituals, ceremonies and festivals associated with it.
3 **Belief and spirituality.** This covered the individual children's thoughts, emotions and personal practices such as private prayer and meditation.

Using this typology, the children were identified as belonging to one of the five following groups:

■ *Highly observant* – these children describe their lives as being significantly shaped by their religion. They are likely to be heavily involved in its practices and are strongly committed to its beliefs and values.

■ *Observant* – children describing religious observance as a compulsory, significant and regular part of their life. They tend to accept their religion's teachings and practices, though may find some of it boring and an imposition.

■ *Occasionally participating* – children who are only rarely taken or sent by their parents to religious activities and are not usually well instructed in their religion. However, they do identify with the religion and enjoy its festivals and feasts.

■ *Implicit individual faith* – these children focus on religion as the 'realm of the supernatural'. They speak of personal spirituality and draw on faith as a resource through prayer, meditation and ritual. Though they may belong to or attend religious institutions, these are not essential to their understanding of faith.

■ *Not religious* – children having little interest in, or understanding of, religion and with little experience of it outside school. They may mock those who are religious.

The researchers found that the amount of time spent on religion by the more devout and observant children affected their out-of-school relationships, with such children having less social interaction with children from outside their particular religion than did less devout children. The children recognised that there were issues of group identity and patterns of exclusion which formed around religious affiliations, and the ethnic term 'Asian' and the religious term 'Christian' were both used by the children as markers of racial difference. The researchers point out that this shows how the categories of ethnicity and religion overlap in children's discourse.

The effect of parental belief

Another study, published in 2005 and led by Dr David Voas of the University of Manchester (Voas and Crockett, 2005), also touches on the issue of the relationship between children's religious beliefs and practice and those of their parents. The research, carried out by the Cathie Marsh Centre for Census and Survey Research, was based on the British Household Panel Study. The Panel now consists of some 10,500 households throughout the UK, and information is collected annually on a range of factors, including employment, income and wealth, health and socio-economic values. Data from the Panel were combined with cross-sectional information from the British Social Attitudes surveys of 1983–2002.

Voas suggests that the accepted idea of people 'believing without belonging', as it is usually understood, is not borne out by the evidence, as his research indicates that religious belief is declining at a faster rate than attendance at religious services in the UK. There are now fewer people who have a real faith than passively 'belong' to a religion.

Parents' beliefs, practices and affiliations, however, do have an impact on their children though, overall, religious faith seems to be declining with each generation. The Voas research indicates that:

- two religious parents have a 50:50 chance of passing on their beliefs to their offspring;
- where there is only one religious parent, the children are only half as likely to be believers as where there are two religious parents;
- where neither parent is religious, it is likely that the children will share the parents' lack of faith.

Voas argues that, 'How children are brought up has an enormous impact on whether they will identify with a religion. Once people become adults, their religious affiliation is less likely to be affected by influences around them.' The report points out, however, that religious parents tend to have more children than do non-religious parents, which might slow down the decline in faith. Steve Jenkins, a spokesman for the Church of England, said that the Voas study had not released 'proper evidence' to support its claims. 'There is an assumption that people "catch" religion from their parents, but many people come to faith through the grandparents, schools, and their friends,' he said.

RELIGION AND HOMOSEXUALITY

An ongoing debate within the Christian church concerns the attitude of the church to homosexuality. Conservative Anglicans say that the Bible is clearly opposed to homosexuality, while liberals argue that Jesus made no reference to the issue. In November 2003 the Episcopal Church of New Hampshire, USA consecrated Gene Robinson as an openly gay bishop and started a controversy in the Anglican Communion that is still raging. Although other bishops have been gay, they were 'closeted' when they came to office; Robinson was the first bishop in a long-term gay relationship ever to be consecrated. So bitter and inflammatory is the issue that Robinson was told that he would not be allowed to take part in the 2008 Lambeth Conference in Canterbury, the ten-yearly gathering of the world's Anglican bishops – the only one out of 880 to be excluded. He stated that he intends to go to Canterbury, but will have no official status and with only the same right of access as a member of the public.

Conservatives in the Anglican church said that the issue of the ordination of gays could lead to a split in the worldwide Anglican Communion. Africa represents the largest single group of worshippers within Anglicanism, and most African churches follow the traditional Christian teaching that outlaws homosexuality. In 2008, the Archbishop of Uganda, Henry Orombi, consecrated two new bishops – one of whom was John Guernsey, a white American priest. Guernsey's parish church in Dale City, Virginia, is one of several in the United States that is opposed to the liberal approach to homosexuality. The feeling in Guernsey's parish was so strong that it voted to leave the Episcopal Church (the official branch of Anglicanism in the United States) and look instead to the Church of Uganda for leadership. Some African bishops are also threatening not to attend the 2008 Lambeth Conference if liberal American bishops play a full part.

Not only did Gene Robinson's consecration alienate the Anglican Church, but it put at risk the ecumenical relationship between the Anglican and the Catholic Church. The Catholic Church is known for its opposition to homosexual relationships, although in *Cherishing Life* it reads: 'The Church utterly condemns all forms of unjust discrimination, violence, harassment or abuse directed against people who are homosexual. Consequently, the Church teaches that homosexual people "must be accepted with respect, compassion and sensitivity"' (Catechism of the Catholic Church 2358). However, it makes clear that homosexuality is problematic: 'In so far as the homosexual orientation can lead to sexual activity which excludes openness to the generation of new human life and the essential complementarity of man and woman, it is, in this particular and precise sense only, objectively disordered' (http//:www. catholic-ew.org.uk). Pope Benedict XVI, who was ordained as Pope in 2005, has taken an uncompromising stand on homosexuality. He wrote that it was incompatible with the priesthood, and inferred that homosexuals were to blame for the problems of child sex abuse in the church. He refers to homosexuality as 'an intrinsic moral evil', and 'an objective disorder'. He went on to say: 'Therefore special concern and pastoral attention should be directed toward those who have this condition, lest they be led to believe that the living-out of this orientation in homosexual activity is a morally acceptable option. It is not' (quoted in Bunting, 2006).

The issue of gay adoption that arose in January 2007 brought Catholic and Anglican sensitivities into the foreground. The Catholic Church expressed concern that equal opportunities legislation would prevent their adoption agencies pursuing their policy of refusing adoptions to gay and lesbian couples, and asked for special exemption on the basis of religious conviction. Ruth Kelly, Communities Secretary in the Labour government and herself a committed Roman Catholic and member of the Catholic organisation Opus Dei, initially seemed to support their viewpoint. Even the Archbishop of Canterbury, Rowan Williams, joined support for the Catholic position. This was an interesting position for Williams to take, coming as it did just before the meeting of the world's Anglican leaders in Dar es Salaam. The African archbishops and bishops were threatening a schism (break) from the Church of England because of the latter's seeming liberal attitude to homosexuality. In the end, government legislation maintained that there were no exemptions and the Catholic adoption agencies were given a period of grace to prepare and monitor existing placements before they made a decision whether to close their agencies or not.

CONCLUSION

Religious belief and practice are associated with a number of social factors, and it is possible to divide populations into different groups to highlight the significance of these factors. However, it is important to remember that the groups are not mutually exclusive – one may be, for example, an elderly Afro-Caribbean woman – and therefore the patterns, while interesting and informative, are just that – patterns. Examining religiosity, or the lack of it, is a complex enterprise and we should tread carefully when interpreting the evidence.

Important concepts

Pentecostalism • evangelicalism • Rastafarianism • cultural transition • cultural defence • New Age Faiths • New Religious Movements

---

Summary points

- Immigration has changed the face of religion in Britain. Not only have immigrants brought different religions and religious practices with them, many show greater religiosity than those in the host society.
- For many ethnic minority groups, religion serves several different purposes, including being an important part of establishing and maintaining one's identity.
- On the whole, women tend to be more religious than men, both in terms of their belief and the practice of their faith. This gender difference is less apparent among those of the Muslim faith.
- The links between religion and social class are complex, but there is a greater tendency for the middle classes to attend services, particularly at Christian churches, than the working classes.

- With regard to age, the Christian churches show that both professed belief and attendance at services is more in evidence among the older age groups. As many immigrants are in the younger age groups, it is more difficult in these cases to establish clear links between religiosity and age.
- The issue of homosexuality threatens to divide branches of the worldwide Christian church.

Critical thinking

(A)

Essay guidance

Read the following essay title carefully, then use the guidance provided to plan an answer.

> Assess the view that the greater religiosity of some ethnic minority groups in Britain might serve to bring them into conflict with the host society.

Introduction

Make this brief, but use it to show that you understand *why* this view might be expressed. Think of an example of a recent situation in which such conflict seemed to be apparent.

Then use the following questions and points to construct a series of paragraphs to develop your arguments. Don't forget to use appropriate evidence, both from sociological research and actual events, to support and illustrate your points.

- What does it mean to say that a group is 'more religious' than another group? How could/should this be decided?
- What is the nature and quality of the evidence on which such an opinion is often based?
- Are there any important differences between different ethnic minority groups? Are members of the host society always aware of these differences?
- How might you make use of the concepts of 'cultural defence' and 'cultural transmission'?
- What are the areas of potential conflict between (or even within) groups of different religious faiths – or between those with faith and those without? (You might consider dress, food, ideas concerning blasphemy and a variety of cultural practices based on religious beliefs – e.g. with regard to marriage, the role of women, the nature of education, the status of older people etc.)

Conclusion

You should have come to a conclusion about the two following issues:

(E)

1 Is there a tendency for members of ethnic minority groups to come into conflict with members of the host society? If so, how great and how widespread is this tendency? Have any situations been triggered by particular events? Are there differences between different groups?

2   If there are examples of conflicts between the groups under discussion, are they actually based solely on the 'greater religiosity' of members of certain groups, or are there other factors at play?

Remember, this is a conclusion – all the evidence for your concluding remarks should have been presented and discussed in the main body of your essay.

Chapter 8

Religion: a Global Context

By the end of this chapter, you will:

- be aware of some of the current arguments concerning religion and global issues such as fundamentalism and intelligent design;
- recognise that the rise in fundamentalism challenges the secularisation thesis;
- have knowledge of some of the religious and ethnic tensions in Britain and other Western countries following the terrorist attacks of 2001 and 2005;
- be able to answer essay questions on these issues.

INTRODUCTION

There are several issues that concern social commentators, sociologists and politicians relating to the role of religion in today's world. In Chapter 6, we looked at the problems that sociologists face when deciding whether secularisation is or is not taking place. We can see that some sociologists of religion have been influenced by a Eurocentric outlook. In arguing that the decline of religion in Western industrialised societies was an inevitable outcome of modernisation, they were ignoring the situations of some non-Western societies with very different relationships to religion and religious belief, as well as possibly misinterpreting or overlooking some evidence from their own society. In this chapter we are going to look at some examples of what some see as the re-emergence of religion, especially in relation to the growth of religious fundamentalism. We will also examine the after-effects of the recent terrorist attacks in the United States and Britain, and see how these link to changes in the way in which Muslims in particular are perceived by many non-Muslims in the West.

FUNDAMENTALISM

While currently applied to many different religions, the term 'fundamentalism' originated in the USA in the first part of the 20th century. Responding to a concern over the loss of influence of traditional American revivalism, leading evangelical Protestant churchmen issued a series of pamphlets between 1910 and 1915 entitled The *Fundamentals: A Testimony to the Truth*. In 1920 an American journalist and Baptist lay preacher, Curtis Lee Laws, used the term 'fundamentalist' to apply to those prepared 'to do battle royal for the Fundamentals'.

The term 'fundamentalist' is often used to describe any ethnic religious group, often extremist, such as those that have emerged since 2003, when Western coalition forces invaded Iraq. However, there is a more precise and sociological definition. A fundamentalist movement is one that challenges modernity and refers its followers back to the original scriptures. Fundamentalists believe that true salvation is possible only through strict adherence to these scriptures. There is a tendency within fundamentalist movements to challenge or resist the larger religious community from which they emerge, because of their view that the original beliefs have become corrupted or compromised in some way. Although we increasingly associate fundamentalism with Islam, there are examples of fundamentalist groups in several of the other major religions, including Hinduism, Buddhism, Christianity and Judaism. Certainly fundamentalism calls into question the assumption that modernisation inevitably leads to secularisation.

Davie (1995) makes an important point about the difficulty of defining fundamentalism as a concept. Although it takes the believers back to what are considered the 'essential truths' of a faith, it does so only as these truths relate to the pressures of an expanding global economy. Bauman (1990) has argued that Christian fundamentalism may be fulfilling a spiritual desire for some people. In a postmodern society some people are made anxious by the erosion of old certainties. Fundamentalism fills the spaces left by this erosion and provides a set of clear, unchallengeable beliefs, practices and moral guidelines – a lifestyle that provides support and security.

FUNDAMENTALISM AND IDEAL TYPES

If we are to use the concept of fundamentalism to refer to similar movements within different faiths, we must create a set of criteria to allow us to do this.

Davie suggests that it would be helpful to construct an ideal type, and she draws on the work of Marty (1988) to outline the following ideal type of fundamentalism:

- ■ Fundamentalism generally emerges out of traditional cultures that have remained undisturbed for many generations and are then challenged or disturbed.
- ■ Threats may be external or internal, but they generate insecurity that may be addressed by a specific leader.
- ■ Reactions of the group to the threats usually make use of selective retrieval from the past, for which particular authority is sought. This authority is often in the form of a sacred text or book.
- ■ An 'us and them' mentality sets in with the group against the rest of society.
- ■ Paradoxically, even though they set themselves up against modernity, fundamentalist groups use often modern technology to spread their beliefs to a wider audience.

Fundamentalism, then, is itself a product of modernity; it is born out of the collision between modernity and traditional cultures. Fundamentalist movements, although they pre-date it, are in fact elements of the postmodern world. In this world, progress has been challenged and generally we have become more concerned about a dystopian future. As Davie (1995, p. 4) argues, there is uncertainty over progress including, for instance, our concerns over environmental pollution and the rapid consumption of natural fossil fuels. A new mood prevails in which religion can be seen to take on a new role. She makes reference to an article by the Archbishop of York (1992) in which he examines the contradictory pressures of the economic and cultural spheres.

> On the one hand there are the inevitable and necessary demands of trade, economic stability and power, factors which require larger and larger economic units in order to survive and which look to the international order for security and justification. But for many people precisely the opposite inclinations – the reassertion of local and national identities and the need for psychological security and rootedness – remain paramount. In other words, we 'need to know that we and our heritage, our language and our culture, count in the scheme of things, and that we are free to make our own choices'. (Habgood, 1992)

As fundamentalism can be seen as a possible response to uncertainty born of social change, we can, therefore, locate it firmly in the debate about modernity and postmodernity. Hervieu-Leger (1993) argues that the growth of fundamentalism is an example of alternative or recreated memories in a situation in which societies have lost their sense of historic tradition. Such 'memories' may not necessarily be harmful in themselves, but may become so where two forms of fundamentalism compete for territory and minds.

The various movements that we would term fundamentalist have thrown into some doubt the assumption that there has been a decline of religion during the latter end of the twentieth century and the beginning of the twenty-first. This was brought into sharp focus as a result of the terrorist attacks on the World Trade Center and the Pentagon on 11 September 2001, and the London bombings of 7 July 2005. The blame for these attacks was laid at the feet of Islamic fundamentalism in the person of Osama bin Laden and the al-Qaeda network. The strength of faith held by people such as 'suicide bombers', who were prepared to sacrifice their lives for a religious cause, called into question the Western idea that religion has become less significant today. The events of 11 September 2001 and 7 July 2005 have served to strengthen the stereotype of Islamic fundamentalism. This is discussed later in the chapter (pp. 169–77).

Over the last three decades we have witnessed the growth and success of two particular forms of fundamentalist faith movements:

- the New Christian Right in the USA;
- Islamic fundamentalism.

CHRISTIAN FUNDAMENTALISM AND THE NEW CHRISTIAN RIGHT IN THE USA

Christian Fundamentalism in the USA emerged in the final decades of the 19th century and the early decades of the 20th. The absolute truths of Protestantism were set down as the Fundamentals of the Faith, affirming the literal evidence of the Bible. Emphasis was laid on the truth of the creation narrative as against the evidence of evolutionary theory, and several states in the USA have challenged the teaching of evolutionism in schools.

In 1925, John Scopes, a biology teacher from Tennessee, was charged with breaking a state law by illegally teaching evolutionary theory. The prosecution was led by William Jennings Bryan, himself a fundamentalist who was responsible for getting legislation introduced into 15 states to ban the teaching of evolution in schools. The American Civil Liberties Union took up the Scopes case, and a brilliant lawyer, Clarence Darrow, led the defence team. Bryan claimed that 'if evolution wins, Christianity goes', while Darrow claimed that it was not evolution, but civilisation itself that was on trial. Although Scopes lost the court case (though this went to appeal at the Tennessee Supreme Court, where the court verdict was overturned), the ground was prepared for evolutionary theory. (See below for a discussion on Intelligent Design). During the next few decades, apart from some small but strong groups, Christian fundamentalism faded from public concern, but came back into prominence in the 1970s.

In the USA, between the 1970s and 1990s, Christian fundamentalist sects started to play an increasing role in society, especially in the political sphere. This was very noticeable during the presidential term of office of Ronald Reagan (1981–9). Some commentators viewed with alarm the increase in the number of believers in millenarianism who were employed by the American government at that time. Although no major international disasters occurred, some observers felt that the people who believed in the Second Coming would not try too hard to work for world peace, especially as they might view international conflict as an opportune way of heralding in the new society.

Christian fundamentalism remains strong in the USA, especially in the Midwest and in the southern 'Bible belt'. Fundamentalists have been instrumental in challenging several liberal reforms including divorce legislation, abortion law reform, gay rights and civil liberties for black and other minority groups. They have also intervened in the teaching of evolution in schools. It was not until 1967 that the Butler Act (which forbade the teaching of evolution in place of the story of Creation) was repealed. In Arkansas, the state legislature passed a law forcing schools to give as much time to the teaching of creation science as to evolution. The American Civil Liberties Union took the case to court on the grounds that the creation story was not a scientific theory. They won their case (see pp. 162–4 below in this chapter).

We can see that this form of religious faith is politically very conservative. For this reason, it has been referred to as the New Christian Right (NCR). Bruce (1992) saw the movement developing from several countervailing trends:

- A perceived threat from federal government into local state affairs, which meant the intrusion of liberal ideas into a traditionally conservative culture.
- The increasing demands from minority groups for civil rights. (Since the 1960s, the southern states had been pressured to promote racial integration and equality.)
- The economic rise of the southern states. They prospered and southerners became more affluent.
- The rise of the 'televangelists', which helped to promote fundamentalism across the USA.

Pray TV: the impact of religious broadcasting

The rise of religious channels on satellite and cable television in different countries has stemmed mainly from American television. These TV stations are often funded by fundamentalist evangelical sects. Until recently, the majority of

American fundamentalists were to be found among the 'dirt poor' or so-called 'trailer trash', (these might also be known as part of the underclass). However, as Bruce (1991) explains, 'the creation of a technically sophisticated and glossy product – the production and distribution facilities of Pat Robertson's Christian Broadcasting Network are the equal of anything in the secular world – allows a previously marginalised group to feel that it has arrived.'

In the early 1980s, American audiences for televised evangelism were estimated to be 15 million, or around 8 per cent of the total audience. However, the sex scandals of the late 1980s associated with two of the leading TV evangelists, Jim Bakker and Jimmy Swaggart, reduced this figure, albeit temporarily.

However, the political impact of the NCR was relatively slight. There were few elections where these voters made a significant difference. Bruce maintains that attitude surveys during the Reagan era showed that, although there was a shift to the right on defence and economic policy, this was not accompanied by a similar shift on social and moral issues. Reagan's administration was followed not by a member of the NCR, but by George Bush (Senior), who held mainstream Christian views.

An article by Mariah Blake (2005) in the *Columbia Journalism Review*, based at Columbia University in the USA, looked at the rise of Christian broadcasting in America. In 2005, the Christian Broadcasting Network employed more than 1000 people, had offices in three American cities and was also present in the Ukraine, the Philippines, India and Israel. Conservative evangelicals control six national television networks, each reaching tens of millions of homes, and virtually all of America's more than 2000 religious radio stations. Evangelical believers can choose to have only Christian programmes beamed into their homes. Sky Angel, one of America's three broadcast satellite networks, carries 36 channels of Christian television and radio – and nothing else. Research has shown that 96 per cent of American evangelicals consume some form of Christian media every month.

In 1944, evangelicals formed the National Religious Broadcasters (NRB) and began to lobby hard against the rule by which the big three networks donated, rather than sold, limited airtime to religious organisations. The lobbying paid off – the government decided to allow religious organisations to buy as much airtime as they could afford. Evangelical ministries were soon flooding the airwaves, while mainstream religious broadcasting virtually disappeared. Since its foundation, NRB has grown to represent 1600 broadcasters and has billions of dollars in media holdings. It also has huge political clout. Despite being tax exempt, and therefore barred from promoting a particular political candidate, it was very active in spreading the Republican message during both the 2000 and 2004 election campaigns of George W. Bush. Since his election, NRB representatives have been regular visitors to the White House.

Over the past decade, Christian TV networks in America have added tens of millions of homes to their distribution lists. The number of religious radio stations almost all of which are evangelical – has grown by 85 per cent since 1998. As a point of comparison, they now outnumber rock, classical, hip-hop, R & B, soul and jazz radio stations combined. Christian radio and television networks experienced a huge growth spurt in the months following 9/11. It was at that time that CBN (the Christian Broadcasting Network) launched Newswatch, the first nightly Christian television news programme. In 2004, FamilyNet TV, part of the Southern Baptist Convention's media empire, also hired a news staff to deliver news programmes. In explaining the success of their news operations, Christian broadcasters refer to the biblical perspective that underpins their news reporting. Frank Wright, President of the NRB, said: 'We don't just tell them what the news is. We tell them what it means. And that's appealing to people, especially in moments of cultural instability' (Blake, 2005, p. 5).

However, despite their growing success, Christian networks still lag behind many secular ones with regard to audience size. About one million US households tune in daily to each of the most popular Christian television shows. About 20 times that number watch the most popular secular shows. Christian radio stations take on average about 5 per cent of the market share, while other news and talk stations attract about three times that percentage. Nevertheless, the current trend is upwards, with more and more Americans tuning in to Christian radio and television networks.

Intelligent design

The powerful Christian conservatives within the Republican Party have also been behind the movement to have Intelligent Design taught in American public (state) schools. President George W. Bush has said himself that he thinks that it should be taught as part of the science curriculum: 'I think that part of education is to expose people to different schools of thought.'

In Dover, Pennsylvania, 9th grade children (aged 14–15) are being taught in their biology lessons that Darwin's theory of evolution provides only one possible explanation of life, and that there are others, including that of Intelligent Design (ID). The reason for this form of teaching lies with the Dover Area School District's Board, which decreed in October 2004 that students were to be made aware of gaps in Darwin's theory and that they should be shown alternatives such as Intelligent Design. Eleven parents took up a lawsuit against the Board because they saw the teaching of ID as a violation of their religious liberties. They argued that promoting particular religious beliefs under the guise of an alternative 'scientific' theory actually contravened the US constitutional separation of church and state.

The main claim of ID is that there are some things in the world that cannot be accounted for by known natural causes and which show features of an intelligent, supernatural designer at work. The proponents of ID see two major inadequacies in Darwin's work:

1   The revolution in molecular biology has revealed a previously unsuspected level of irreducible complexity in minute, microscopic organisms.
2   The premise of natural selection cannot explain all natural development.

Supporters of ID argue that they do not wish to prevent the theory of evolution being taught in schools, but that students should be presented with alternative theories and allowed to make up their own mind.

The debate between evolutionism and ID is being carried out by eminent scientists. Although many scientists and civil liberties lawyers have attacked the decision to treat ID as a theory on the same level as that of evolution, there are other highly respected scientists arguing for its inclusion as an alternative scientific explanation. However, there are clear links between those supporting ID and religious faith. Their literature regularly insists that Darwinism is simply a thinly veiled attempt to present secular religion (atheistic materialism) to the western world. Those who have attacked the decision to treat ID as a scientific theory point out that the idea of ID is fundamentally untestable and unprovable, as it relies on inserting a supernatural force – God, or an 'intelligent designer' – into a scientific theory. They argue that ID has no explanatory or predictive power. It simply says that some things that seem very complex could not have happened on the basis of natural causes, so must have been created by a supernatural entity.

Opponents of ID in the United States claim that making the teaching of it compulsory in public (i.e. state) schools entangles government with religion and therefore violates the US constitutional separation of church and state. In 1987, the US Supreme Court ruled that the belief that a supernatural creator was responsible for the creation of humans is a *religious* viewpoint, and therefore it cannot be taught in state schools alongside the scientific theory of evolution. However, many polls have shown that believers in Intelligent Design are in the majority in America. Surveys repeatedly show that most Americans prefer creationist versions of the origins of human life to scientific ones. A poll by the Pew Research Center in September 2005 showed that 64 per cent of Americans were in favour of teaching some form of creationism in publicly funded schools, with only 26 per cent wishing to keep the idea of divine intervention out of science classes (*http://people-press.org/commentary/display.php3?AnalysisID=118*).

Intelligent Design in British Schools

It is interesting to see what part ID is playing in British schools. In September 2006 a teaching pack, including two DVDs and a teachers' manual, was sent to the head of science at all secondary schools in England by a privately funded group calling itself Truth in Science. The OCR Exam Board encourages students to debate creationist ideas alongside evolutionism. However, as an OCR spokesperson said: 'Creationism and intelligent design are not to be regarded by OCR as scientific theories. They are beliefs that do not lie within scientific understanding.' Nevertheless, the government decided to write to all schools telling them that the materials should not be used in science lessons. The Education Minister, Jim Knight, said that 'neither intelligent design nor creationism are recognised scientific theories'. This is not the case, however, for the Emmanuel Schools Foundation sponsored by the Christian millionaire car dealer Sir Peter Vardy. The Foundation has set up three secondary academies in the north-east of England and concern has been expressed about the evangelical bias of the teachers and the teaching within these schools.

According to a BBC MORI poll of 2112 adults, carried out in January 2006 for the *Horizon* programme, 40 per cent of people in the UK agreed that alternatives to Darwin's theory should be taught as science in schools. When asked what should be taught in science lessons, 69 per cent said evolution, 44 per cent said creationism and 41 per cent said ID. When asked to decide which of the three explanations they would choose, 48 per cent said evolution without God, 22 per cent said creationism, and 17 per cent said ID (*www.ipsos-mori.com/polls/2006/bbc-horizon.shtml*).

ISLAMIC FUNDAMENTALISM

The rise of Islamic fundamentalism is yet another challenge to the view of the inevitability of secularisation in modern societies. It would have been almost impossible to have predicted that Islam, a traditional religious system, would have undergone such a tremendous revival and would have had such an enormous impact on countries from Iran in the Middle East across North Africa as far as Egypt.

The Islamic Revolution started in Iran (formerly Persia) in the late 1970s. Under the Shah, Iran was one of the more 'Westernised' of the Middle Eastern states, having a close relationship with the USA. The Shah's government had been introducing elements of what became known as his 'White Revolution', namely all-embracing state-wide institutions of party, youth and women's movements, land reforms and the introduction of secular education. There was some opposition to these reforms, but it was not unified. As Bruce (2000, p. 5) argued:

> Oil wealth promised great material prosperity and delivered it to some but it did so in ways that undermined socially significant parts of the traditional economy, in particular the small traders and craftsmen of the bazaar. Far from liberating Iran, oil increased its dependence on the West. Instead of promoting indigenous and sustainable development, it further distorted the economy.

Opposition from the religious clerics was growing, but not necessarily targeted against the Shah. However, in 1962 criticism became so vehement against the Local Council Laws (allowing women and non-Muslims to vote) that the laws had to be abandoned. As a result the Shah's rule became increasingly repressive until in 1978 Ayatollah Khomeini, an exiled mullah living in Paris, was brought back to lead a concerted movement against the Shah's regime. The Shah fled and Ayatollah Khomeini became the leader of the new Islamic state of Iran.

The Ayatollah's government reversed the previous trend of liberalisation in Iran, reintroducing Islamic law and beliefs according to the Qur'an. Males and females were segregated in education, which was now to be based on Islamic teachings, women had to go veiled in public, adulterers were to be stoned and practising homosexuals to be executed. Zubaida (1996) argues that the process of Islamicisation has not been completed; there are forces acting against it. He has distinguished three groups whose conflicting interests prevent the completion process:

- radicals – who want to export the revolution across the world;
- conservatives – who want to concentrate the revolution in Iran;
- pragmatists – who want to liberalise and open Iran to foreign investment and trade.

Gellner (1992) asks an important question about the Islamic faith, namely why is it seemingly so resistant to secularisation? In his opinion, there are several reasons:

■ The central doctrines of Islam contain an emphatic and severe monotheism, which produces both doctrine and law. This has profound
implications for Muslim life as the leaders of the faith become givers
of the law.

■ Like Christianity, it is a pre-industrial faith, a doctrinal world religion,
which is effectively challenging the secularisation thesis.

■ The effect of Western impact on Muslim countries between the 18th and
20th centuries was not to produce a polarisation amongst Muslim
intellectuals, between Westernisers and those choosing the popular faith,
but instead a move 'back' to High Islam. This had previously only been
practised by a minority of Muslims; now it could be practised by all.

Therefore, a Muslim who returns to this High or Reformist Islam is reaffirming
what is considered best in the local culture.

Kepel (1994, p. 2) wrote the following with regard to Islamic fundamentalism:

> Around 1975 the whole process went into reverse. A new religious
> approach took shape, aimed no longer at adapting to secular values but at
> recovering a sacred foundation for the organisation of society – by chang-
> ing society if necessary. Expressed in a multitude of ways, this approach
> advocated moving on from a modernism that had failed, attributing its
> setbacks and dead ends to separation from God. The ... aim was no longer
> to modernise Islam, but to 'Islamize modernity'. Since that date this
> phenomenon has spread all over the world.

Gellner (1992, p. 22) wrote: 'Things may yet change in the future. But on the
evidence available so far, the world of Islam demonstrates that it is possible to
run a modern, or at any rate modernising, economy, reasonably permeated by
the appropriate technological, educational, organisational principles, and
combine it with a strong, pervasive, powerfully internalised Muslim conviction
and identification.'

Salman Rushdie and *The Satanic Verses*: a case study

When *The Satanic Verses* was published in October 1988, it met with acclaim
from the British literati and criticism from British Muslims. The book was seen
as offensive and even blasphemous to Islam, especially in relation to its
treatment of Muhammad. However, according to Bhikhu Parekh (1989), the
response of religious leaders was measured; it was the press which actually

exacerbated the situation by ridiculing Muslim fanatics. In December 1989, a small group of Muslims burned a copy of the book and attracted considerable attention both nationally and internationally. As Muslim protest grew, in February 1989 the Ayatollah Khomeini imposed a death sentence (a fatwa) on Rushdie that lasted for ten years. During this period Rushdie was in hiding, though he did appear from time to time on the British media. It is Parekh's view that the exacerbation of the incident was primarily down to sensationalist reporting:

- The press made little attempt to explain the initial complaints of Muslims against the book.
- Muslim spokespeople were unable to argue their case coherently and they spoke in ways that alienated some non-Muslims.
- Many of the press reports oversimplified the issues involved and focused on the issue of free speech.
- The press discussed the Muslim protest in narrow legal terms and did not criticise Rushdie's possible lapse of good taste.
- Finally, the national press did little to bridge the racial divide opened up by the imposition of the fatwa.

We can see then that despite the attraction of traditional beliefs, fundamentalism is essentially a modern phenomenon. Its links to global politics and world economies are as significant as its links to religion. 'In wealthy countries, it appears to give confidence to minorities who are persecuted or discriminated against, and has been used by those in power to wage war against the non-believers. The more that this goes on the more polarised the world becomes' (Dowd, 2006).

RELIGIOUS RESURGENCE: CATHOLICISM IN BRITAIN

A *Guardian*/ICM Poll (December 2006) showed that in answer to the question 'Are you religious?', 33 per cent of the 1006 respondents said yes, 63 per cent said no and 3 per cent were unsure. Other interesting statistics are worth noting here: 82 per cent of respondents believed that religion causes division between people, while 57 per cent thought it was a force for good (Glover and Topping, 2006).

These data seem to support the view that religion is really in decline in Britain today. However, such figures hide pockets of considerable religious revival. One of these is the revival of the Roman Catholic churches as a side-effect of recent immigration, particularly from Eastern European countries such as Poland. This has happened since Poland acceded to the European Union in 1994. Catholic churches have seen a significant increase in numbers of worshippers, especially by young Poles, and although numbers are not exact, it is estimated that Britain has seen an influx of around 300,500 Polish migrants. These migrants have also boosted the Roman Catholic Church in Scotland by 50,000. Around one-third of recent migrants are said to be practising Catholics. Monsignor Tadeusz Kukla, vicar-delegate to the Polish Mission in England, said: 'The Poles who come here are searching for a community, just as they are in France and Germany, Spain and Italy. We think 50 per cent to 60 per cent are going to mass. They are setting a very good example to the English. ... They will remind the English of what they have lost.' However, other Catholic clergy are more circumspect and do not see the Polish congregations as likely to have any effect on the indigenous population, as the two communities are very separate (quoted in Bates, 2006).

Evangelicalism

Another example of religious resurgence in Britain is Pentecostalism. It is estimated to be the fastest growing Christian denomination in the world. In Britain its followers are around 1.7 million, but globally it is estimated to attract 120 million believers. Pentecostalists are generally evangelical and charismatic. Around half of the congregations are black and many of the churches in Britain are London-based. For example, the Kingsway International Christian Centre in Hackney, East London claims to have 12,000 people attending its Sunday services. As David Voas says, 'Black churchgoers in inner London are an important source of growth in the context of the national decline in church attendance ... the Pentecostals have appeared out of nowhere in the last couple of decades, but it remains to be seen whether they can make inroads into the white population' (quoted in Bates, 2006).

The rise in evangelical congregations is paralleled by the increased interest in creationism and we have already shown (p. 164) how this issue is of particular concern because of its effect on education.

The evangelical movement has given rise to controversy in both Britain and the USA. Some see it as a movement against liberal reform and go as far as to suggest that it is a challenge to democracy. This was part of the concern in the debate about freedom of speech when evangelical Christians wanted to take *Jerry Springer, the Opera* off the stage because they saw it as blasphemous. Although it was screened on BBC2 television, the outcry from the evangelicals threatened the sponsorship for the stage show from one charity, and two major stores withdrew the DVDs from their shelves.

The *Jerry Springer* incident links to another aspect of evangelicalism and that is the emphasis on Christian morality, especially in its opposition to homosexuality. The movement is extremely homophobic and most see same-sex relationships as sinful practice. With little acceptance of gay and lesbian practices as lifestyle choices, evangelicals believe that homosexuality is a learned attitude and that it can be 'cured' through the power of prayer. The opposition to homosexuality is not confined to small groups of fanatics; the issue has come to prominence in the Catholic and Anglican Churches over the recent past.

ISLAM AND MUSLIMS IN THE POST-9/11 WORLD

While it can be argued that religion can have a cohesive effect in society, drawing people together, there is evidence that under certain circumstances it can have the opposite effect, leading to conflict within and between societies. The effects of events such as the terrorist attacks of 9/11, the London bombings of July 2005 and the war in Iraq have been far-reaching, for Muslims and non-Muslims alike. This section will look at the extent to which British Muslims are, and, perhaps more importantly, are perceived to be, integrated into British society, together with the part played by their religion in the identity of some Muslims. We will also examine the extent to which there has been a rise in Islamophobia, a word which is often used to go beyond its literal meaning of 'fear of Islam' to encompass dislike – or even hatred – of Islam.

Muslims in Europe

A feature of many European countries over the last 30 years or so has been the inward migration of Muslim populations. In December 2005, the BBC News website published statistics on the Muslim population in certain European countries. It was pointed out that the exact number of Muslims is difficult to establish, as census figures are sometimes queried and many countries chose not to compile the information. The point was also made that immigration and above-average birth rates have contributed to a rapid increase in the Muslim population, growing at a faster rate than that of the host country. Data from some selected countries are shown in Table 8.1.

As an update to those figures, the Home Secretary, Jacqui Smith, during a visit to Pakistan in April 2008, said that the Mulim population of the UK had risen to 2 million. Of course, the nature of immigrant settlement patterns means that these Muslim populations are not spread evenly throughout the host country. Table 8.2 lists some European towns and cities, showing the percentage of their inhabitants who are Muslim.

Table 8.1 Muslim populations of selected European countries

Country	Total population (millions)	Muslim population (millions)	Muslim population as a percentage of the total
Albania	3.1	2.2	70.0
Austria	8.2	0.34	4.1
Belgium	10.3	0.4	4.0
Denmark	5.4	0.27	5.0
France	62.3	5.0–6.0	8.0–9.6
Germany	82.5	3.0	3.6
Italy	58.4	0.83	1.4
Macedonia	2.1	0.63	30.0
Netherlands	16.3	0.95	5.8
Spain	43.1	1.0	2.3
Sweden	9.0	0.3	3.0
Turkey	68.7	68.0	99.0
United Kingdom	58.8	1.6	2.8

Source: adapted from BBC News: Muslims in Europe Country Guide (23 December 2005) *http://news.bbc.co.uk/1/hi/world/europe/4385768.stm*

Table 8.2 Muslim populations in selected European towns and cities

Town/city	Muslims as % of population
Marseilles	25
Malmö	25
Amsterdam	24
Stockholm	20
Brussels	20
Moscow	16–20
London	17
Birmingham	14.3
The Hague	14.2
Rotterdam	13
Copenhagen	12.6
Leicester	11
Paris	7.4
Antwerp	6.7
Hamburg	6.4
Berlin	5.9

Source: Danish Affairs http://danishaffairs.wordpress.com

Islam and the West

The 2006 Pew Global Attitudes survey referred to earlier (see Chapter 7, p. 145) revealed that there were deep mutual suspicions between the Muslim world and the West. According to the findings, many Westerners saw Muslims as fanatical, violent and intolerant, while Muslims tended to believe that

Westerners were selfish, immoral and greedy – and also fanatical and violent. The BBC Islamic affairs analyst Roger Hardy said that a string of events, including terrorist attacks and the publication of Danish cartoons satirising the Prophet Muhammad appeared to have taken their toll on relations between Islam and the West. The Pew survey spoke of 'a great divide' between Muslim countries and the West, adding that Muslims and Westerners blamed each other for deteriorating relations between the two. However, the researchers also pointed out that attitudes were not uniformly negative. For example, in the West, a majority of respondents in France, Britain and the USA retained overall favourable opinions of Muslims. While 80 per cent of respondents in Spain and Germany associated Islam with fanaticism, this view was less prevalent in the USA (43 per cent), Britain (48 per cent) and France (50 per cent). Again, Muslim opinion was far from uniform, with Muslims living in Europe often attributing positive attributes to Westerners, including tolerance, generosity and respect for women.

The 'Danish cartoons' affair

This illustrates the problems that can ensue, often unintentionally, between people of different faiths, and highlights the often fragile and sensitive nature of relationships between some Muslim and non-Muslim countries. In September 2005 the Danish newspaper *Jyllands-Posten* published a series of 12 cartoons depicting the prophet Muhammad, in what it said was an attempt to promote freedom of expression. This refers to remarks by the Danish author Kare Bluitgen that he was unable to find an author to illustrate his children's book on the prophet Muhammad. It is considered unacceptable – actually blasphemous – by Muslims to make any representation of the prophet, even favourable ones, for fear that it could lead to idolatry. One of the Danish cartoons in particular caused great offence to many Muslims, namely that showing the prophet with a turban shaped like a bomb.

Initially, the reaction against the cartoons was restricted to Denmark, with the Islamic Society of Denmark demanding an apology and the withdrawal of the cartoons. There was also a peaceful protest by 5000 people at the Copenhagen offices of the *Jyllands-Posten* newspaper on 14 October. The Danish Prime Minister refused to meet with ambassadors from 11 Islamic countries to discuss the cartoons, giving as his reasons the importance of free speech and the government's unwillingness to influence editorial opinion. Muslim organisations in Denmark then filed a complaint against the newspaper, citing blasphemy under a rarely invoked section of the Danish criminal code.

A delegation of imams then headed off to Egypt with a 43-page document entitled 'Dossier about championing the Prophet Muhammad peace be upon him'. The dossier, which was then widely distributed throughout the Muslim world, contained, among other things, the original 12 cartoons, examples of anti-Muslim hate mail, and three additional images. One of these was a picture of a bearded man with a pig's snout held onto his face with elastic. This was later shown to be nothing at all to do with Islam but a photograph of the winner of a French pig-squealing contest.

Early in 2006, a Norwegian newspaper republished the cartoons, as did papers in France, Germany, Spain, Italy and the United States. Violent protests followed in several countries, including Pakistan, Iraq, Lebanon, Jordan, Indonesia and Syria. The Danish flag was publicly burned, Danish goods were boycotted, Christian churches were burned and Libya closed its embassy in Denmark. In January 2006 the editor of *Jyllands-Posten* issued two apologies for hurting Muslim feelings – though significantly not for publishing the cartoons. The row gradually subsided, only to be reignited in February 2008 (though with far less violence) when Danish newspapers reprinted the cartoon that caused the greatest offence. This followed the arrest of three people accused of plotting to kill the man who drew it.

The issue of the veil

In October 2006, Jack Straw, a former Foreign Secretary and MP for Blackburn, wrote in a local newspaper, the *Lancashire Evening Telegraph*, that women who wore the full veil (niqab) covering their face could make community relations more difficult. He said that the full veil is 'a visible statement of separation and difference', and that he asked veiled women to consider showing their face when they came to speak to him as their MP. He added that he made sure that when he asked this he had a female colleague with him in the room, and his constituents had so far always agreed to do as he asked. Mr Straw, who has publicly defended the right of Muslim women to wear headscarves, said that revealing the full face enabled him 'to see what the person means, not just what they say'.

His remarks attracted strong criticism from some Muslim groups, though the Muslim Council of Britain said that it understood Mr Straw's discomfort. Dr Daud Abdullah, a member of the Council, pointed out that individual Muslim women could choose to remove part of the veil, but that covering their hair remained 'obligatory'.

Following Jack Straw's remarks and the heated debate that they engendered, the *Guardian*/ICM undertook a poll of public opinion (Glover, 2006). ICM interviewed a random sample of 1023 adults by telephone on 11 October. The interviews were conducted across the country, and the results were weighted to a profile of all adults.

The results of the poll showed that there was a widespread acceptance of Britain's Muslim community, alongside fears about the development of a divided society. Only 22 per cent of respondents thought that British Muslims had done all they needed to do to fit into mainstream society. However, there was a clear generational gap in social attitudes, with young people much less concerned than their parents about Muslim integration. Fifty-three per cent of people thought that Jack Straw was right to suggest that the full veil creates a barrier between Muslim women and other people, with only 36 per cent saying that he was wrong. The generational gap was again apparent in this response, with only 31 per cent of 18–24-year-olds agreeing with Jack Straw, as against 65 per cent of over-65s. Despite concerns that the threat of Islamist terrorism has fuelled fear and intolerance among non-Muslims, 88 per cent said that they would not be anxious about sitting on a train or bus near to someone who appeared to be Muslim. Again, only 11 per cent said that they would feel anxious about a Muslim family moving into a nearby house.

Muslim attitudes

In April 2007 the Gallup Organisation published the results of a global survey of Muslim attitudes, which was based on face-to-face interviews with people aged 15 and older in 40 Muslim countries. As part of this wider survey, Gallup had looked in 2006 at how integrated Muslims were in three European countries – Britain, France and Germany – and how much they identified with their nations, their faith and their ethnicity. The British poll was carried out in Greater London only, and Gallup admits that this may not be entirely typical of the British Muslim community as a whole. However, the British results pointed to a much more hopeful outlook for integration than some reports of extremism, alienation and a 'ghetto mentality' have suggested.

The British survey showed that more than half of those surveyed identify very strongly with Britain, and about four in five believe that it is important to master the English language, get a good education and find a job. The poll also found that nine out of ten Muslims surveyed believe that attacks that target civilians are unjustified and are morally wrong. About 81 per cent also condemn violence even if used in a noble cause – a figure that is 9 per cent higher than the view of the general public. There were some interesting comparisons between Muslims and the wider population: 82 per cent of British Muslims believed in respect for other religions, compared with 45 per cent of non-Muslims, and Muslims were much more likely to identify very strongly or extremely strongly with their religion – 69 per cent compared with 30 per cent of non-Muslims. However, only 13 per cent of Muslims thought that it was necessary to remove the face veil (niqab) for integration into British society, compared with the 55 per cent of non-Muslims who see this as essential. The report showed strong differences between London's Muslims and non-Muslims on moral issues. Only 10 per cent of Muslims believed that sex outside marriage was acceptable, compared with 80 per cent of non-Muslims. Even fewer – less than 5 per cent – found homosexual acts acceptable, compared with 65 per cent (Binyon, 2007).

British Muslims today

In February 2007, a report was published (Mirza et al. 2007) based on research which explored the attitudes of Muslims in Britain today, and the reasons why there has been a significant rise in Islamic fundamentalism among the younger generation. The report was entitled *Living Apart Together: British Muslims and the Paradox of Multiculturalism*. An important section of the report consists of findings from original research conducted between July 2006 and January 2007. The authors give a detailed description of the methodology used:

> The polling company, Populus, conducted a quantitative survey of 1003 Muslims in the UK, though telephone and Internet questionnaires. Telephone interviews were generally conducted in English but in a minority of cases the interview was conducted in a different language if requested by the respondent. The answers were weighted to represent the demographic of the Muslim population in the UK. Some further questions were asked to 1025 people from the general population for points of comparison. We also conducted 40 semi-structured, hour-long interviews with younger British-born Muslims, exploring their attitudes towards religion, British society and values. The respondents were either university students or recent graduates, were of either Pakistani or Bangladeshi origin, and came from a range of socio-economic backgrounds. This smaller sample was not intended to be demographically representative of the entire Muslim population, but it provided useful data about the complex attitudes of younger Muslims.

The authors of the report point out the important distinction that should be made between 'Islam' and 'Islamism'. Islam is a world religion, while Islamism refers to the *politicisation* of religion, an ideology which draws upon religion but pursues a particular political programme and set of goals. In a letter to the *Guardian* newspaper (2 February 2007), Munira Mirza, one of the authors of the report, said that one of its aims was to get past the sensational portrayal of Muslims as 'the problem' – either as terrorists or as victims of Islamophobia.

While 86 per cent of Muslims agreed that 'My religion is the most important thing in my life', the research showed a growing religiosity among the younger generation of Muslims. Rather than simply following their parents' cultural traditions, younger Muslims' interest in religion is more politicised. The research revealed some interesting differences between younger British Muslims and their parents' generation (Mirza et al., 2007, p. 5):

- 62 per cent of 16–24 year olds feel that they have as much in common with non-Muslims as Muslims, compared to 71 per cent of those aged 55+.
- 27 per cent of 16–24 year olds would prefer to send their children to a mixed state school (rather than an Islamic one) compared to 19 per cent of those aged 55+.
- 37 per cent of 16–24 year olds would prefer to live under Sharia law, compared to 17 per cent of those aged 55+.
- 74 per cent of 16–24 year olds would prefer Muslim women to choose to wear the veil, compared to 28 per cent of those aged 55+.

The report emphasises that there is considerable diversity amongst Muslims, with many adopting a much more secular approach. For example, the research found that 21 per cent of Muslims had consumed alcohol, 65 per cent had paid interest on a mortgage, 19 per cent had gambled and 9 per cent admitted to taking drugs, all of which are forbidden under Islamic law.

Muslim identity

The authors of the report suggest that the emergence of a strong Muslim identity in Britain is partly a result of the particular multicultural policies implemented in Britain since the 1980s, policies which have emphasised difference at the expense of a shared national identity. They believe that such policies have divided people along ethnic, religious and cultural lines. Islamist groups have gained influence by playing what the authors call 'the politics of identity' and demanding for Muslims the 'right to be different'. Both the authorities and some Muslim groups have exaggerated the problem of Islamophobia, which the authors believe has led to a sense of victimhood amongst some Muslims. The research showed that, despite the widespread concerns about Islamophobia, 84 per cent of Muslims said that they had been treated fairly in British society.

In their search to find the reasons for the growing religiosity among many younger British Muslims, the authors point out that in British society generally there has been a weakening of older, collective forms of identity, such as the decline of traditional communities, working-class politics, trades unions and an undermining of 'Britishness'. This has led to a feeling of disengagement among young people generally, and not just Muslims. However, some younger Muslims are turning to religion as part of their search for meaning and community. Wider political trends in Britain have led to 'diversity policies', which has resulted in a social fragmentation, with different ethnic and religious groups encouraged to 'look after their own'. According to a 2006 report by the Office for National Statistics about religion in the UK, more than half of Jewish, Muslim, Sikh and Hindu adults living in England and Wales in 2001 said that their religion was important to their self-identity (*www.statistics. gov.uk/focuson/ethnicity/*)

Conversations with younger Muslims during the *Living Apart Together* research process suggested that they spent more time reading the Qur'an and attending religious lectures than their parents did. Some reported that their parents actually disapproved of this increased religiosity, preferring their children to concentrate instead on educational achievement and getting a good job. The authors of the report suggest that perhaps the turn to greater religiosity among many young Muslims might be seen as a kind of 'teenage rebellion' against the cultural traditions of their community. However, they point out that the heightened degree of religiosity was also apparent among those aged 25–34, so was not simply a teenage phenomenon, something that they would 'grow out of'. They conclude that this new religiosity 'represents a very definite shift in attitudes to identity and religion.' (2007, p. 87) For many young Muslims, religion has become the backbone of a strong personal identity.

Many young Muslims, therefore, are committed to Islam because they feel that it satisfies their quest for meaning and identity. However, the report points out that this commitment to Islam does not always lead young Muslims to the mosque or to the traditional community elders. Dr Siddiqui, the head of the Muslim Parliament, told a conference of 3000 Muslims in Birmingham in 2005 that: 'Most mosques are not equipped to deal with young people … Our mosques are largely tribal and controlled by old men on the dole with no understanding of the changing world around them' (quoted in Mirza et al., 2007, p. 40). Indeed, the researchers found that many young Muslims found their local mosques irrelevant. The imams often do not speak English and rarely encourage critical discussion about aspects of the Qur'an. The radicalisation of the more violent Islamists often takes place in private spaces, even abroad, and can even encourage a move away from traditional community ties and social networks.

The research also revealed another major difference between generations, with younger Muslims desiring a return to a 'purer' Islam, which does not rely on certain cultural traditions passed down through the generations – in other words, Islamic fundamentalism.

The French academic Olivier Roy (2004), claims that Islam in Europe is undergoing a fundamental change. There is a paradox between growing secularisation and increasing religiosity. Roy argues that religion has become more important at an individual level, but less important in regulating the cultural life of the community. This means that older forms of religious authority, such as the mosque and community elders, no longer exercise the level of control that policy makers often assume. Younger Muslims have developed a more individualised approach to their religion, acting out of personal choice. The effect of this is that while many younger Muslims develop a deeper interest in their religion, others adapt it in a more flexible way to adjust to a largely secular society.

A new Muslim organisation was launched in Britain in May 2008, claiming to represent the 'silent majority who feel no conflict between their faith and democracy'. Its name is British Muslims for Secular Democracy, and its chair and co-founder is the journalist Yasmin Alibhai-Brown. At the launch, she made the interesting point that her group thought that the government's attempts to 'placate' Muslims by offering various concessions (e.g. separate schools) would actually cause long-term damage to communities by fuelling Muslims' separation from the rest of society (Butt, 2008).

MANAGING RELIGIONS

There is little doubt that the twin effects of growing immigration from Muslim countries and the so-called 'war on terror' pose considerable problems for both the stability and harmony of many Western countries.

Turner (2007) points out that one largely unintended consequence of the globalisation of the labour market has been the increase in social diversity. The establishment of diasporic communities has also resulted in greater religious diversity. (A diasporic community is one whose people have relocated from their original homeland.) Turner's argument is that the generally liberal social policies and institutions of modern Western democratic societies are ill equipped to manage the resulting social tensions. Following the collapse of communism and the rise of fundamentalism, religious diversity has become a major political issue in democratic societies. The consequence, according to

Turner, is that the states of advanced societies can no longer rely on the conventional separation between politics and religion, and have thus entered into a new phase involving the direct management of religions.

In the post-9/11 world, there is a general sense of a crisis of liberalism and secularism, and of the need for greater security and surveillance. Turner argues that to deal with this sense of crisis, diasporic Muslim communities have become the target of government interventions and investigations. The various government strategies have led to what he terms 'the management of Muslims'. This is in contrast to the earlier traditional strategies of 'benign neglect' of Muslim communities. The process of 'managing Muslims' is often undertaken under the banner of pluralism and multiculturalism.

Why should religions and religious groups need to be managed in this way? Turner's answer is that it is important to the state, particularly when applied to those religions that offer an alternative vision of power and truth. The state needs to assert (or reassert) its authority over civil society if it is to try to command the loyalty of its citizens over and above other, possibly competing, claims of membership.

Turner identified two forms of the management of religions. He makes use of Foucault's concept of 'governmentality', since managing religions has become a recent addition to the more general functions of the administrative state. The first form of governmentality applied to religions is the *liberal model*, which Turner sees as having a strategy of 'upgrading' religions. When applied to Islam, this liberal model tends to assume that Islam needs to be 'modernised' in order to be compatible with liberal democratic regimes. The intended outcome is to produce 'moderate Muslims'. The strategies of this approach include:

- raising the educational level of Muslim communities, including their leaders and mullahs;
- providing legislation to give Muslim women security, educational opportunities and freedom to reject arranged marriages, and possibly inducement to abandon the veil or other forms of modesty and seclusion;
- opposition to what are seen as brutal aspects of criminal law, such as amputations.

In short, argues Turner, the liberal management of modernising Islam is intended to bring about its partial secularisation. He believes that, although a small group of Muslim modernists might welcome such strategies, the majority of Muslims would regard them as deeply problematic, because they appear to change the nature of individual piety.

The second model of the management of religions is what Turner calls '*enclavement*'. The word 'enclave' comes from the Latin word for 'key', so to enclave a group or society is to lock it up. However, the modern enclave is not simply a walled society (although these exist), because with new technologies, governments can exercise surveillance and control without physical barriers. Turner believes that since 9/11, enclavement has become the dominant paradigm, as liberal 'upgrading' policies are subject to political criticism. He gives as the ultimate example of modern enclavement Guantanamo Bay, 'an area of extra-legal containment and rendition' (2007, p. 125).

Turner distinguishes between two forms of enclavement, spontaneous and institutional. Spontaneous enclavement occurs when a group voluntarily adopts social practices that result in social closure, for example inter-group marriage. However, he is, of course, more concerned with the second form, institutional enclavement. This refers to the involuntary social closure of a group with the specific aim of social exclusion.

Institutional enclavement can, however, be either benign or malicious. Examples of benign institutional enclavement would include the quarantine of groups carrying an infectious disease that might harm others, such as SARS. Turner points out that this kind of enclavement would tend to be short-term responses to environmental risks. Malevolent enclavement covers enclosure, bureaucratic barriers, police surveillance, legal exclusions and registrations. Turner sees the effect of many such enclavements as resulting in the immobility of sections of the population, and gives as examples gated communities for the elderly, ghettoes for migrants (both legal and illegal), imprisonment, tagging for criminals and so on. He points out that modern information technology has provided states with a range of new techniques to implement forms of enclavement. Turner believes that policies of enclavement will inevitably produce greater alienation of Muslim communities from their host societies, but what he terms 'management through exclusion' seems to be the dominant pattern associated with the 'war on terror'.

So – is the enclavement of Muslim communities inevitable? Turner obviously hopes not, but says that positive state policies towards minority groups cannot succeed without parallel changes in society that will create new patterns of social solidarity strong enough to cross enclaves. He suggests that the following are needed to bring this about:

- a strong legal framework and effective citizenship to create an environment in which racism is not tolerated;
- government policies that convey the message that no ethnic or religious group is favoured above others, and hence minority rights are clearly protected by law;

■ the redistribution of economic resources to ensure that second-generation immigrant children are not systematically disadvantaged;

■ a social climate that allows inter-marriage, social reciprocity and the emergence of overlapping social groups such as clubs, churches and voluntary associations to help create an overlapping social consensus of value and belief;

■ a cultural sphere, including sport and other leisure activities, to counteract the tendency towards group loyalty, localism, tribalism or ethnic solidarity.

It is Turner's belief that in the absence of such overlapping social groups, there can be no overlapping consensus in society, and enclavement will follow.

CONCLUSION

Despite the evidence which points to a decline in religious practices, and to some extent, in religious belief, in many Western countries, religion continues to play an important part in many countries throughout the world. If secularisation is taking place (and many sociologists do not agree on this point), it is neither universal nor uniform. The 'clash of cultures' that can occur when groups of people with sometimes widely differing beliefs and cultural practices live in the same country can be extremely damaging, both to individuals and to the communities in which they live. The rise of fundamentalism, particularly so-called Islamic fundamentalism, is of great concern to many Western governments. Ironically, it is sometimes their attempts to control and 'manage' this that increases both its likelihood and the severity of its effects.

Important concepts
fundamentalism • New Christian Right • televangelism • intelligent design • Islamicisation • evangelicalism • Islamophobia • governmentality • enclavement

Summary points
• Despite several indices pointing to the decline of religious belief and practice in many advanced industrial societies, there is also evidence of a growth in fundamentalist beliefs, in both Christian and Muslim societies.

- In the USA, members of the so-called New Christian Right have become a powerful force in politics, and their conservative views on a number of issues receive widespread publicity, not least through the growing number of Christian radio and television networks.
- The increase in Islamic fundamentalism has raised concerns about the perceived growth in the radicalisation of young British-born Muslims.
- Following the terror attacks of 9/11 in the USA and other attacks in Britain and Spain, there has been much debate concerning the extent to which ethnic minority communities, particularly Muslims, are integrated into the host society. In Britain, concern has been raised that some multicultural policies have served to emphasise the differences between ethnic groups, which may have been at the expense of a shared national identity.
- Turner fears that as governments increasingly turn to 'managing' religions, the greater enclavement of Muslims will follow.

Critical thinking

- If you wish to explore the debate about Intelligent Design, look up the article that appeared in the *Observer* on 2 October 2005 (*www.guardian.co.uk/Archive*).
- Another interesting site for the ID debate is that of the American Civil Liberties Union (*www.aclu.org/ReligiousLiberty*).
- It would also be useful to look up some of the other websites mentioned in this chapter, particularly the Pew Global Attitudes Report, the Muslim Women's Network and the report by Mirza et al., *Living Apart Together: British Muslims and the Paradox of Multiculturalism*.
- For each of these, consider how and where the information fits into the various ongoing debates within the sociology of religion.

Essay guidance

Use the notes and tasks below to plan an answer to the following essay question.

> 'The growth of religious fundamentalism challenges the view that modern societies are inevitably becoming more secular.' Assess the sociological arguments and evidence for this statement.

A note of caution is necessary here. The essay is not simply about *secularisation*, but how far *religious fundamentalism* can be seen as producing a challenge to the secularisation process.

Deconstructing the essay title might produce these questions:

1 *'growth of religious fundamentalism'*:
   What is fundamentalism?
   Are there different kinds?
   Where is it growing?
   What evidence is there for this?
   What reasons have been suggested for its growth?

2 *'challenges the view'*
   Whose view?
   Is there only one?
   Is the view universally accepted?
3 *'that modern societies'*
   To which societies are we referring?
   What do we take to be modern?
   Is there any useful evidence from contemporary societies that are non-industrial, or
     less developed than most Western societies?
4 *'are inevitably becoming more secular'*
   What do we mean by 'inevitably'? Does this presuppose a theory that says secularisa-
     tion must take place?
   Which theorists would hold this position?
   Who might argue against such a theory?
   How should we measure and assess the evidence for secularisation?
5 *'Assess the sociological arguments and evidence'*
   Remember the important distinction between 'arguments' and 'evidence'.

The essay gives you the opportunity to demonstrate the skills of evaluation and analysis.
Once you have deconstructed an essay question like this, it makes the process of planning the essay much simpler.

References

Abbott, P. and Wallace, C. (1990) *An Introduction to Sociological Theory: Feminist Perspectives* (London: Routledge & Kegan Paul).

Abercrombie, N., Baker, J., Brett, S. and Foster, J. (1970) 'Superstition and Religion: the God of the Gaps', in D. Martin and M. Hill (eds), *A Sociological Yearbook of Religion in Britain*, 3 (London: SCM), pp. 91–129.

Abrams, M., Gerard, D. and Timms, N. (eds) (1985) *Values and Social Change in Britain* (London: Macmillan).

Aldridge, A. (2000) *Religion in the Contemporary World* (Cambridge: Polity Press).

Aron, R. (1967) *Main Currents in Sociological Thought* (London: Weidenfeld and Nicolson).

BBC/MORI Poll, January 2006, *www.ipsos-mori.com/polls/2006/bbc-horizon.shtml*.

BBC news item, November 2005, *http://news.bbc.co.uk/go/pr/fr/-/hi/world/europe/4375910.stm*.

BBC news website: Statistics on Muslim population in European countries, December 2005, *http://news.bbc.co.uk/1hi/world/europe/4385768.stm*.

Barker, E. (1984) *The Making of a Moonie* (Oxford: Blackwell).

Bates, S. (2006) 'Devout Poles show Britain how to keep the faith', *Guardian* 23 December 2006.

Bauman, Z. (1990) 'Postmodern Religion', in P. Heelas (ed.), *Religion, Modernity and Postmodernity* (Oxford: Blackwell).

Beck, U. (1992) *Risk Society: Towards a New Modernity* (London: Sage).

Beckford, J. (1989) *Religion and Advanced Industrial Society* (London: Sage).

Beckford, J. (1996) 'Postmodernity, High Modernity and New Modernity', in K. Flanagan and P. Jupp (eds) (1996), *Postmodernity, Sociology and Religion* (Basingstoke: Macmillan).

Beckford, J. (2003) 'Religion, Consensus and Conflict', in *Sociology Review* 13:2 (Oxford: Philip Allan updates).

Beckford, J. (2004) 'Religion and Postmodernity', in *Sociology Review* 14:2 (Oxford: Philip Allan updates).

Beliefnet (2004) *http://www.beliefnet.com*.

Beliefnet (2004) US Presidential Election Voting by Religious Groups, *http://beliefnet. com/story/153/story_15355.html*.

Bell, D. (2005) (speech to Hansard Society, delivered 17 January 2005, *http:// education.guardian.co.uk/faithschools/story/0,,1392281,00.html*.

Bellah, R. (1970) *Beyond Belief* (New York: Harper and Row).

Berger, P. (1973) *The Social Reality of Religion* (Harmondsworth: Penguin).

Berger, P. (1990) *The Sacred Canopy: Elements of a Sociological Theory of Religion* (New York: Anchor Books).

Berger, P. (2006) 'Religion and Global Civil Society', in M. Juergensmeyer (ed.), *Religion in Global Civil Society* (New York: Oxford University Press).

Berger, P. and Luckmann, T. (1969) 'Sociology of Religion and Sociology of Knowledge', in R. Robertson (ed.), *Sociology of Religion* (Harmondsworth: Penguin).

Bilton, T. et al. (1996) *Introductory Sociology*, 3rd edition (Basingstoke: Macmillan).

Blake, M. (2005) 'Stations of the Cross', in *Columbia Journalism Review Issue*, 3 May/ June 2005 (Columbia University Graduate School of Journalism).

Bloom, W. (1991) *The New Age* (London: Rider).

Bocock, R. (1985) 'Religion in Modern Britain', in R. Bocock and K. Thomson (eds), *Religion and Ideology* (Manchester: Manchester University Press).

Bocock, R. and Thomson, K. (eds), (1985) *Religion and Ideology* (Manchester: Manchester University Press).

Bottomore, T. (1964) *Karl Marx: Early Writings* (New York: McGraw-Hill).

Brierley, P. (2005) *Religious Trends No. 5* (Swindon: Christian Research).

Bruce, S. (1985) *Religion in Modern Britain* (Oxford: Oxford University Press).

Bruce, S. (1991) 'Pray TV: Observations on Mass Median Religion', in *Sociology Review* 1:2 (Oxford: Philip Allan Publishers).

Bruce, S. (1992) 'Religion in the Modern World', in *Developments in Sociology*, vol. 8 (London: Causeway Press).

Bruce, S. (1995a) 'Religion and the Sociology of Religion', in *Developments in Sociology*, vol. 11 (London: Causeway Press).

Bruce, S. (1995b) *Religion in Modern Britain* (Oxford: Oxford University Press).

Bruce, S. (1996) *Religion in the Modern World: From Cathedrals to Cults* (Oxford: Oxford University Press).

Bruce, S. (1998) 'Religion and Ethnic Conflict', in *Developments in Sociology*, vol. 5 (London: Causeway Press).

Bruce, S. (2000) *Fundamentalism* (Cambridge: Polity Press).

Bruce, S. (2002) 'God and Shopping', in *Sociology Review* 12:2 (Oxford: Philip Allan Updates).

Butler, C. (1995) 'Religion and Gender: Young Muslim Women in Britain', in *Sociology Review* 4:3 (Oxford: Philip Allan Updates).

Casanova, J. (1994) *Public Religions in the Modern World* (Chicago: University of Chicago Press).

Celsing, C. (2006) *Are Swedes Losing Their Religion? www.sweden.se/templates/cs/ Article_15193.aspx*.

Charity Commissioners (2006) *www.charity-commission.gov.uk/spr/corcom1.asp.*

Christian Research: *http://www.christian-research.org.uk.*

Church Census and Evangelicanism (2005) *http://www.eauk.org/resources/info/statistics/2005englishchurchcensus.*

Church of England Electoral Roll (2002) *www.cofe.anglican.org/info/statistics/churchstatistics2002.*

Crompton, R. and Lyonette, C. (2007), 'Are We All Working Too Hard? Women, Men and Changing Attitudes to Employment', in A. Park, J. Curtice, K. Thomson, M. Phillips and M. Johnson (eds), *British Social Attitudes, 23rd Report* (London: Sage).

Davie, G. (1989) 'Religion', in *Developments in Sociology*, vol. 5 (London: Causeway Press).

Davie, G. (1994) *Religion in Britain since 1945* (Oxford: Blackwell).

Davie, G. (1995) 'Competing Fundamentalisms', in *Sociology Review* 4:4 (Oxford: Philip Allan Updates).

Dowd, M. (2006) *Fundamentalism*, Channel 4 Television.

Durkheim, E. (1965) *The Elementary Forms of the Religious Life* (New York: Free Press).

Eder, K. (1990) 'Environmentalism', paper presented at the XIIth World Congress of Sociology, Madrid.

Engels, F. (1984) 'On the History of Early Christianity', in L. S. Feuer (ed.), *Marx and Engels: Basic Writings on Politics and Philosophy* (Englewood Cliffs, NJ: Fontana).

English Church Census (2005) *www.christian-research.org.uk/pr180906.htm.*

Equality Act 2006 Guidance Notes, *www.religionlaw.co.uk/07relguide.pdf.*

Fact File (2002) Carel Press.

Gellner, E. (1992) *Postmodernism, Reason and Religion* (London: Routldege).

Giddens, A. (1991) *The Consequences of Modernity* (Cambridge: Polity Press).

Giddens, A. (1997) *Sociology*, 3rd edition (Cambridge: Polity Press).

Glock, C. and Stark, R. (1965) 'On the Origin and Evolution of Religious Groups', in C. Glock and R. Stark (eds), *Religion and Society in Tension* (New York: Rand McNally).

Goodkin, J. and Citron, J. (1994) *Women in the Jewish Community: Reviews and Recommendations* (London: Office of the Chief Rabbi).

Gorard, S. et al. (2008) 'Developing a sense of justice among disadvantaged students: the role of schools', Birmingham University European Group for Research on Equity in Educational Systems (EGREES).

Gramsci, A. (1971) *Selections from the Prison Notebooks* (London: New Left Books).

Habgood, J., Archbishop of York (1992) 'Viewpoint', in *The Independent*, 12 March 1992.

Hall, S. (1985) 'Religious Ideologies and Social Movements', in R. Bocock and K. Thompson (eds), *Religion and Ideology* (Manchester: Manchester University Press).

Hallsworth, S. (1994), 'Understanding New Social Movements', in *Sociology Review*, 4:1 (Oxford: Philip Allan Updates).

Hamilton, M. B. (1995) *The Sociology of Religion: Theoretical and Comparative Perspectives* (London: Routledge).

Hannigan, J. (1993) 'New Social Movement Theory and the Sociology of Religion', in L. Harvey and M. MacDonald (eds), *Doing Sociology: A Practical Introduction* (Basingstoke: Macmillan).

Harvey, L. and MacDonald, M. (1993) *Doing Sociology: A Practical Introduction* (London: Macmillan).

Heelas, P. (1990) (ed.) *Religion, Modernity and Postmodernity* (Oxford: Blackwell).

Heelas, P. (1996) *The New Age Movement* (Oxford: Blackwell).

Heelas, P. (2000) 'Turning within', in M. Percy (ed.), *Previous Convictions: An Anatomy of Conversion* (London: SPCK).

Heelas, P. and Woodhead, L. (2003) 'The Kendal Project', in *Sociology Review* 13:2 (Oxford: Philip Allan Updates).

Herbert, W. (1960) *Protestant, Catholic, Jew* (New York: Anchor Books).

Hervieu-Leger, D. (1993) *La Religion pour Memoire* (Paris: Cerf).

Hirschi, T. and Stark, R. (1969) 'Hell Fire and Delinquency', *Social Problems* 17:2, pp. 202–13.

Holden, A. (2002) 'Witnessing the Future? Millenarianism and Postmodernism', in *Sociology Review* 11:3 (Oxford: Philip Allan Updates).

Holden, A. (2007) 'Ethnicity, Religion and Community', in *Sociology Review* 17:4 (Oxford: Philip Allan Updates).

Hunt, S. (2003) 'Religion and Postmodernity', in *Sociology Review* 13:1 (Oxford: Philip Allan Updates).

Hutnik, N. (1991) *Ethnic Minority Identiy: A Social Psychological Perspective* (Oxford: Clarendon Press).

Huxley, A. (1965) *Brave New World* (Harmondsworth: Penguin Books).

ICM Poll on Religion (2006) for *Guardian* 23 December 2006.

Jones, M. (1996) 'Insights: The Protestant Ethic Revisited', in *Sociology Review* 6:1 (Oxford: Philip Allan Updates).

Jones, P. (1993) *Studying Society: Sociology Theories and Research Practices* (London: Collins Educational).

Kepel, G. (1994) *The Revenge of God* (Cambridge: Polity Press).

Knight, J. (2006) *www.publications.parliament.uk/pa/cm200607/cmhansard/cm061211/ text/6121w0035.htm.*

Kosmin, B., Meyer, E. and Keysar, A. (2001) *American Religious Identification Survey 2001*, Graduate Center of the City University of New York published online, *www.gc.cuny.edu/faculty/researchbriefs/aris.pdf.*

Land, R. (2004) 'How Religion Defines America', on BBC News Website 'What the World Thinks of God', *http://news.bbc.co.uk/hi/programmes/wtwtgod/ default.stm.*

Lawson, T. and Garrod, J. (1996) *The Complete A–Z Sociology Handbook* (London: Hodder & Stoughton).

Lyon, D. (1996) 'Religion and the Postmodern: Old Problems, New Prospects', in K. Flanagan and P. Jupp (eds) (1996) *Postmodernity, Sociology and Religion* (Basingstoke: Palgrave).

Lyon, D. (2000) *Jesus in Disneyland: Religion in Postmodern Times* (Cambridge: Polity Press).

Maduro, O. (1982) *Religion and Social Conflicts* (New York: Orbis Books).

Marshall, G. (1991) 'The Protestant Ethic', in *Sociology Review* 1:1 (Oxford: Philip Allan Updates).

Martin, D. (1969) *The Religious and the Secular* (London: Routledge & Kegan Paul).

Martin, D. (1978) *A General Theory of Secularisation* (Oxford: Blackwell).

Martin, D. (1991) 'The Secularisation Issue: Prospect and Retrospect', *British Journal of Sociology* 42:3.

Marty, M. (1988) 'Fundamentals of Fundamentalism', in L. Kaplan (ed.), *Fundamentalism in a Comparative Perspective* (Boston, MA: University of Massachusetts Press).

McGuire, M. (1981) *Religion: The Social Context* (Belmont, CA: Wadsworth).

Merton, R. (1968) *Social Theory and Social Structure* (New York: Free Press).

Mirza, M., Senthilkumaran, S. and Ja'far, Z. (2007) *Living Apart Together* (London: Policy Exchange).

Modood, T., Beishon, S. and Virdee, S. (1994) *Changing Ethnic Identities* (London: Policy Studies Institute).

Modood, T., Berthoud, R. and Lakey, L. (1997) *Ethnic Minorities in Britain: Diversity and Disadvantage* (London: Policy Studies Institute).

More magazines (London: EMAP Elan).

Neitz, M. J. (1993) 'Inequality and Difference: Feminist Research in the Sociology of Religion', in W. H. Swatos (ed.), *A Future for Religion? New Paradigms for Social Analysis* (Berkeley, CA: Sage).

Nelson, G. (1986) 'Religion and Social Change', in M. Haralambos (ed.), *Developments in Sociology* (Ormskirk: Causeway Press).

Nesbitt, E. (1990) 'Pitfalls in Religious Taxonomy: Hindus and Sikhs, Valmokis and Ravidasis', in *Religion Today*, October 6:1; reprinted 1994 in J. Wolffe (ed.), *The Growth of Religious Diversity in Britain from 1945: A Reader* (London: Hodder for Open University).

Neibuhr, H. (1929) *The Social Sources of Denominationalism* (New York: World Publishing).

O'Dea, T. (1966) *The Sociology of Religion* (Englewood Cliffs, NJ: Prentice Hall).

O'Dea, T. (1970) *Sociology and the Study of Religion* (New York: Basic Books).

Office for National Statistics Report 2006 *www.statistics.gov.uk/focuson/ethnicity/*.

Pahl, R. (1996) 'The Future of Success', *Sociology Review*, 5:4 (Oxford: Philip Allan Updates).

Palmer, S. (1994) *Moon Sisters, Krishna Mothers, Rajneesh Lovers* (Syracuse, NY: Syracuse University Press).

Parekh, B. (1989) 'The Rushdie Affair and the British Press', *Social Studies Review*, 5:2 (Oxford: Philip Allan Publishers).

Parsons, T. (1960) *Structure and Process in Modern Society* (New York: Free Press).

Parsons, T. (1966) *Societies: Evolutionary and Comparative Perspectives* (Englewood Cliffs, NJ: Prentice Hall).

Parsons, T. (1971) *The System of Modern Societies* (Englewood Cliffs, NJ: Prentice Hall).

Pattman, R. (1988) 'The Social Construction of AIDS', in P. Langley (ed.), *Discovering Sociology* (London: Causeway Press).

Pew Forum on Religion and Public Life, statement, December 2007, *http://pewforum. org/religion-politics*.

Pew Research Center Poll, September 2006, *http://people-press.org/commentary/display. php3?AnalysisID=118*.

Pew Research Council, Survey 2002 *http://pewforum.org/publications/reports/ poll2002.pdf*.

Pryce, K. (2001) *Endless Pressure* (Harmondsworth: Penguin).

Richter, P. and Francis, L. J. (1988) *Gone but not Forgotten: Church Leaving and Returning in the Twenty-first Century* (London: Darton, Longman and Todd).

Roy, O. (2004) *Globalized Islam: The Search for a New Ummah* (London: Hurst).

'She who Disputes' (2006) *www.thenwc.org.uk/wnc_work/muslim_women.html*.

Shiner, L. (1967) 'The Concept of Secularisation in Empirical Research', in K. Thompson and J. Tunstall (eds), *Sociological Perspectives* (Harmondsworth: Penguin).

Smith, G. (2005) *Children's Perspectives on Believing and Belonging*, National Children's Bureau in conjunction with the Joseph Rowntree Foundation.

Stanton, E. Cady (1985) *The Woman's Bible: The Original Feminist Attack on the Bible* (Edinburgh: Polygon Books).

Stark, R. and Bainbridge, W. (1987) *A Theory of Religion* (New York: Peter Lang).

Stark, R. and Glock, C. (1965) *Religion and Society in Tension* (Chicago: Rand McNally).

Stark, R. and Glock, C. (1968) *American Piety: The Nature of Religious Commitment* (Berkeley: University of California Press).

Stark, R., Kent, L. and Doyle, D. (1982) 'Religion and Delinquency: The Ecology of a "Lost Relationship"', *Journal of Research in Crime and Delinquency* 19: 4–24.

Svennevig, M. et al. (1988) *Godwatching: Viewers, Religion and Television* (London: John Libby).

Swatos, W. H. (1993) *A Future for Religion? New Paradigms for Social Analysis* (Berkeley, CA: Sage).

Taylor, M. (2005) 'Two-Thirds Oppose State-Aided Faith Schools', *Guardian*, 23 August.

Troeltsch, E. (1958) *Protestantism and Progress* (Boston, MA: Beacon Press).

Turner, B. S. (1983) *Religion and Social Theory: A Materialistic Perspective* (Atlantic Highlands, NJ: Humanities Press).

Turner, B. S. (1991) *Religion and Social Theory*, 2nd edition (London: Sage).

Turner, B. S. (2007) 'Managing Religions: State Responses to Religious Diversity', *Contemporary Islam*, 1:2 (Netherlands: Springer).

UN Office on Drugs and Crime: Afghan opium survey (2007), *www.unodc.org/unodc/en/frontpage/afghan-opium-report.html*.

University of Michigan (1997) *www.ns.umich.edu/htdocs/releases/story.php?id=1835*.

Valls, M. and Malabard, V. (2005) *La Laïcité en Face* (France: Broché).

Voas, D. and Bruce, S. (2006) 'Is Religion Giving Way to Spirituality?', *Sociology Review* 15:4 (Oxford: Philip Allan Updates).

Voas, D. and Crockett, A. (2005) 'Religion in Britain: Neither Believing Nor Belonging', *Sociology* 39:1.

Wahid, S. (2007) quoted in J. Van Dyk (2007) *Islamic Fundamentalism in South Asia*, *www.strategicstudiesinstitute.army.mil/pdffiles/of-interest-2.pdf*, p. 8.

Wallis, R. (1984) *The Elementary Forms of the New Religious Life* (London: Routledge).

Wallis, R. (1985) 'The Sociology of the New Religions', *Social Studies Review* 1:1 (Oxford: Philip Allan Publishers).

Wallis, R. and Bruce, S. (1984) 'The Stark–Bainbridge Theory of Religion: a Critical Analysis and Counter-proposals', *Sociological Analysis 45*: pp. 11–48.

Wallis, R. and Bruce, S. (1992) 'Secularization: the Orthodox Model', in S. Bruce (ed.), *Religion and Modernization* (Oxford: Clarendon Press).

Ward, D. (2001) 'Alternative Spirituality Rising Fast', *Guardian* 18 June.

Weber, M. (1971) *The Protestant Ethic and the Spirit of Capitalism* (London: Unwin University Books).

Williams, J. (2000) 'The Church in the UK', *Sociology Review* 10:1 (Oxford: Philip Allan Updates).

Wilson, B. (1966) *Religion in a Secular Society* (London: Watts).

Wilson, B. (1970) *Religious Sects* (London: Weidenfeld and Nicolson).

Wilson, B. (1982) *Religion in Sociological Perspective* (Oxford: Oxford University Press).

Wilson, B. (1985) 'A Typology of Sects', in R. Bocock and K. Thompson (eds), *Religion and Ideology* (Manchester: Manchester University Press).

Wilson, B. (1992) *The Social Dimensions of Sectarianism* (Oxford: Clarendon Press).

Worsley, P. (1987) *The Trumpet Shall Sound*, 2nd edition (New York: Schocken).

YouGov Poll, December 2004, *www.yougov.com/archives/pdf/STI040101003_2.pdf*.

Zubaida, S. (1996) 'How Successful is the Islamic Republic in Islamizing Iran?', in J. Beinin and J. Stork (eds), *Political Islam: Essays from the Middle-East* (Berkeley: University of California).

Index